The Kitchen Yearbook

CHARTWELL
BOOKS INC.

Published by Chartwell Books Inc.,
A division of Book Sales Inc.
110 Enterprise Avenue
Secaucus, New Jersey 07094

© Marshall Cavendish Limited 1979

Printed in Singapore

ISBN 0 89009 173 0

Introduction

Throughout the year, as the seasons change so do our needs and tastes for food. A bleak Winter conjures up thoughts of steaming soups and piping hot stews. Spring brings new flavors, crisp vegetables, fish and poultry. The lazy salad days of Summer mean long evenings and eating outdoors. The rich harvests of Autumn bring new fruits, fish and game. Inevitably, the nights grow shorter, the cycle moves on and Winter frost returns. These natural events are taken for granted, but even in today's urbanized society, our tastes are still guided by the natural elements and our ancient instincts: rich, warming food to keep out the chill and sustain us in our work; the fresh, healthful Spring vegetables; in warmer days, cool salads; and as the harvest comes in, with abundant produce, it also brings our deep-rooted and traditional enjoyment of all the natural gifts the land still provides.

Note: Measurements are given in Metric and Standard, separated by a slash. These measurements should not be used interchangeably when following a recipe as they are not direct conversions. Follow one or the other.

Herbs, when in season, are specified as fresh. If they are not available, dried herbs may be substituted using one-third of the quantity given. For example, for 1 tablespoon freshly chopped basil, use 1 teaspoon dried basil.

All flour is all-purpose and all sugar granulated unless otherwise specified. Ovens should be preheated to the temperature given in the recipe.

CONTENTS   *Spring*   *Summer*

Autumn

Winter

Feast Days

Spring

The arrival of Spring has always been an excuse for feasting. As the days gradually lengthen, and the appearance of the sun becomes less unpredictable, new life (much of it edible!) suddenly becomes apparent wherever we look. Tender young lambs, fresh green vegetables, fruit blossoms – all reflect not only the change in our surroundings, but also a change in our eating habits. We want to eat food that is lighter in color and flavor, to lose some of the weight we put on in the winter and, as the season progresses, to make the most of the fresh scenery by eating outside. So Spring food has to be flexible, making the best of what's around but using it both in cold and hot dishes, for picnics or for chilly evenings. Spring is, above all, a gay and carefree time, so whatever you're eating, enjoy it.

What's best in season

Fruit:	Apples	Grapes	Mandarins	Pineapples
	Apricots	Grapefruit	Melons	Rhubarb
	Bananas	Lemons	Oranges	Tangerines
	Gooseberries	Limes	Pears	

Vegetables:	Asparagus	Cucumbers	Mushrooms	Scallions
	Avocados	French or Belgian endive	Okra (ladies' fingers)	Shallots
	Beets	Globe artichokes	Onions	Snow peas
	Broccoli	Green beans	Parsnips	Spinach
	Cabbages	Kale	Peas	Tomatoes
	Carrots	Leeks	Potatoes	Turnips
	Cauliflowers	Lettuces	Radishes	Watercress
	Celery	Lima beans	Rutabaga	

Herbs:	Basil	Coriander	Marjoram	Sage
	Bay	Dill	Mint	Summer savory
	Chervil	Fennel	Parsley	Tarragon
	Chives	Lemon balm	Rosemary	Thyme

Nuts:	Almonds

Fish:	Bass	Flounder	Mackerel	Shrimp
	Carp	Grouper	Mullet	Sole
	Cockles	Haddock	Oysters	Trout
	Cod	Hake	Red snapper	Tuna
	Crab	Halibut	Salmon	Turbot
	Crayfish	Herring	Sardines	Whiting
	Eel	Lobster		

Poultry:	Available fresh or frozen all year round

Game:	Pigeon	Quail	Rabbit

Meat and variety meats	Available fresh or frozen all year round

Appetizers

Sicilian stuffed tomatoes

8 large tomatoes
6 Tbsp olive oil
2 medium onions, finely chopped
1 garlic clove, crushed
125g/1⅓ cups fresh breadcrumbs
8 anchovies, chopped
3 Tbsp black olives, pitted and chopped
2 Tbsp parsley, freshly chopped
2 tsp oregano, freshly chopped
2 Tbsp Parmesan cheese, grated
1 Tbsp butter, cut into 8 pieces

Cut off the tops of the tomatoes. Scoop out and discard the seeds, being careful not to pierce the skins.

Heat the oil in a frying pan. Add the onions and garlic and fry until the onions are soft, but not brown. Remove from the heat and stir in the breadcrumbs, anchovies, olives, parsley and oregano. Fill the tomatoes with the anchovy mixture, piling it up slightly. Place the tomatoes side by side in a baking dish. Sprinkle over the Parmesan cheese and put a piece of butter on each tomato.

Bake in a moderate oven (180°C/350°F) for 20 to 25 minutes or until the tops are lightly browned. Serve hot, straight from the oven, or allow to cool and serve chilled.
Serves 4

Sardine Eggs

6 eggs, hard-cooked
175g/6oz can sardines, drained
4 Tbsp mayonnaise
1 Tbsp lemon juice
1 Tbsp parsley, freshly chopped
salt and white pepper

Cut the eggs in half lengthwise. Cut a thin slice off the bottom of each one so they will sit flat. Remove the yolks and press through a strainer into a small mixing bowl.

Add the remaining ingredients with seasoning to taste to the egg yolks and mash together well. Fill the whites with the sardine mixture. Serve chilled with brown bread and butter.
Serves 6

Sicilian Stuffed Tomatoes makes a colorful and appetizing first course, served hot or cold.

Oysters Kilpatrick – simple to prepare and exotic to taste.

garlic clove, tarragon, anchovies, parsley, cayenne and seasoning to taste. Add three-quarters of the shrimp to the mayonnaise and mix well. Chill well in the refrigerator.

Cut the stalks off the artichokes. Pull off any bruised or tough outer leaves, then slice off the top third of the artichokes. Trim the tips of the remaining leaves using scissors. Rub the cut edges with the remaining lemon juice to prevent discoloration.

Half fill a large saucepan with water and add 1 teaspoon salt. Bring to a boil. Place the artichokes in the water and simmer for 30 minutes or until tender. Test by pulling out a leaf. Remove the artichokes from the pan and place upside-down on paper towels to drain and cool.

Pull the leaves of each artichoke apart and remove the yellow inner core. Scrape out the hairy choke and discard it. Fill the center with the shrimp mayonnaise. Garnish with the remaining shrimp.

Serve on individual plates garnished with lemon slices. Serve any extra sauce separately.
Serves 6

Oysters Kilpatrick

60g/¼ cup butter, softened
32 oysters, on the half shell
2 tsp Worcestshire sauce
12 bacon slices, broiled until crisp and crumbled
2 Tbsp parsley, freshly chopped

Carefully spread a thin layer of butter over each oyster. Sprinkle with the Worcestershire sauce and bacon. Broil the oysters for 2 minutes. Serve hot, garnished with the parsley.
Serves 4

Globe artichokes with shrimp and spicy mayonnaise

625ml/2½ cups mayonnaise
4 Tbsp lemon juice
2 Tbsp chives, finely chopped
1 tsp capers, chopped
1 garlic clove, crushed
1 Tbsp tarragon, freshly chopped
6 anchovies finely chopped
2 Tbsp parsley, freshly chopped
pinch cayenne pepper
salt and pepper
500g/2½ cups shrimps (shelled) deveined
6 globe artichokes
2 lemons, sliced

Mix together the mayonnaise, 1 tablespoon of the lemon juice, the chives, capers,

Fried shrimp balls

750g/1½lb shrimp (shelled), deveined and finely chopped
30g/⅓ cup fresh brown breadcrumbs
1 garlic clove, crushed
1 small onion, finely chopped
3 Tbsp ginger wine
black pepper
90g/1½ cups dry breadcrumbs
vegetable oil for deep frying
lemon wedges to serve
FRITTER BATTER
60g/¼ cup flour
¼ tsp salt
pinch sugar
4 Tbsp water
2 tsp vegetable oil
1 egg white

Mix the shrimp with the fresh breadcrumbs, garlic, onion, ginger wine and pepper to taste. With floured hands form the mixture into 24 balls.

To make the fritter batter, sift the flour, salt and sugar into a mixing bowl. Stir in the water and oil to make a smooth batter. Beat the egg white until it will form a soft peak and fold into the batter. Dip the shrimp balls in the batter, then roll them in the dry breadcrumbs to coat on all sides. Shake off any excess.

Half-fill a deep-fat fryer with oil and heat to 190°C/375°F on a deep-fat thermometer, or until a cube of stale bread dropped into the oil turns light brown in 40 seconds.

Put the shrimp balls, five or six at a time, in the frying basket and lower into the oil. Fry, shaking occasionally, for 3 to 5 minutes or until crisp and golden brown. Drain the shrimp balls on paper towels and keep hot while you fry the remaining shrimp balls.

Serve hot, garnished with the lemon wedges.

Serves 4-6

Kipper pâté

375g/12oz kipper fillets, boned
2 Tbsp butter, melted
1 Tbsp sweet sherry
4 Tbsp heavy cream
1 tsp worcestershire sauce
black pepper
2 Tbsp clarified butter, melted

Put the kippers in a bowl and pour over boiling water. Leave for 15 minutes, then drain well. Skin the fillets and flake the flesh. Put the flesh in a blender with the melted butter, sherry, cream, Worcestershire sauce and pepper to taste. Blend, off and on, for 1 to 2 minutes or until the mixture is smooth. Alternatively, pound the ingredients together with a pestle in a mortar.

Spoon the pâté into a small serving dish and smooth the top. Pour over the clarified butter and chill for at least 2 hours before serving, with Melba toast.

Serves 4

Deep-fried smelts

50g/½ cup flour
salt and black pepper
1 Tbsp parsley, freshly chopped
500g/1lb smelts
vegetable oil for deep frying
lemon wedges for serving

Mix together the flour, salt and pepper to taste and the parsley in a plastic bag. Add the smelts to the bag and shake well to coat them with the seasoned flour.

Half fill a deep-frying pan with oil and heat to 185°C/360°F on a deep-fat thermometer, or until a cube of stale bread dropped into the oil turns golden brown in 50 seconds. Put half the smelts in the frying basket and lower into the oil. Fry for 2 to 3 minutes or until crisp and light brown. Shake the basket occasionally. Drain the fried smelts on paper and keep them hot while you fry the remaining smelts.

Serve hot with lemon wedges and tartar sauce.

Serves 4

Kipper Pâté, served in individual dishes, makes a tasty start to a meal.

Soups

Creamy asparagus soup

2 Tbsp butter
1 medium onion, finely
chopped
3 Tbsp flour
1.2l/2½ pints chicken stock
Salt and white pepper
½ tsp celery salt
¼ tsp grated nutmeg
500g/1lb asparagus, chopped
300ml/1¼ cups light cream

Melt the butter in a saucepan. Add the onion and cook until soft, but not brown. Remove from the heat and sprinkle over the flour. Stir well, then gradually stir in the chicken stock. Add salt and pepper to taste, the celery salt, nutmeg and asparagus. Return to the heat and bring to a boil, stirring constantly. Cover and simmer gently for 20 to 30 minutes or until the asparagus is very tender.

Remove from the heat. Purée the soup in a blender or food mill or rub it through a strainer using the back of a wooden spoon. If you are serving the soup hot, return it to the saucepan and reheat gently. Stir in the cream just before serving.

To serve the soup cold, stir the cream into the purée and chill for at least 2 hours before serving.
Serves 4-6

Iced watercress and almond soup

1 bunch watercress, finely chopped
1 celery stalk, finely chopped
300ml/1¼ cups light cream
grated rind of 1 lemon
300ml/1¼ cups milk
500ml/1 pint chicken stock
3 Tbsp ground almonds
1 Tbsp butter
2 Tbsp flour
salt and black pepper

Put the watercress, celery, cream, lemon rind and milk in a large saucepan and bring to just under boiling point. Remove from the heat and stir in the stock and almonds. Mix the butter with the flour to make a smooth paste (*beurre manié*) and stir into the soup in small pieces. Return to the heat and cook for 2 to 3 minutes, stirring constantly, or until the soup is thick and smooth. Season to taste and cook gently for a further 2 minutes.

Remove from the heat and allow to cool, then chill for at least 1 hour before serving.
Serves 4

Creamy Asparagus Soup makes a rich, delicately flavored first course for a dinner party, served hot or cold.

Minestrone

1l/2 pints water
125g/⅔ cup dried kidney beans
60g/⅓ cup garbanzos
175g/¾ cup salt pork, cut into cubes
4 Tbsp olive oil
2 medium onions, finely chopped
1 garlic clove, crushed
2 medium potatoes, peeled and diced
4 carrots, scraped and cut into 1cm/½in lengths
4 celery stalks, cut into 1cm/½in lengths
½ small head cabbage, finely shredded
6 medium tomatoes, peeled, seeded and chopped
2.5l/5 pints chicken stock
1 bouquet garni
salt and black pepper
250g/1½ cups green peas (shelled)
125g/4oz macaroni
60g/½ cup Parmesan cheese, grated

Bring the water to a boil in a saucepan. Add the beans and garbanzos and boil for 2 minutes. Remove from the heat and leave to soak for 1½ hours.

Return to the heat and bring back to a boil. Simmer for 1½ hours or until the beans and garbanzos are almost tender. Drain well.

Fry the salt pork in a large saucepan until it is golden brown and has rendered most of its fat. Remove the salt pork cubes from the pan. Add the oil, onions and garlic to the pan and fry until the onions are soft but not brown. Stir in the potatoes, carrots and celery and continue to cook for 5 minutes, stirring. Add the cabbage and tomatoes and cook for a further 5 minutes.

Add the stock, bouquet garni, garbanzos, beans, salt pork and salt and pepper to taste. Bring to a boil, then cover and simmer for 35 minutes.

Discard the bouquet garni. Add the peas and macaroni and continue to simmer, uncovered, for 10 to 15 minutes or until the macaroni is *al dente*, or just tender.

Ladle the soup into bowls and sprinkle with the Parmesan. Serve hot.
Serves 8

Iced Watercress and Almond Soup – a creamy spring appetizer.

Avgolemono is a traditional Greek soup with an unusual and delicious lemon flavor.

Avgolemono

90g/½ cup long-grain rice
1.9l/7½ cups chicken stock
4 eggs
juice of 2 lemons
pepper
2 Tbsp parsley, freshly chopped

Wash the rice, then soak in cold water for 30 minutes. Drain. Bring the stock to a boil in a saucepan and add the rice. Reduce heat, cover and simmer for 15 minutes or until the rice is tender. Remove from the heat.

Beat the eggs together in a mixing bowl. Gradually beat in the lemon juice, then a few spoonfuls of the stock mixture. Stir the egg mixture into the remaining stock mixture in the saucepan.

Return to the heat and cook gently for 2 to 3 minutes. Do not let the soup boil or it will curdle. Add pepper to taste. Ladle into soup bowls and sprinkle with parsley.
Serves 6

Herb and potato soup

4 medium potatoes, peeled
2 Tbsp butter
2 medium onions, thinly sliced and pushed out into rings
1 Tbsp chervil, freshly chopped
2 Tbsp parsley, freshly chopped
2 Tbsp chives, freshly chopped
salt and black pepper
1 Tbsp paprika
1.2l/2½ pints chicken stock

Cook the potatoes in boiling salted water until tender. Drain and mash.

Melt the butter in a large saucepan. Add the onions and cook until they are soft, but not brown. Remove from the heat and stir in the potato purêe, chervil, parsley, chives, salt and pepper to taste and the paprika. Gradually stir in the stock. Return to the heat and bring to a boil, stirring frequently. Cover and simmer gently for 30 minutes. Serve hot.
Serves 4

Green pea and sausage soup

1 Tbsp butter
500g/3 cups green peas (shelled)
4 lettuce leaves, shredded
3 scallions, chopped
½ tsp sugar
salt and black pepper
1.2l/2½ pints water
300ml/1¼ cups milk
1 Vienna sausage, thinly sliced
300ml/1¼ cups heavy cream

Melt the butter in a large saucepan. Add the peas, lettuce, scallions, sugar and salt and pepper to taste. Cook, stirring, for 2 minutes. Add the water and milk and bring to a boil. Simmer gently for 15 minutes or until the peas are tender. Remove from the heat.

Puree the soup in a blender of food mill, or by pushing through a strainer, and then strain. Alternatively, rub the soup through a strainer.

Return the pureed soup to the saucepan and bring to a boil, stirring. Add the sausage and simmer gently for 2 minutes. Stir in the cream and heat through without boiling. Serve hot.

Serves 6

Spinach soup

2 Tbsp butter
1 large onion, finely chopped
2 Tbsp flour
1.2l/2½ pints chicken stock
salt and black pepper
½ tsp paprika
½ tsp grated nutmeg
2 Tbsp lemon juice
750g/1½lb spinach, coarsely chopped
6 Tbsp heavy cream
6 bacon slices, broiled until crisp and crumbled

Melt the butter in a large saucepan. Add the onion and fry until it is soft but not brown. Remove from the heat and sprinkle over the flour. Stir well, then gradually stir in the stock. Add salt and pepper to taste, the paprika, nutmeg, lemon juice and spinach and return to the heat. Bring to a boil. Cover and simmer for 20 o 25 minutes or until tender.

Purée the soup in a blender or food mill, then return to the saucepan. Reheat gently, stirring frequently. Ladle into soup bowls and top each serving with a tablespoon of cream and crumbled bacon.

Serves 6

Green Pea and Sausage Soup is an economical and filling start to a meal.

Main Dishes

Whiting stuffed with shrimp

juice of 1 lemon
6 medium whiting, boned and cleaned
salt and black pepper
125g/½ cup butter
300g/2½ cups button mushrooms, sliced
300g/1⅔ cups shrimp (shelled) deveined
6 Tbsp parsley, freshly chopped

Sprinkle the lemon juice over the fish, then rub inside and out liberally with salt and pepper.

Melt 2 tablespoons of the butter in a frying pan. Add the mushrooms with salt and pepper to taste and fry for 2 to 3 minutes. Stir in the shrimp and parsley and cook for 2 to 3 minutes longer. Remove from the heat. Stuff the cavities in the whiting with the mushroom mixture. Cut half the remaining butter into small pieces and dot over the bottom of a baking dish. Place the whiting in the dish, side by side, and dot with the remaining butter.

Bake in a moderate oven (180°C/350°F) for 20 to 30 minutes or until the fish is cooked. Test with a fork: the flesh should flake easily. Serve hot.
Serves 6

Flounder with artichoke sauce

1kg/2lb flounder fillets, skinned
salt and black pepper
1 small onion, sliced and pushed out into rings
1 celery stalk, chopped
1 mace blade
1 bouquet garni
6 white peppercorns, crushed
300ml/1¼ cups fish stock
185ml/¾ cup dry white wine
1 Tbsp lemon juice
1 Tbsp parsley, freshly chopped
SAUCE
3 globe artichokes
juice of 1 lemon
2 Tbsp butter
30g/¼ cup flour
salt and white pepper
pinch cayenne pepper
4 Tbsp heavy cream

First prepare the artichokes for the sauce. snap the leaves off the artichokes and cut off the stalks. Trim the base of all pieces of green to expose the white heart. As each heart is prepared, drop it into a saucepan of water to which the lemon juice has been added. Bring the water to a boil and simmer for 30 to 40 minutes or until the artichoke hearts are tender.

Flounder with Artichoke Sauce makes a satisfying and delicious main course.

Meanwhile, rub the flounder fillets with salt and pepper. Lay them in a flameproof casserole and add the onion, celery, mace blade, bouquet garni and peppercorns. Pour over the stock, wine and lemon juice. Bring to a boil, then cover and cook gently for 8 to 12 minutes or until the fish is cooked. Test with a fork: the flesh should flake easily.

Transfer the fish fillets to a warmed serving dish. Fold them over or roll up and keep hot. Strain the cooking liquid and reserve 300ml/1¼ cups.

Melt the butter in a saucepan. Stir in the flour to make a smooth paste and cook for 1 minute, stirring. Remove from the heat and gradually stir in the reserved cooking liquid. Return to the heat and cook, stirring, for 2 to 3 minutes or until the sauce is thickened and smooth. Stir in salt and pepper to taste and the cayenne. Remove from the heat.

Drain the artichoke hearts and chop finely. Add to the sauce with the cream. Heat through gently without boiling, then pour over the fish fillets. Sprinkle with the parsley and serve.
Serves 6

Fillets of sole with spinach and Mornay sauce

750g-1kg/1½-2lb sole fillets, skinned
salt and black pepper
125ml/½ cup fish stock, boiling
125ml/½ cup white wine, boiling
1kg/2lb spinach
60g/¼ cup butter
SAUCE
2 Tbsp butter
4 Tbsp flour
300ml/1¼ cups milk
300ml/1¼ cups fish stock
60g/½ cup Parmesan cheese, grated
60g/½ cup Gruyere cheese, grated
4 Tbsp heavy cream
salt and white pepper

Lay the sole fillets in a baking dish. Sprinkle with salt and pepper and pour over the boiling fish stock and wine. Cover the dish and bake in a moderate oven (180°C/350°F) for 8 to 12 minutes or until the fish is cooked.

Meanwhile, put the spinach in a saucepan. (Do not add any water: there should be enough left on the leaves after washing.) Cook for about 6 minutes or until the spinach is tender.

While the spinach is cooking, make the sauce. Melt the butter in a saucepan. Stir in the flour and cook, stirring, for 1 minute. Gradually stir in the milk, then the fish stock and bring to a boil, stirring

constantly. Simmer, stirring, until the sauce is thick and smooth. Remove from the heat and add the Parmesan, Gruyère, cream and seasoning to taste. Stir well.

When the spinach is cooked, drain it, pressing to remove all excess moisture. Chop the spinach and add the butter and salt and pepper to taste. Mix well. Spread the spinach over the bottom of a flame-proof serving dish. Top with the drained sole fillets and pour over the sauce. Broil until the top is lightly browned.
Serves 4

Halibut steaks with cucumber and sour cream sauce

300ml/1¼ cups dry white wine
2 Tbsp lemon juice
1 Tbsp dill, freshly chopped
1 small onion, halved
4 peppercorns, crushed salt
4 medium halibut steaks
60g/½ cup flour
1 tsp paprika
black pepper
1 small cucumber, peeled, seeded and finely chopped
150ml/⅔ cup sour cream
2 Tbsp butter
1 Tbsp vegetable oil

Put the wine, lemon juice, dill, onion, peppercorns and 1 teaspoon salt in a shallow dish. Add the fish steaks and marinate for 2 hours, basting occasionally.

Put the cucumber in a colander, sprinkle with salt and leave to drain for 30 minutes. Rinse and pat dry with paper towels.

Mix together the flour, paprika, a pinch of black pepper and ¼ teaspoon salt. Remove the halibut steaks from the marinade and coat with the flour.

Discard the onion from the marinade. Put the marinade in a saucepan and add the cucumber. Bring to a boil and boil until it has reduced to about 150ml/⅔ cup. Strain into a bowl, rubbing the cucumber through the strainer until only a dry pulp remains. Discard the pulp.

Return the strained mixture to the saucepan and stir in the sour cream. Heat through gently, stirring occasionally.

Meanwhile, melt the butter with the oil in a frying pan. Add the halibut steaks and fry for about 8 minutes on each side or until the fish is cooked. Test with a fork: the flesh should flake easily. Transfer the steaks to a warmed serving dish and pour over the cucumber sauce. Serve hot.
Serves 4

Spinach is a healthy, colorful accompaniment to many dishes, and is particularly good with fish.

Broiled Sardines with Watercress Sauce is a simply cooked dish with a special flavor.

Fried trout with sour cream and mushroom sauce

90g/¾ cup flour
salt and black pepper
6 medium trout, cleaned and eyes removed
125g/½ cup butter
2 Tbsp vegetable oil
375g/3 cups button mushrooms, halved
1 tsp lemon juice
1 tsp paprika
300ml/1¼ cups sour cream
1 Tbsp parsley, freshly chopped

Mix the flour with salt and pepper to taste in a plastic bag. Add the fish and shake gently to coat them with the seasoned flour.

Melt 60g/¼ cup of the butter with the oil in a frying pan. Add the fish, in batches, and fry for about 5 minutes on each side or until lightly browned and cooked.

Transfer the fish to a warmed serving dish and keep hot.

Melt the remaining butter in a saucepan. Add the mushrooms and cook for 3 minutes. Stir in the lemon juice, paprika, sour cream and salt and pepper to taste and cook, stirring, for 2 to 3 minutes or until the mixture is hot but not boiling.

Pour the sauce over the fish and sprinkle with the parsley. Serve hot.
Serves 6

Broiled sardines with watercress sauce

12 sardines, cleaned
2 Tbsp olive oil
1 bunch watercress, finely chopped
1 Tbsp parsley, freshly chopped
250ml/1 cup mayonnaise
salt and black pepper

Arrange the sardines, in one layer, in a shallow flameproof casserole or serving dish. Brush with half the olive oil. Broil for 3 to 5 minutes or until lightly browned. Turn the sardines and brush the other sides with the remaining oil. Broil for a further 3 to 5 minutes or until lightly browned and cooked. Test with a fork: the flesh should flake easily.

Meanwhile, mix together the watercress, parsley, mayonnaise and salt and pepper to taste. Put this sauce into a serving bowl.

Serve the sardines hot accompanied by the sauce.
Serves 4

Baked salmon steaks with hollandaise sauce

1 Tbsp butter, softened
4 salmon steaks, thick
salt and black pepper
1 bouquet garni
12 large mushrooms
125ml/½ cup dry white wine
300ml/1¼ cups fish stock
8 large shrimp (shelled), deveined
6 parsley sprigs
SAUCE
3 Tbsp dry white wine
2 large egg yolks, slightly beaten
125g/½ cup unsalted butter, diced
2 tsp lemon juice
salt and pepper

Grease a flameproof dish with the softened butter. Rub the salmon steaks with salt and pepper and place in the dish. Add the bouquet garni. Remove the mushroom stalks from the caps and add the stalks to the dish. Reserve the mushroom caps. Pour the wine and the stock over the salmon. Bring to a boil, then transfer to a moderate oven (180°C/350°F). Bake for 30 minutes, basting the salmon twice during the cooking period with pan juices.

Arrange the mushroom caps and shrimp around the salmon and bake for a further 5 minutes or until the salmon is cooked.

Transfer the salmon steaks to a warmed serving dish. Arrange the mushroom caps and shrimp around and on top. Keep warm while you make the sauce.

Pour the wine into a heavy pan and boil rapidly until it has reduced by one third. Cool. Place the egg yolks in the top of a double boiler, or a heatproof bowl placed over a pan filled one-third full with simmering water. Beat until thick and creamy and pale yellow in color. Add the wine and whisk again. Add the butter, piece by piece, whisking constantly until each piece has melted. When the sauce will just hold its shape, remove from the heat and whisk in the lemon juice and season to taste with salt and pepper. Spoon a little of the sauce over the steaks and serve the rest separately in a sauceboat. Garnish with the parsley sprigs and serve.
Serves 4

Beef and cheese roll with tomato sauce

3 thick white bread slices, crusts removed
4 Tbsp milk
750g/1½lb ground beef
2 eggs, lightly beaten
2 tsp dry mustard
salt and black pepper
1 tsp thyme, freshly chopped
1 onion, finely chopped
2 Tbsp parsley, freshly chopped
1 Tbsp flour
250g/8oz mozzarella cheese, sliced
2 Tbsp butter, melted
SAUCE
3 Tbsp butter
2 onions, finely chopped
1 garlic clove, crushed
500g/1lb tomatoes, peeled and quartered
1 tsp sugar
salt and black pepper
4 Tbsp red wine (optional)

Put the bread in a bowl and pour over the milk. Soak for 3 minutes. Gently squeeze the bread and pour off any excess milk. Add the beef, eggs, mustard, salt and pepper to taste, the thyme, onion and parsley. Knead well together, then turn out onto a piece of wax paper or foil that has been sprinkled with the flour. Using a fork, press the meat out into a thin rectangle. Cover and chill for 1 hour.

Cover the top of the meat rectangle with the cheese slices. Roll up the meat like a jelly roll, using the paper to lift it. Place in a

shallow roasting pan with the join underneath and brush with the melted butter. Bake in a moderate oven (180°C/350°F) for 50 minutes.

Meanwhile, make the sauce. Melt the butter in a saucepan and add the onions and garlic. Fry until the onions are soft but not brown. Add the tomatoes, sugar, salt and pepper to taste and the red wine, if using. Simmer for 45 minutes, stirring occasionally.

Transfer the meat roll to a warmed serving dish and pour over the sauce, or serve it separately in a sauceboat.
Serves 4-6

Beef carbonnade

60g/½ cup flour
salt and black pepper
1kg/2lb chuck steak, cut into 2.5cm/1in cubes
4 Tbsp vegetable oil
6 medium onions, thinly sliced
2 garlic cloves, chopped
500ml/1 pint beer
1 Tbsp brown sugar
1 bouquet garni

Sift the flour and salt and pepper to taste into a plastic bag. Add the steak cubes and shake the bag to coat them with the seasoned flour.

Heat the oil in a flameproof casserole. Add the meat cubes and brown quickly on all sides. Remove from the casserole. Add the onions and garlic to the casserole and fry until the onions are soft but not brown. Return the meat to the casserole with the beer, brown sugar and bouquet garni. Cover and simmer for 2 hours or until the meat is tender.

Above: Beef and Cheese Roll with Tomato Sauce makes a wholesome and tasty supper dish.

Overleaf: Marinated Beef Tenderloin – succulent and satisfying served with new potatoes and broccoli.

Thirty minutes before the end of the cooking, remove the lid so that the liquid will reduce. Discard the bouquet garni and serve hot, from the casserole.
Serves 4

Sirloin steaks teriyaki

4 sirloin steaks, about 6mm/¼in thick
2 Tbsp butter
1 Tbsp vegetable oil
MARINADE
4 Tbsp sweet sake or pale dry sherry
2 Tbsp soy sauce
1 garlic clove, crushed
4 Tbsp chicken stock

Mix together the ingredients for the marinade in a shallow dish. Add the steaks and baste them well with the marinade. Leave to marinate for 30 minutes, basting occasionally.

Remove the steaks from the marinade and pat dry with kitchen paper towels. Reserve 4 tablespoons of the marinade.

Melt the butter with the oil in a frying pan. Add the steaks and fry for 1 minute on each side. Pour off all but a thin film of fat from the pan and add the marinade. Fry the steaks for a further 3 minutes on each side, basting occasionally with the pan juices. This will produce rare steaks; increase time for medium or well-done.

Transfer the steaks to warmed serving dishes and spoon over the pan juices.
Serves 4

Marinated beef tenderloin

1 x 2kg/4lb beef tenderloin
salt and black pepper
8 bacon slices
MARINADE
300ml/1¼ cups red wine
125ml/½ cup tarragon vinegar
1 tsp grated nutmeg
1 tsp ground cloves
2 bay leaves
1 onion, sliced and pushed out into rings
½ lemon, thinly sliced
1 large carrot, scraped and thinly sliced
SAUCE
2 Tbsp vegetable oil
2 onions, finely chopped
1 large carrot, scraped and finely chopped
4 Tbsp brandy
375ml/1½ cups beef stock
1 bouquet garni
3 Tbsp butter
1 Tbsp flour

Rub the beef with salt and pepper and place in a shallow dish. Mix together all the marinade ingredients and pour over the beef. Leave to marinate for 24 hours.

Remove the beef from the marinade and pat dry with kitchen paper towels. Place the beef in a roasting pan. Strain the marinade and reserve 125ml/½ cup.

Lay the slices of bacon over the meat and roast in a hot oven (220°C/425°F) for 1 hour. This will produce rare meat. If you prefer it well-done, increase the cooking time by 30 minutes.

Meanwhile, make the sauce. Heat the oil in a saucepan. Add the onions and carrot and fry until the onions are soft but not brown. Stir in the reserved marinade and brandy and bring to a boil. Boil until the liquid has reduced to one-third the original quantity. Add the stock, bouquet garni and salt and pepper to taste. Cover and simmer for 30 minutes.

Mix ½ tablespoon of the butter with the flour to make a smooth paste (beurre manié). Add in small pieces to the sauce, stirring constantly, and cook until the sauce is thickened and smooth. Discard the bouquet garni and stir in the remaining butter. Pour the sauce into a sauceboat.

Transfer the meat to a carving board and discard the bacon. Carve into thick slices and serve with the sauce.
Serves 8

Spiced meatballs

1kg/2lb veal or beef, finely ground
1 medium onion, very finely chopped
60g/⅔ cup fresh white breadcrumbs
1 egg, lightly beaten
2 Tbsp parsley, freshly chopped
1 Tbsp mint, freshly chopped
2 tsp oregano, freshly chopped
2 garlic cloves, crushed
½ tsp ground allspice
salt and black pepper
2 Tbsp olive oil
1 Tbsp wine vinegar
125g/1 cup flour
125ml/½ cup vegetable oil

Mix together the meat, onion, breadcrumbs, egg, parsley, mint, oregano, garlic, allspice and salt and pepper to taste. Add the olive oil and vinegar and knead together with your hands. Shape the mixture into 32 walnut-sized balls. Coat the balls with half the flour, then chill for 1 hour.

Coat the balls with the remaining flour. Heat the vegetable oil in a frying pan. Add the balls, in batches, and fry for 6 to 8 minutes or until browned and cooked through. Drain on paper towels.

Serve hot, with a tomato sauce.
Serves 4

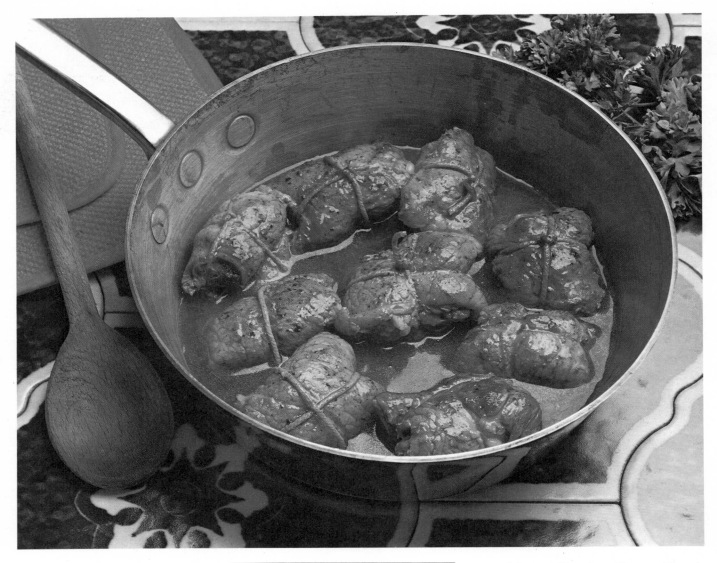

Veal Rolls Stuffed with Chicken Livers and Herbs makes an unusual and sophisticated supper dish.

Veal rolls stuffed with chicken livers and herbs

500g/1lb veal scallops, pounded thin
6 Tbsp flour
3 Tbsp butter
2 Tbsp vegetable oil
250ml/1 cup Marsala
250ml/1 cup chicken stock
STUFFING
2 Tbsp butter
125g/½ cup chicken livers, finely chopped
60g/¼ cup proscuitto, diced
1 small onion, finely chopped
1 tsp chives, freshly chopped
1 tsp parsley, freshly chopped
1 tsp marjoram, freshly chopped
1 tsp thyme, freshly chopped
salt and black pepper

First prepare the stuffing. Melt the butter in a saucepan. Add the chicken livers and fry until they are lightly browned but still soft. Remove from the heat and add the remaining stuffing ingredients with salt and pepper to taste. Mix well and leave to cool.

Cut the scallops into 10cm/4in squares. Place a heaped tablespoonful of the chicken liver filling in the center of each square and roll up, tucking in the sides. Tie with strong thread. Coat the veal rolls with the flour.

Melt the butter with the oil in a frying pan. Add the rolls, in batches, and fry for about 10 minutes or until they are well browned on all sides. Remove the rolls from the pan.

Pour off all but 1 tablespoon of the fat from the pan. Add the Marsala and chicken stock and bring to a boil. Return the veal rolls to the pan and simmer gently for 15 minutes or until the meat is cooked through and very tender.

Transfer the veal rolls to a warmed serving dish and keep hot. Boil the cooking liquid for about 10 minutes or until it has reduced to about 125ml/½ cup. Pour over the veal rolls and serve hot.

Serves 4

Greek roast veal

1 x 3kg/6lb shoulder of veal, boned
1 garlic clove, thinly sliced
salt and black pepper
finely grated rind of 1 lemon
finely grated rind of 1 orange
1 Tbsp marjoram, freshly chopped
2 Tbsp butter
1 Tbsp olive oil
2 Tbsp lemon juice
2 Tbsp orange juice
300ml/1¼ cups dry white wine (preferably resinated Greek wine)
1 bay leaf, crumbled
lemon wedges to garnish

Lay the veal flat on a working surface. Make incisions all over the meat and insert the garlic slivers. Rub the meat with salt and pepper and sprinkle with the orange and lemon rinds and marjoram. Roll up the meat and tie with string at 2.5cm/1in intervals.

Melt the butter with the oil in a flame-proof casserole. Put the veal roll in the casserole and brown on all sides. Remove from the heat.

Mix together the lemon and orange juice, the wine and bay leaf and pour over the veal. Return to the heat and bring to a boil. Cover and simmer gently for 2 hours or until the veal is tender.

Transfer the veal to a carving board. Remove the string. Garnish with the lemon wedges. Keep hot.

Skim any fat off the surface of the cooking liquid and strain it into a saucepan. Boil until it has reduced to half its original quantity. Pour into a sauceboat and serve with the meat.
Serves 6

Cantonese roast pork

1 x 1kg/2lb pork tenderloin
2 Tbsp vegetable oil
2½ Tbsp clear honey
MARINADE
4 Tbsp soy sauce
1 Tbsp sugar
3 Tbsp dry sherry
½ tsp ground cinnamon
½ tsp rosemary, freshly chopped
½ tsp marjoram, freshly chopped
½ tsp monosodium glutamate (optional)
salt and black pepper
SAUCE
125ml/½ cup soy sauce
4 Tbsp chili sauce

Cut the pork tenderloin along the grain into strips about 15cm/6in long and 2.5cm/1in wide. Mix together the in-gredients for the marinade, with salt and pepper to taste, in a shallow dish. Add the pork strips and turn them over in the marinade until well coated. Leave to marinate for 3 hours, turning the strips every 20 minutes.

Put enough water in a roasting pan to make a 2.5cm/1in layer. Place a wire rack in the pan. Arrange the pork strips on the rack, reserving the marinade. Roast in a hot oven (220°C/425°F) for 12 minutes.

Mix the oil into the reserved marinade and brush this mixture over the pork strips. Reduce the oven temperature to moderate (180°C/350°F) and roast the pork for a further 10 minutes.

Brush the pork strips with the honey and continue roasting for 5 minutes.

To make the sauce, mix the ingredients together well and pour into a medium-size serving bowl.

Cut the pork strips crosswise into 1cm/½in slices and serve hot with the sauce, rice and hot mustard.
Serves 4

Pork tenderloin in sour cream and vermouth sauce

4 medium pieces pork tenderloin
salt
60g/¼ cup butter
1 garlic clove, crushed
6 black peppercorns
300ml/1¼ cups dry vermouth
2 tsp cornstarch
150ml/⅔ cup sour cream
1 Tbsp chives, freshly chopped

Rub the pork with the salt. Melt the butter in a frying pan. Add the pork, in batches, and fry until they are lightly browned on all sides. Transfer the pork to an ovenproof casserole.

Sprinkle the garlic and peppercorns over the pork and pour over all but 1 tablespoon of the vermouth. Cover and bake in a moderate oven (180°C/350°F) for 45 minutes or until the pork is cooked through and tender.

Transfer the pork to a warmed serving dish and keep hot. Skim off any fat from the surface of the cooking liquid and strain it into a saucepan. Dissolve the corn-starch in the reserved tablespoon of vermouth and stir into the cooking liquid into it. Pour into cooking liquid in a thin stream. Cook, stirring, for 2 minutes or until thickened and smooth. Add the sour cream and stir well. Heat through gently without boiling.

Pour the sauce over the pork and sprinkle with the chives. Serve hot.
Serves 4

Fresh orange juice is just one of the ingredients in the piquant and refreshing recipe for Greek roast veal.

Pork chops with white wine and herbs

1 Tbsp oregano, freshly chopped
1 Tbsp marjoram, freshly chopped
1 garlic clove, crushed
salt and black pepper
4 large pork loin chops
60g/¼ cup butter
125ml/½ cup dry white wine
1 tsp cornstarch
1 Tbsp parsley, freshly chopped

Mix together the oregano, marjoram, garlic and salt and pepper to taste. Coat both sides of the pork chops with the herb mixture, pressing it on well.

Melt the butter in a frying pan. Add the chops and fry for 3 minutes on each side, using tongs to turn them. Pour in half the wine and bring to a boil. Cover and cook for 30 to 40 minutes or until tender.

Transfer the chops to a warmed serving dish and keep hot. Dissolve the cornstarch in the remaining wine, stir in a little of the hot liquid and add to the pan, stirring constantly. Bring to a boil, stirring well. Simmer for 3 to 5 minutes or until thickened and smooth and pour over the chops. Sprinkle with the parsley and serve.
Serves 4

Pork and pineapple casserole

1 x 1kg/2lb pork tenderloin, beaten thin
1 garlic clove, halved
salt and black pepper
1 Tbsp finely grated orange rind
1½ tsp marjoram, freshly chopped
1½ tsp sage, freshly chopped
2 Tbsp butter
2 medium green peppers, pith and seeds removed and cut into thin strips
300ml/1¼ cups dry white wine
½ medium pineapple, peeled, cored and coarsely chopped
1 Tbsp cornstarch
2 Tbsp orange juice

Rub the escalopes with the cut sides of the garlic and with salt and pepper. Discard the garlic. Lay the pork flat on a working surface and sprinkle over the orange rind, marjoram and sage. Roll up the escalopes and tie with string.

Melt the butter in a flameproof casserole. Add the green pepper strips and fry for 4 minutes, stirring frequently. Remove from the casserole.

Add the pork rolls to the casserole and brown on all sides. Add the wine, pineapple, green pepper strips and salt and pepper to taste. Bring to boil, then cover and simmer for 30 to 40 minutes or until the pork is cooked and tender.

Transfer the pork rolls to a warmed serving dish. Remove the string. Arrange the pineapple pieces and green pepper strips around the pork rolls. Keep hot.

Skim any fat off the surface of the cooking liquid, then strain into s saucepan. Dissolve the cornstarch in the orange juice. Stir a little of the hot cooking liquid into this mixture. Return the mixture to the saucepan and stir into the cooking liquid. Bring to a boil and simmer for 5 minutes or until thickened and smooth.
Pour the sauce over the pork rolls.
Serves 4

Lamb with cider sauce

1 rack of lamb, consisting of 8 chops
(carré d'agneau)
salt and black pepper
1 garlic clove, halved
2 Tbsp olive oil
2 carrots, scraped and chopped
2 small turnips, peeled and quartered
2 leeks, white part only, chopped
2 small onions, chopped
2 bacon slices, chopped
2 tsp chervil, freshly chopped
300ml/1¼ cups chicken stock
300ml/1¼ cups hard cider
4 Tbsp fresh white breadcrumbs
2 Tbsp butter
4 Tbsp flour

Rub the lamb with salt and pepper and the cut sides of the garlic. Discard the garlic. Heat the oil in a large flameproof casserole. Put the meat in the casserole and brown on each side. Remove from the casserole.

Add the carrots, turnips, leeks, onions and bacon to the casserole and fry for 10 minutes, stirring frequently. Return the meat to the casserole and add the chervil. Pour in the stock and cider and bring to a boil. Cover and transfer to a moderate oven (180°C/350°F). Bake for 1 hour.

Remove the casserole from the oven and transfer the meat to the rack in the broiler pan, fat side up. Coat with the breadcrumbs and broil for 5 minutes or until the crumbs are evenly browned.

Meanwhile, strain the cooking liquid from the casserole into a saucepan. Discard the vegetables. Mix together the butter and flour to make a smooth paste (beurre manié) and add in small pieces to the cooking liquid. Cook, stirring constantly, for 5 minutes or until the sauce thickens and is smooth.

Place the meat on a warmed serving dish and serve with the sauce.
Serves 4

Pork and Pineapple Casserole is a deliciously flavored combination of fruit and meat which makes an ideal lunch or supper dish.

Loin of Lamb with Peas and Beans is a fresh tasting dish which tastes as good as it looks.

Loin of lamb with peas and beans

60g/¼ cup butter
1 Tbsp olive oil
1 medium onion, thinly sliced
6 bacon slices, diced
1 x 2kg/4lb loin of lamb, chined
500g/3 cups green peas (shelled)
250g/8oz green beans, trimmed
150ml/⅔ cup sour cream

Melt the butter with the oil in a roasting pan. Add the onion and bacon and fry until the onion is soft but not brown and the bacon has rendered its fat. Add the lamb and cook for 5 to 10 minutes, or until it is brown on all sides.

Transfer to a fairly hot oven (200°C/400°F) and roast for 20 minutes.

Add the peas and beans to the roasting pan and reduce the oven temperature to warm (170°C/325°F). Roast for a further 1 hour 10 minutes, or until the meat and vegetables are tender.

Transfer the lamb to a carving board. Strain off all but about 1 tablespoon of fat from the roasting pan. Stir the sour cream into the vegetable mixture and spoon into a warmed serving dish.

Carve the meat into thick slices and serve with the vegetables.
Serves 4-6

Saddle of lamb with mint

1 x 3kg/6lb saddle of lamb
salt and black pepper
8 lemon thyme sprigs
60g/⅔ cup fresh brown breadcrumbs
2 Tbsp mint, freshly chopped
1 small onion, grated
1 Tbsp butter, melted
185ml/¾ cup chicken stock
½ Tbsp butter
1 Tbsp flour

Rub the meat with salt and pepper. Insert the lemon thyme sprigs between the meat and the fat. Place the saddle, fat side uppermost, on a rack in a roasting pan.

Mix together the breadcrumbs, mint, onion and salt and pepper to taste. Stir in the melted butter. Spread this mixture evenly over the fat on the saddle.

Roast in a moderate oven (180°C/350°F) for 1 hour. Reduce the oven temperature to cool (150°C/300°F) and continue roasting for a further 1 to 1¼ hours or until the meat is cooked and tender.

Transfer the meat to a carving board. Keep hot.

Skim any fat from the surface of the cooking juices in the roasting pan. Strain the juices into a saucepan and stir in the stock. Bring to a boil. Mix the butter with the flour to make a smooth paste (beurre manié) and add to the saucepan in small pieces. Cook, stirring, until the gravy is thickened and smooth.

Serve the meat, accompanied by the sauce.
Serves 6-8

Roast leg of lamb with lemon and lima bean sauce

1 x 2kg/4lb leg of lamb
4 garlic cloves, cut into slivers
salt and black pepper
2 Tbsp vegetable oil
2 egg yolks
4 Tbsp lemon juice
250ml/1 cup chicken stock
500g/2 cups lima beans (shelled)
2 tsp thyme, freshly chopped

Make slits in the lamb and insert the garlic slivers. Rub the meat with salt and pepper and place on a rack in a roasting pan. Pour over the oil and roast in a moderate oven (180°C/350°F) for 1½ hours or until the lamb is cooked. Baste occasionally with the drippings in the roasting pan.

Meanwhile, mix together the egg yolks, lemon juice and stock in a small bowl. Cook the lima beans in boiling salted water for 10 to 15 minutes or until just tender.

Drain the lima beans well and put them aside.

Transfer the lamb to a carving board. Remove the garlic slivers, if you like. Keep hot.

Skim off any fat from the cooking juices in the roasting pan. Add the juices to the egg yolk mixture and pour into a saucepan. Add the lima beans, thyme and salt and pepper to taste and cook gently, stirring occasionally, until the sauce is thickened and smooth. Do not let the sauce boil or it will curdle. Pour the sauce into a sauce-boat and serve with the lamb.

Serves 6

Ham with tarragon cream sauce

1 x 2kg/4lb smoked ham
2 bay leaves
6 peppercorns
2 thyme sprigs
SAUCE
1 medium onion, finely chopped
4 Tbsp white wine
60g/¼ cup butter
2 Tbsp flour
300ml/1¼ cups chicken stock
1 Tbsp tarragon, freshly chopped
salt and black pepper
150ml/⅔ cup heavy cream

Put the ham in a saucepan with the bay leaves, peppercorns and thyme spring. Cover with cold water and bring slowly to a boil. Simmer for 2 hours, skimming off any scum that rises to the surface and adding more water, if necessary. Turn off the heat and leave the ham in the water for 30 minutes.

Meanwhile, prepare the sauce. Put the onion and wine in a saucepan and bring to a boil. Simmer until the wine has evaporated, then remove the sauce-pan from the heat.

Melt 3 tablespoons of the butter in another saucepan. Remove from the heat and stir in the flour to make a smooth paste. Gradually stir in the stock. Return to the heat and cook, stirring, for 3 to 4 minutes or until the mixture is thickened and smooth. Stir in the onion and tarragon with salt and pepper to taste. Cook for 2 minutes, stirring constantly.

Stir in the cream and remaining butter and heat through without boiling. Keep warm.

Remove the ham from the pan. Peel off the skin and fat and carve the meat into thin slices. Arrange on a warmed serving dish and pour over the sauce.

Serve hot.

Serves 6-8

Marinated liver in red wine sauce

75ml/⅓ cup olive oil
300ml/1¼ cups dry red wine
1 garlic clove, crushed
1 bay leaf
salt and black pepper
1kg/2lb calf's or lamb's liver, thinly sliced
6 bacon slices, very thinly sliced into strips
1 Tbsp parsley, freshly chopped

Mix together 4 tablespoons of the oil, the wine, garlic, bay leaf and salt and pepper to taste in a shallow dish. Add the liver slices and marinate for 30 minutes.

Heat the remaining oil in a frying pan. Add the bacon and fry until it is crisp. Drain on paper towels and keep hot. Remove the liver slices from the marinade and pat dry with paper towels. Add to the pan, in batches, and fry until lightly browned on all sides. Remove from the pan, transfer to a warmed serving dish and keep hot.

Add the marinade to the pan. Bring to a boil for 10 minutes or until reduced to about one-third of the original quantity. Add the bacon to the liver and strain over the marinade. Sprinkle with the parsley and serve hot.

Serves 4

A well-known Portuguese dish, Marinated Liver in Red Wine Sauce tastes simply delicious.

Spiced chicken with honey

60g/¼ cup butter
125ml/½ cup clear honey
4 Tbsp prepared German mustard
1 tsp salt
1 tsp mild curry powder
2kg/4lb chicken, cut into 8 serving pieces

Spiced Chicken with Honey is very simple to prepare but tastes magnificent. Serve for lunch or supper.

Melt the butter in a saucepan and stir in the honey, mustard, salt and curry powder. Pour half the mixture into a roasting pan. Place the chicken pieces in the pan and pour over the remaining honey mixture.

Bake in a fairly hot oven (190°C/375°F) for 1 hour or until the chicken is tender. Baste the chicken with the honey mixture in the pan at least twice during the cooking period.

Transfer the chicken to a warmed serving dish and spoon over any honey mixture in the pan. Serve hot.

Serves 4

Mozzarella chicken

2 Tbsp vegetable oil
1 medium onion, finely chopped
500g/1lb tomatoes, peeled and chopped
2 Tbsp tomato paste
3 Tbsp water
1 Tbsp oregano, freshly chopped
salt and black pepper
6 bacon slices
25g/1oz butter
1 tsp tarragon, freshly chopped
6 chicken breasts, skinned and boned
125g/4oz mozzarella cheese, sliced

Heat the oil in a saucepan. Add the onion and fry until it is soft but not brown. Add the tomatoes, tomato paste, water, oregano and salt and pepper to taste. Simmer for 20 minutes, stirring occasionally.

Meanwhile, fry the bacon in a frying pan until it is crisp. Drain on paper towels. Add the butter to the bacon fat in the pan. When it has melted stir in the tarragon. Add the chicken breasts and fry for 15 to 20 minutes or until tender and cooked through.

Transfer the chicken breasts to a flameproof serving dish. Place a slice of bacon on each breast and pour over the tomato sauce. Cover with the cheese slices. Broil for 4 to 5 minutes or until the cheese has melted and is lightly browned. Serve hot.

Serves 6

Chicken with shrimp and asparagus

2 Tbsp butter
1 x 2.5kg/5lb chicken, cut into 8 serving pieces
2 small onions, finely chopped
3 Tbsp flour
500ml/1 pint chicken stock
Salt and black pepper
½ tsp paprika
¼ tsp cayenne pepper
2 tsp dill, freshly chopped
1 bay leaf
2 Tbsp Madeira
500g/1lb asparagus
250g/1⅓ cups shrimp (shelled), deveined
150ml/⅔ cup heavy cream

Melt the butter in a flameproof casserole. Add the chicken pieces, in batches, and brown on all sides. Remove from the casserole.

Add the onions to the casserole and fry until they are soft but not brown. Remove from the heat and sprinkle over the flour. Stir well, then gradually stir in the stock. Add salt and pepper to taste, the paprika, cayenne, dill, bay leaf and Madeira and mix well. Return to the heat and bring to a boil, stirring.

Return the chicken pieces to the casserole. Cover and cook for 30 minutes. Add the asparagus and shrimp to the casserole. Re-cover and cook for a further 30 minutes or until the chicken is tender.

Transfer the chicken pieces to a warmed serving dish. Arrange the asparagus around the chicken. Keep hot.

Stir the cream into the casserole and heat through without boiling. Discard the bay leaf and pour the sauce over the chicken and asparagus. Serve hot.

Serves 4-6

Chicken stuffed with chicken livers, cream cheese and herbs

6 Tbsp butter, softened
1 large onion, finely chopped
1 x 2.5kg/5lb chicken or capon
4 chicken livers, finely chopped
2 tsp thyme, freshly chopped
2 tsp marjoram, freshly chopped
2 tsp chervil, freshly chopped
1 Tbsp parsley, freshly chopped
125g/½ cup cream cheese
60g/1 cup fine dry breadcrumbs
Salt and black pepper
SAUCE
150ml/⅔ cup dry white wine
150ml/⅔ cup chicken stock
150ml/⅔ cup light cream

Melt 2 tablespoons of the butter in a frying pan. Add the onion and fry until it is soft but not brown. Add the chicken livers, thyme, marjoram, chervil and parsley. Fry for a further 3 minutes, stirring frequently. Remove from the heat and allow to cool slightly, then stir in the cream cheese, breadcrumbs and salt and pepper to taste.

Stuff the chicken with the cream cheese mixture and truss. Place the chicken in a roasting pan and rub with salt and pepper. Spread with the remaining butter. Roast in a medium oven (190°C/357°F) for 1½ hours.

Mix together the wine, stock and cream and pour into the pan around the chicken 30 minutes before the end of the cooking time.

Transfer the chicken to a warmed serving dish and untruss. Skim any fat from the surface of the cooking liquid, adjust the seasoning and pour into a sauceboat. Serve this gravy with the chicken.

Serves 6

Marmalade duck

1 x 3kg/5lb duck
salt and black pepper
1 orange, peeled and quartered
1 bouquet garni
500g/1lb marmalade
juice of 2 oranges
1 Tbsp brandy
1 tsp cornstarch
1 Tbsp water
GARNISH
2 large oranges, sliced
8 watercress sprigs

Marmalade Duck – succulent duck roasted with bitter sweet marmalade and served with an orange and brandy sauce is the perfect dinner party dish.

Rub the cavity in the duck with salt and pepper. Put the orange quarters and bouquet garni inside and truss the duck. Place it on a large piece of aluminum foil and spread the duck with the marmalade. Wrap the foil loosely around the duck and place on a rack in a roasting pan. Make several cuts in the bottom of the foil to allow the duck fat to drip into the roasting pan.

Roast in a very hot oven (220°C/425°F) for 15 minutes. Reduce the oven temperature to moderate (190°C/350°F) and continue roasting for 1½ hours, or until the juices run clear when the thigh is pierced.

Remove the foil 20 minutes before the end of roasting to allow the skin to brown. Transfer the duck to a warmed serving dish. Untruss and keep hot.

Skim any fat off the surface of the liquid in the roasting pan. Stir in the orange juice and brandy and place over heat on top of the stove. Bring to a boil, stirring. Boil for 5 minutes. Dissolve the cornstarch in the water and stir a little of the hot liquid into the mixture. Stir back into the gravy. Simmer for 2 minutes, stirring, or until thickened and smooth. Strain the gravy into a sauceboat.

Arrange the orange slices and watercress around the duck and serve at once, with the gravy.

Serves 4

Vegetables

Souffléd carrots

625ml/2½ cups chicken stock
500g/1lb carrots, scraped and quartered
salt and white pepper
2 tsp marjoram, freshly chopped
1 tsp flour
3 eggs, separated

Bring the stock to a boil in a saucepan. Add the carrots and cook for 10 to 15 minutes or until they are tender. Drain the carrots, reserving 2 tablespoons of the stock. Purée the carrots in a blender or food mill or push them through a strainer into a mixing bowl. Alternatively, use a potato masher. Season the carrot purée well and stir in the marjoram, flour and reserved stock. Lightly beat the egg yolks together and stir into the carrot mixture.

Beat the egg whites until they will hold a stiff peak. Fold them into the carrot mixture. Spoon into a buttered shallow baking dish and bake in a moderate oven (180°C/350°F) for 15 minutes.

Remove from the oven and serve hot, from the dish.
Serves 4

Green beans with tomato sauce

2 Tbsp butter
1 Tbsp olive oil
1 garlic clove, crushed
1 onion, finely chopped
1 small red pepper, pith and seeds removed and chopped
1 small carrot, scraped and chopped
750g/1½lb tomatoes, peeled and chopped
1 Tsp sugar
salt and black pepper
500g/1lb green beans
1 Tbsp parsley, freshly chopped

Melt the butter with the oil in a saucepan. Add the garlic, onion, red pepper and carrot and fry until the onion is soft but not brown. Add the tomatoes, sugar and salt and pepper to taste. Simmer gently for 40 minutes.

Fifteen minutes before the sauce is ready, cook the beans in boiling salted water for about 10 minutes or until they are just tender. Drain well and stir them into the tomato sauce. Simmer for a further 2 minutes.

Pour the beans and sauce into a warmed serving dish and sprinkle with the parsley. Serve hot.
Serves 4

Mixed vegetables in cream sauce

1 small cauliflower, broken into flowerets
125g/¾ cup green peas (shelled)
125g/1 cup green beans
4 small carrots, diced
250g/8oz asparagus
4 small button mushrooms
3 Tbsp butter
2 Tbsp flour
300ml/1¼ cups light cream
150ml/⅔ cup milk
salt and black pepper
2 tsp chervil, freshly chopped
1 tsp lemon juice

Cook the cauliflower, peas and beans in boiling salted water for 10 to 15 minutes or until they are tender. Add the carrot dice after about 7 minutes cooking. Meanwhile, cook the asparagus, with the tips just above the water, in gently simmering water for 10 to 15 minutes or until tender. Do not overcook the vegetables; they should be tender but still firm.

Meanwhile, cook the mushrooms in 1 tablespoon of the butter in a small saucepan for 2 to 3 minutes.

Drain all the vegetables. Cut the asparagus into 2.5cm/1in pieces. Put all the vegetables in a warmed serving dish and keep hot.

Melt the remaining butter in a saucepan. Stir in the flour and cook for 1 minute. Remove from the heat and gradually stir in the cream and milk. Return to the heat and simmer, stirring constantly, until the sauce is thickened and smooth. Stir in salt and pepper to taste and the chervil.

Remove from the heat and stir in the lemon juice. Pour the sauce over the vegetables and mix well. Serve hot.
Serves 4

Rice with peas, Venetian style

1 Tbsp olive oil
10 bacon slices, chopped
60g/¼ cup butter
1 onion, thinly sliced
500g/3 cups green peas (shelled)
500g/1lb Italian rice, such as Avorio
75ml/⅓ cup dry white wine
1.2l/2½ pints chicken stock, boiling
salt and black pepper
125g/1 cup Parmesan cheese, grated

Heat the oil in a saucepan. Add the bacon and fry until it is crisp and golden brown. Drain the bacon on paper towels.

Add 2 tablespoons of the butter to the

Fresh, crunchy carrots and cauliflowers are ideal for serving with spring dishes.

Oysterplant Sautéed with Herbs is an unusual vegetable dish, but one that's well worth trying.

fat in the pan and when it has melted add the onion. Fry until the onion is soft but not brown. Add the peas and rice and cook gently, stirring, for 5 minutes. Stir in the wine and about one-third of the boiling stock. Regulate the heat so that the mixture is bubbling all the time, and stir occasionally with a fork. When the rice swells and the liquid has been absorbed, add another one-third of the boiling stock. Add the remaining stock when that has been absorbed.

Stir in the bacon, remaining butter, salt and pepper to taste and the cheese. Mix well, reduce the heat to low and cook gently for 1 minute.

Transfer to a warmed serving dish.
Serves 4-6

Oysterplant sautéed with herbs

500g/1lb oysterplant, scraped and cut
into 7.5cm/3in pieces
2 Tbsp butter
1 garlic clove, crushed
1 tsp chervil, freshly chopped
1 tsp oregano, freshly chopped
2 Tbsp parsley, freshly chopped
Salt and black pepper
1 tsp lemon juice

Cook the oyster plant in boiling salted water for about 20 minutes or until it is just tender. Drain well and keep warm.

Melt the butter in a frying pan. Add the garlic and fry for 1 minute. Add the oyster plant, chervil, oregano, parsley and salt and pepper to taste and fry, stirring, for 6 to 8 minutes or until the oyster plant is lightly browned.

Transfer to a warmed serving dish and sprinkle over the lemon juice. Serve hot.
Serves 4

Chinese fried cucumber and pineapple

2 medium cucumbers, thinly sliced
2 Tbsp vegetable oil
½ tsp salt
1 Tbsp vinegar
½ small pineapple, peeled, cored and
cut into cubes
175ml/¾ cup water
2 tsp flour
1 tsp sugar
1 tsp soy sauce

Salt the cucumber slices and leave for 30 minutes in a colander. Rinse, drain and pat the cucumber slices dry with paper towels. Heat the oil in a frying pan. Add the cucumber slices, salt and vinegar and cook for 4 minutes. Add the pineapple and cook for 2 minutes longer.

Mix together the water, flour, sugar and soy sauce in a small bowl, stirring well to dissolve the flour. Pour into the frying pan and cook, stirring constantly, for a further 5 minutes or until the liquid has thickened. Serve hot.

Serves 4

Spinach baked with noodles

125g/½ cup butter
2 onions, finely chopped
1.5kg/3lb spinach
salt and black pepper
2 eggs, lightly beaten
375g/12oz egg noodles, cooked
90g/¾ cup Parmesan cheese, grated
90g/1½ cups dry white breadcrumbs
SAUCE
3 Tbsp butter
3 Tbsp flour
500ml/1 pint milk

Melt half the butter in a frying pan. Add the onions and fry until they are soft but not brown.

Meanwhile, put the spinach in a saucepan. (Do not add any water: there should be enough left on the leaves after washing.) Cook for about 6 minutes or until the spinach is tender.

Drain the spinach well, pressing to remove all excess moisture. Chop the spinach finely and add to the onions with salt and pepper to taste. Stir in the eggs and cook gently, stirring, for 2 minutes or until the eggs are just beginning to set. Remove from the heat.

Arrange half the egg noodles in a baking dish. Sprinkle with half the cheese and cover with half the spinach mixture. Add layers of the remaining egg noodles, cheese and spinach mixture.

To make the sauce, melt the butter in a saucepan. Stir in the flour and cook, stirring, for 1 minute. Gradually stir in the milk and bring to a boil, stirring constantly. Simmer, stirring, until the sauce is thickened and smooth. Add salt and pepper to taste, then pour over the top of the spinach and noodle mixture.

Melt the remaining butter in a frying pan. Add the breadcrumbs and remove from the heat. Spoon over the sauce. Bake in a fairly hot oven (190°C/375°F) for 20 minutes or until the breadcrumb topping is golden brown. Serve hot, from the dish.

Serves 4-6

Spinach Baked with Noodles makes a filling lunch or supper dish, ideal for vegetarians.

Above: Snow peas are a variety of pea of which the pod is also eaten.
Right: Thinly sliced pickled cucumbers in a vinegar and dill dressing can be used as a garnish, or served with meat and poultry dishes.

Salads

Pickled cucumber salad

8 cucumbers
salt and black pepper
1 Tbsp sugar
125ml/½ cup white vinegar
1 Tbsp lemon juice
3 Tbsp dill, freshly chopped

Score down the skin of the cucumbers with a fork to make ridges. Cut the cucumbers into very thin slices. Put the slices in a shallow dish and sprinkle generously with salt. Cover and leave for 1 hour.

Meanwhile, mix together the sugar, vinegar, lemon juice and salt and pepper to taste. Stir well to dissolve the sugar.

Drain the cucumber slices and pat dry with paper towels. Arrange the slices in a serving dish and pour over the vinegar dressing. Sprinkle with the dill and chill for at least 3 hours before serving.
Serves 4

Snow pea salad

4 dried Chinese mushrooms, soaked in cold water for 30 minutes
1 Tbsp vegetable oil
175g/6oz can bamboo shoots, drained and thinly sliced
375g/12oz snow peas
1 celery stalk, cut into 5cm/2in pieces
1 tsp salt
½ tsp sugar
1 tsp white wine vinegar

Drain the mushrooms, reserving 1 tablespoon of the soaking liquid. Thinly slice the mushrooms. Heat the oil in a frying pan. Add the mushroom slices and bamboo shoots and fry for 2 minutes, stirring constantly. Add the snow peas and celery and cook, stirring, for 2 minutes.

Sprinkle the salt, sugar, vinegar and reserved soaking liquid over the vegetables. Cook, stirring, for a further 2 minutes.

Transfer the vegetables to a serving dish and allow to cool. Then chill for at least 1 hour before serving.
Serves 4

Avocado chervil salad

4 avocados
125ml/½ cup lemon juice
salt and black pepper
1 Tbsp chervil, freshly chopped

Halve the avocados and remove the seeds. Peel off the skin and cut the flesh into thin slices. Place the slices in a shallow glass dish and pour over the lemon juice. Season with salt and pepper and toss the slices so they are well coated with the lemon juice.

Sprinkle with the chervil and serve.
Serves 4

Fennel, endive and tomato salad

1 head, Florence fennel, thinly sliced
1 head French or Belgian endive, thinly sliced
4 tomatoes, thinly sliced
4 Tbsp olive oil
2 Tbsp white wine vinegar
1 garlic clove, crushed
salt and black pepper

Put the fennel, endive and tomato slices in a salad bowl. Mix together the oil, vinegar, garlic and salt and pepper to taste in a screwtop jar and shake well. Pour this dressing over the vegetables and toss. Chill for 30 minutes before serving.
Serves 4-6

Picnic Fare

Veal cake

500g/1lb lean veal, cut into 1cm/½in
cubes
500g/1lb (2 cups) cooked ham, cubed
salt and black pepper
2 Tbsp parsley, freshly chopped
1 tsp celery salt
2 tsp thyme, freshly chopped
6 eggs, hard-cooked and sliced
500ml/1 pint veal or chicken stock,
jellied

Mix together the veal, ham, salt and pepper to taste, the parsley, celery salt and thyme in a mixing bowl. Layer the meat mixture and egg slices in a 1.2l/2½ pint capacity steaming mold, beginning and ending with the meat mixture. Pour over the stock. Cover with foil and secure with string.

Put the mold in a saucepan and add enough water to come halfway up the sides. Bring to a boil and simmer for 2 hours, adding more water when necessary.

Remove the mold from the pan and take off the foil cover. Cool, then chill for at least 4 hours or until set. Dip the bottom of the mold quickly in hot water and turn out the cake onto a plate. Wrap carefully and chill until you leave for the picnic.
Serves 4-6

Meat loaf

1.5kg/3lb lean beef, ground
4 bacon slices, finely chopped
2 tsp thyme, freshly chopped
salt and black pepper
1 garlic clove, crushed
4 Tbsp red wine
1 Tbsp wine vinegar
1 tsp prepared French mustard

Mix together the beef, bacon, thyme, salt and pepper to taste, the garlic, wine, vinegar and mustard in a mixing bowl. Knead well together with your hands. Put the meat mixture into a greased large loaf pan and smooth the top. Place the pan in a roasting pan and add enough water to come halfway up the pan.

Bake in a warm oven (170°C/325°F) for 1 hour. Cover the loaf pan with foil to prevent the top browning too much and continue baking for 30 minutes.

Remove the pan from the oven and pour off any fat. Leave to cool for 1 hour, then turn out of the pan and wrap in aluminum foil. Chill for at least 6 hours before packing in the picnic basket.
Serves 6-8

Bean salad

250g/¾ cup dried red kidney beans,
soaked overnight
175g/½ cup dried white beans, such as
navy or pea beans, soaked
overnight
125g/½ cup dried garbanzos, soaked
overnight
1 red pepper, pith and seeds removed
and chopped
3 scallions, chopped
1 garlic clove, crushed
2 Tbsp chives, freshly chopped
2 Tbsp white wine vinegar
6 Tbsp olive oil
1 Tbsp lemon juice
salt and black pepper

Drain the beans and garbanzos and put in a saucepan. Cover with fresh water and bring to a boil. Simmer for 40 minutes or until the beans and garbanzos are tender. Remove from the heat, drain well, set aside and allow to cool.

Put the beans and garbanzos in a salad bowl and add the red pepper, scallions, garlic and chives. Mix together the vinegar, oil, lemon juice and salt and pepper to taste in a screwtop jar. Shake well and pour over the bean mixture. Toss well so all the ingredients are thoroughly coated with the dressing.

Spoon into a plastic container and chill for at least 30 minutes before packing into the picnic basket.
Serves 6-8

Ideal for a spring picnic, this cold Meat Loaf goes well in sandwiches or with salads.

Potato salad with herbs

500g/1lb potatoes
8 scallions, chopped
1 Tbsp parsley, freshly chopped
2 tsp marjoram, freshly chopped
1 tsp lemon thyme, freshly chopped
1 tsp chervil, freshly chopped
6 Tbsp olive oil
2 Tbsp wine vinegar
salt and black pepper
½ tsp sugar

Cook the potatoes in boiling salted water until tender, then drain well and slip off the skins. Allow to cool until you are able to handle them comfortably. Cut the potatoes into 1cm/½in cubes.

Put the potato cubes in a mixing bowl and add the scallions, parsley, marjoram, lemon thyme and chervil. Mix together the oil, vinegar, salt and pepper to taste and the sugar in a screwtop jar, shaking well to dissolve the sugar. Pour this dressing over the potato mixture and toss well until all the potato cubes are thoroughly coated with the dressing.

Pack into a plastic container and chill well before transferring the mixture to the picnic basket.
Serves 4

Pissaladières

PASTRY
250g/2 cups flour
½ tsp salt
60g/¼ cup butter
60g/¼ cup shortening
3-4 Tbsp iced water
FILLING
4 Tbsp olive oil
6 medium onions, thinly sliced
2 garlic cloves, crushed
3 large tomatoes, peeled, seeded and finely chopped
1 Tbsp tomato paste
50g/2oz can anchovies, drained and chopped
27 black olives, pitted
salt and black pepper

First make the pastry cases. Sift the flour and salt into a mixing bowl. Add the butter and shortening and cut them into small pieces, then rub into the flour until the mixture resembles breadcrumbs. Mix in enough water to form a dough. Chill for 30 minutes.

Roll out the dough to an oblong about 2cm/¾in thick. Cut out nine circles using a 10cm/4in cookie cutter. Use the circles to line nine greased tartlet pans or shallow muffin pans. Place the pans on a baking sheet and line each with crumpled wax paper.

Bake the pastry cases in a fairly hot oven (190°C/375°F) for 10 minutes, then remove the crumpled wax paper. Bake for a further 5 minutes or until the pastry is golden brown. Cool in the pans for 5 minutes, then carefully remove and cool completely on a wire rack.

Meanwhile, make the filling. Heat the oil in a frying pan. Add the onions and garlic and fry until the onions are soft but not brown. Stir in the tomatoes, tomato paste, anchovies, olives and salt and pepper to taste. Cook for a further 2 to 3 minutes.

Remove from the heat and spoon the filling into the pastry shell. Allow to cool before wrapping in foil for the picnic.
Makes 9 tartlets

Picnic patties

3 Tbsp butter
½ small onion, finely chopped
125g/1 cup mushrooms, sliced
2 Tbsp flour
salt and black pepper
¼ tsp grated nutmeg
1 tsp oregano, freshly chopped
¼ tsp Tabasco sauce
125ml/½ cup light cream
250g/1 cup cooked chicken, diced
125g/½ cup cooked ham, diced
PASTRY
350g/3 cups flour
¼ tsp salt
300g/1¼ cups butter
6-7 Tbsp iced water
1 egg yolk
2 Tbsp milk

First make the pastry. Sift the flour and salt into a mixing bowl. Add ¼ cup of the butter and cut it into small pieces with a knife. Rub the butter into the flour until the mixture resembles breadcrumbs. Stir in enough of the water to bind the mixture, then knead to a dough. Chill for 15 minutes.

Roll out the dough to an oblong about 6mm/¼in thick. Place the remaining butter, in an oblong piece about 6mm/¼in thick, in the center of the dough. Fold over the dough in half to enclose the butter. Turn so the open end faces you and roll out to an oblong. Fold the oblong in three and turn again so the open end faces you. Roll out to an oblong once again and fold in three. Chill for 15 minutes.

Repeat the rolling, folding, turning and chilling twice.

During the final chilling, prepare the filling. Melt 2 tablespoons of the butter in a saucepan. Add the onion and fry until it is soft but not brown. Add the mushrooms

Delicious savory tartlets, Pissaladieres are ideal for picnics but make tasty snacks any time of the day.

and cook for 3 to 4 minutes. Remove the vegetables from the pan with a slotted spoon.

Add the remaining butter to the pan. When it has melted, stir in the flour, salt and pepper to taste, the nutmeg, oregano and Tabasco. Cook, stirring, for 1 minute. Remove from the heat and gradually stir in the cream. Return to the heat and cook, stirring, until the mixture is thickened and smooth. Remove from the heat.

Stir the cooked onion and mushrooms into the sauce with the chicken and ham. Leave to cool slightly.

Roll out the dough to a circle about 3mm/⅛in thick. Cut out twelve 13cm/5in circles with a cookie cutter. Mix together the egg yolk and milk. Brush around the edges of the circles. Spoon equal amounts of the mushroom filling onto the center of each pastry circle and fold over the dough to make half-moon shapes. Press the edges together to seal. Brush with the egg-yolk glaze.

Place the patties on a baking sheet and bake in a hot oven (220°C/425°F) for 20 to 25 minutes or until the pastry is puffed up and golden brown.

Cool on a wire rack before wrapping in aluminum foil.

Makes 12 patties

Picnic Patties, stuffed with mushrooms, chicken and ham, are ideal for spring picnics, especially when served with a chilled wine.

Stuffed cucumbers

2 cucumbers, peeled and halved lengthwise
salt and black pepper
125g/4oz can tuna fish, drained and flaked
125g/½ cup cooked ham, diced
2 eggs, hard cooked and finely chopped
60g/¼ cup cream cheese
10 cocktail onions, finely chopped
2 Tbsp mayonnaise
1 Tbsp prepared mustard

Scoop the seeds from the cucumber using the point of a teaspoon. Cut away some of the flesh, leaving a shell about 6mm/¼in thick. Rub the cucumber shells with salt and leave for 15 minutes.

Meanwhile, mix together the tuna fish, ham, eggs, cream cheese, onions, mayonnaise, prepared mustard and salt and pepper to taste.

Rinse the cucumber shells in cold water and wipe dry with paper towels. Fill each half with the tuna fish mixture and place the halves together again. Wrap in foil and chill for at least 2 hours before the picnic.

To serve, slice crosswise on a slant into 2.5cm/1in thick slices.

Serves 4-6

Light Dishes

Jellied grape and cheese salad

juice of 2 lemons
2 envelopes unflavored geletin
2 Tbsp hot water
175g/6oz black grapes, halved and seeded
CHEESE GELATIN
185g/¾ cup cream cheese
125g/½ cup cottage cheese, strained
150ml/⅔ cup sour cream
2 envelopes unflavored gelatin
2 Tbsp hot water
2 tsp grated orange rind
4 Tbsp orange juice
4 Tbsp white wine
1 tsp sugar

Add enough water to the lemon juice to make it up to 550ml/2¼ cups. Dissolve the gelatin in the hot water and strain into the lemon juice mixture. Pour about a 6mm/¼in layer of the lemon juice mixture into a greased 2l/4 pint capacity mold. Chill until set, then arrange the grape halves, cut sides up, on the lemon gelatin. Pour over another 6mm/¼in layer and chill until set. Cover with the remaining lemon mixture and chill until set.

Meanwhile, mix together the cream cheese, cottage cheese and sour cream. Dissolve the gelatin in the hot water and strain into the cheese mixture. Add the orange rind, orange juice, wine and sugar. Mix well and chill until on the point of setting.

Spoon the cheese gelatin on top of the lemon gelatin in the mold and return to the refrigerator. Chill for a further 2 hours or until completely set.

To unmold, dip the bottom of the mold quickly in hot water. Turn the salad out onto a serving dish.
Serves 6

Baked potatoes stuffed with blue cheese

4 large potatoes
150ml/⅔ cup sour cream
125g/1 cup blue cheese, crumbled
2 Tbsp chives, freshly chopped
pinch cayenne pepper
salt and black pepper

Bake the potatoes in a fairly hot oven (190°C/375°F) for 1½ hours or until they are tender. Remove from the oven and allow to cool slightly, then cut off a thin slice from the top of each one. Scoop out the

cooked potato to within 6mm/¼in of the skin, being careful not to break the skin.

Mash together the cooked potato, sour cream, cheese, chives, cayenne and salt and pepper to taste. Stuff the potato skins with the potato and cheese mixture.

Place the filled potatoes on a baking sheet and return to the oven. Bake for 10 to 15 minutes or until the filling is lightly browned. Serve hot.
Serves 4

Lobster Newburg

2 x 1kg/2lb cooked lobsters, shells split, claws cracked and stomach and intestinal vein removed
3 Tbsp butter
125ml/½ cup sherry
¼ tsp grated nutmeg
salt and black pepper
3 egg yolks
250ml/1 cup heavy cream
8 hot slices of buttered toast

Remove the lobster meat from the shells and claws and dice it. Melt the butter in a frying pan. Add the lobster meat and fry for 4 minutes, stirring frequently. Pour over the sherry and simmer for 3 minutes. Stir in the nutmeg and salt and pepper to taste.

Beat the egg yolks and cream together in a small bowl. Gradually stir into the lobster mixture and cook for 3 to 4 minutes or until the mixture is thick. Do not boil or the mixture will curdle.

Spoon over the hot toast and serve.
Serves 4

The fruit and cheese in this Jellied Grape and Cheese Salad make a light and refreshing main course for a springtime luncheon or buffet table.

Shrimp chow mein

oil for deep frying
250g/8oz thin egg noodles, cooked and
drained
10 dried Chinese mushrooms, soaked
in hot water for 20 minutes
2 Tbsp vegetable oil
2 carrots, scraped and thinly sliced on
the diagonal
250g/8oz bean sprouts
250g/8oz can water chestnuts, drained
and sliced
125ml/½ cup chicken stock
1 Tbsp sake or dry sherry
1 Tbsp soy sauce
375g/2 cups shrimps (shelled)
deveined

Heat the oil in a deep-fat fryer until it
reaches 185°C/360°F on a deep fat thermometer, or until a cube of stale bread dropped
into the oil turns golden in 50 seconds.

Lower the noodles into the oil and fry
for 3 to 4 minutes or until they are golden
brown. Drain on paper towels and arrange
on a warmed serving dish. Keep hot while
you cook the vegetables.

Drain the mushrooms and slice into
strips. Heat the oil in a frying pan. Add the
mushrooms, carrots, bean sprouts and
water chestnuts. Fry for 5 minutes stirring
constantly. The vegetables should be
tender but still crisp.

Stir in the stock and sake or sherry and
bring to a boil. Stir in the soy sauce and
shrimp. Cover and simmer for 3 to 5
minutes or until the fish are heated
through.

Make a well in the center of the noodles
and spoon in the fish mixture.

Serve hot.
Serves 2-3

Cheese and ham soufflé

125g/½ cup butter
2 Tbsp fine dry white breadcrumbs
90g/¾ cup flour
500ml/1 pint milk, scalded
125g/⅔ cup Cheddar cheese, grated
75g/1 cup cooked ham, finely
chopped
6 eggs, separated
salt
½ tsp paprika
pinch cayenne pepper

Place a double piece of wax paper around
the outside of a 1.2l/2½ pint capacity
soufflé dish and tie on with string. The
paper should come 5cm/2in above the rim
of the dish. Use 2 tablespoons of the butter
to grease the inside of the paper collar and

the dish. Place the breadcrumbs in the dish
and swirl around so that all sides are
coated. Tip out excess.

Melt the remaining butter in a saucepan.
Stir in the flour and cook, stirring, for 1
minute. Remove from the heat and
gradually stir in the milk. Return to the
heat and cook, stirring, until the mixture is
thickened and smooth. Remove from the
heat and add the cheese and ham. Stir
until the cheese has melted.

Lightly beat the egg yolks in a small
bowl. Add to the cheese mixture. Season
with salt, the paprika and cayenne.

Beat the egg whites until they will hold a
stiff peak. Fold into the cheese and ham
mixture and spoon into the soufflé dish.
Bake in a fairly hot oven (190°C/375°F) for
35 minutes or until the top is puffed up and
lightly browned.

Remove the paper collar and serve
immediately.
Serves 4

Ricotta cheese omelet with tomato sauce

1½ Tbsp olive oil
1 small onion, finely chopped
250g/8oz tomatoes, peeled and
chopped
4 Tbsp tomato paste
1 tsp oregano, freshly chopped
½ tsp sugar
salt and black pepper
250g/1 cup ricotta cheese
4 Tbsp Parmesan cheese, grated
4 large eggs
1 Tbsp butter

Heat the oil in a frying pan. Add the onion
and fry until it is soft but not brown. Stir
in the tomatoes, tomato paste, oregano,
sugar and salt and pepper to taste and
simmer gently for 20 minutes, stirring
occasionally.

Meanwhile, mix together the ricotta
cheese, 3 tablespoons of the Parmesan
cheese and salt and pepper to taste in a
mixing bowl. Beat the eggs with the
remaining Parmesan and salt and pepper to
taste in another bowl.

Melt the butter in a frying pan or
omelet pan. Pour in the egg mixture and
cook the omelet for about 5 minutes, lifting
the set edges to allow the liquid egg mixture to run onto the pan. Spoon the cheese
mixture onto half of the omelet and fold
over the other half. Continue cooking for
about 3 minutes.

Slide the omelet onto a warmed serving
dish and pour over the tomato sauce.
Serve hot.
Serves 2

Shrimp Chow Mein is something slightly different – and delicious – for a special occasion.

Desserts

Golden gooseberry bake

1kg/2lb gooseberries
125g/½ cup sugar
4 Tbsp water
60g/2 cups cornflakes
60g/⅓ cup rolled oats
6 Tbsp butter
2 Tbsp light corn syrup
1 Tbsp brown sugar

Put the gooseberries, sugar and water in a saucepan and boil for 4 minutes to make a syrup. Add the gooseberries and poach gently for 15 minutes or until the fruit is just softening. Remove from the heat and pour the gooseberries into a baking dish.

Put the cornflakes in a mixing bowl and crush them lightly with your hand. Stir in the rolled oats.

Melt the butter with the light corn syrup in a saucepan. Stir into the cornflake mixture and spoon on top of the gooseberries. Sprinkle with the brown sugar and bake in a moderate oven (180°C/350°F) for 20 minutes or until the top is lightly browned.

Serve hot, with cream or custard sauce.
Serves 4-6

Green melon mousse

1 medium honeydew melon
300ml/1¼ cups heavy cream
4 Tbsp Grand Marnier
finely grated rind of 1 lemon
pinch ground ginger
4 eggs, separated
125g/⅔ cup brown sugar
2 envelopes unflavored gelatin
4 Tbsp warm water

Halve the melon and discard the seeds. Scoop out the flesh and purée it in a blender or food mill, or push it through a nylon strainer. Stir in the cream, Grand Marnier, lemon rind and ginger.

Beat the egg yolks and brown sugar together in the top of a double boiler or in a heatproof bowl placed over a saucepan of hot water. Beat until the mixture is thick and pale and will make a ribbon trail on itself when the beater is lifted.

Stir the egg yolk mixture into the melon mixture. Dissolve the gelatin in the warm water and strain into the melon mixture. Mix well.

Beat the egg whites until they will hold a stiff peak. Fold them into the melon mixture. Spoon into a serving dish and chill for a least 3 hours or until set.
Serves 8

Rum babas

1 cake compressed yeast
1 Tbsp lukewarm milk
250g/2 cups flour
pinch salt
2 Tbsp sugar
2 eggs
60g/¼ cup butter, melted
SAUCE
185g/¾ cup sugar
375ml/1½ cups water
150ml/⅔ cup rum
12 candied cherries, halved
60g/½ cup blanched almonds, slivered

Mash the yeast and milk together to make a smooth paste. Leave in a warm, draft-free place for 15 minutes or until frothy. Sift the flour into a mixing bowl and add the salt and sugar. Make a well in the center and add the yeast mixture, eggs and melted butter. Mix together well, then beat the dough with your hand, lifting and slapping it vigorously. The dough should be quite sticky, but if it is too difficult to handle, add a little flour.

When the dough begins to lose its stickiness, turn it out onto a lightly floured surface and continue kneading until it is elastic. Roll the dough into a ball and place n a greased bowl. Cover and let rise in a warm place for 1½ to 2 hours or until almost idoubled in bulk.

Punch down and knead the dough for 2 minutes. Divide the dough into 12 portions. Gently press each portion into a greased baba mold, filling it only two-thirds full. Leave in a warm place to rise for 35 to 45 minutes or until the dough has risen to the tops of the molds.

Bake in a fairly hot oven (190°C/375°F)

for 15 minutes or until lightly browned and cooked. Test by inserting a skewer: it should come out clean. Unmold the babas onto a wire rack, set aside and allow to cool slightly.

Meanwhile, make the sauce. Dissolve the sugar in the water in a small saucepan. Bring to a boil and boil for 5 minutes. Remove from the heat and allow to cool slightly.

Stir most of the rum into the syrup. Arrange the babas, in one layer, in a shallow dish. Pour over the rum syrup and leave to soak for 30 to 40 minutes, basting occasionally.

Carefully transfer the babas to a wire rack and allow to drain. Place the babas on a serving dish and sprinkle with the remaining rum. Decorate with the candied cherries and slivered almonds.

Makes 12

Rich and light-textured, Rum Babas are soaked in a rum-flavored syrup and glazed with apricot jam. Although strictly pastries, they make mouth-watering desserts.

Steamed banana pudding

125g/½ cup butter
125g/½ cup sugar
185g/1½ cups flour
¼ tsp salt
1 tsp baking powder
2 eggs
3 large bananas, mashed
2 Tbsp milk
grated rind of 1 orange

Cream the butter and sugar together until the mixture is light and fluffy. Sift the flour, salt and baking powder into a mixing bowl. Add the eggs to the butter mixture, one at a time, adding a tablespoonful of the flour mixture with each one. Beat well. Fold in the remaining flour mixture, then mix in the mashed bananas, milk and orange rind.

Spoon into a greased 1.2l/2½ pint capacity steaming mold and cover with a piece of greased wax paper and aluminum foil. Make a pleat in the center of the paper and foil top to allow the pudding to expand. Tie on securely with string.

Steam for 1½ hours, adding more water as necessary.

Turn the pudding out of the mold onto a warmed serving dish. Serve hot with custard sauce.
Serves 4-6

Steamed Banana Pudding is a warm, filling dessert for one of those chillier spring days.

Honey and cream cheese pie

250g/1 cup cream cheese
2 Tbsp sugar
3 Tbsp clear honey, warmed
2 eggs, lightly beaten
1 tsp ground cinnamon
PASTRY
185g/1½ cups flour
pinch salt
6 Tbsp butter
2-3 Tbsp iced water

First make the pastry. Sift the flour and salt into a mixing bowl. Add the butter and cut into small pieces with a knife. Then rub the butter into the flour until the mixture resembles breadcrumbs. Stir in enough water to bind the mixture together and knead to a dough. Chill for 30 minutes.

Roll out the dough and use to line a 20cm/8in pie plate. Bake shell for 5 minutes in an oven pre-heated to fairly hot (190°C/375°F).

Beat the cream cheese, sugar and honey together with a wooden spoon. Add the eggs and mix well. Pour into the pastry case and bake in a fairly hot oven (190°C/375°F) for 30 to 35 minutes or until the filling is lightly browned.

Sprinkle over the cinnamon and leave to cool before serving.
Makes one 20cm/8in pie

Coffee soufflé

6 ladyfingers broken into small pieces
75ml/⅓ cup coffee-flavored liqueur
3 Tbsp butter
3 Tbsp confectioners' sugar
30g/¼ cup flour
185ml/¾ cup hot milk
4 Tbsp strong black coffee
1 Tbsp sugar
5 egg yolks
6 egg whites
125g/1 cup walnuts, chopped

Put the ladyfingers in a shallow dish and sprinkle over half the liqueur. Leave to soak for 30 minutes, then mash with a fork. Grease a 1.5l/3 pint capacity soufflé dish with 1 tablespoon of the butter. Sprinkle in the confectioners' sugar and tip and rotate the dish to coat the sides and bottom completely.

Melt the remaining butter in a saucepan. Remove from the heat and stir in the flour. Gradually stir in the milk. Return to the heat and cook, stirring, until the mixture is thickened and smooth. Stir in the remaining liqueur, the black coffee and the mashed ladyfingers. Leave to cool to lukewarm.

Beat the sugar into the egg yolks, then add to the coffee mixture and beat well together. Beat the egg whites until they will form a stiff peak. Fold into the coffee mixture. Spoon the mixture into the soufflé dish and sprinkle the walnuts on top.

Bake in a moderate oven (180°C/350°F) for 30 to 45 minutes or until well risen and lightly browned.

Serve immediately.

Serves 4-6

Rhubarb and banana cream

1kg/2lb rhubarb, cut into 2.5cm/1in pieces
250g/1 cup sugar
4 Tbsp water
2 bananas, mashed
250ml/1 cup heavy cream
2 egg whites

Put the rhubarb, sugar and water in a saucepan and cook the rhubarb for 15 minutes or until it is soft. Remove from the heat and drain the rhubarb. Put it in a mixing bowl and allow to cool.

Stir the mashed bananas and cream into the rhubarb. Beat the egg whites until they will hold a stiff peak, then fold them into the rhubarb mixture. Spoon into a serving dish and chill for at least 4 hours before serving.

Serves 6

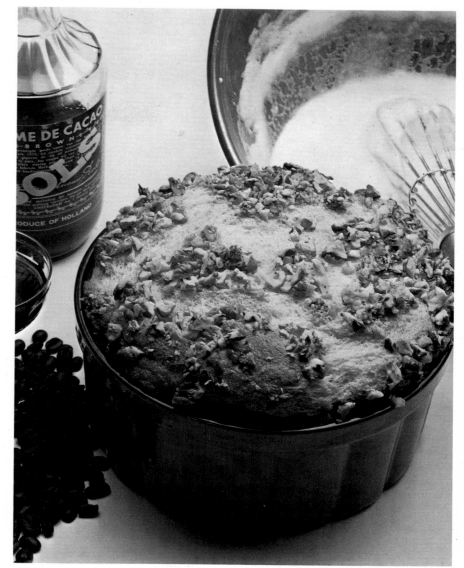

Orange rice mold

250g/1 cup short-grain rice, soaked in cold water for 30 minutes and drained
500ml/1 pint milk
juice and grated rind of 1 orange
3 oranges, peel and pith removed, segmented and chopped
2 Tbsp sugar
250ml/1 cup heavy cream, stiffly whipped

Put the rice and milk in a saucepan and bring to a boil. Cover and cook gently for 15 minutes or until the rice is tender and all the water has been absorbed.

Turn the rice into a mixing bowl and stir in the orange juice and rind. Leave to cool for 5 minutes. Stir in half the orange segments and the sugar, then fold in the cream. Spoon into a plain or decorative greased 1l/2 pint capacity ring mold. Smooth the top.

Chill for at least 2 hours or until the mixture feels firm. Turn out on to a

Coffee Soufflé makes a delicate light dessert for a dinner party.

Grasshopper Pie – a marvelous combination of cookies, marshmallows, liqueurs and cream go together to make this rich, elegant pie.

mixture into the paper circle to make a layer about 6mm/¼in thick. Using a 2.5cm/1in nozzle, pipe the remaining meringue mixture around the edge of the circle in decorative swirls to form a case.

Bake in a cool oven (150°C/300°F) for 1 hour. Turn off the oven and leave the meringue inside for a further 30 minutes.

Remove from the oven and leave to cool, then carefully peel off the paper. Place the meringue case on a serving plate.

To make the filling, cream the butter until it is soft, then beat in the confectioners' sugar until the mixture is light and fluffy. Stir in the egg yolks, food coloring, orange rind, liqueur, if using, and cream. Spoon into the meringue case and arrange the orange slices on top. Serve immediately.

Serves 6-8

Grasshopper pie

36 chocolate cream sandwich cookies, crushed
2 Tbsp butter, melted
30 large marshmallows
185ml/¾ cup milk
4 Tbsp creme de menthe
4 Tbsp creme de cacao (clear)
250ml/1 cup heavy cream, stiffly whipped

Combine the crushed cookies and melted butter and press into the bottom and sides of a greased 23cm/9in pie pan.

Melt the marshmallows in the milk in a saucepan, stirring frequently. Remove from the heat and stir in the liqueurs. Allow the mixture to cool, then fold in the whipped cream. Spoon into the crumb shell and chill for at least 4 hours before serving.

Makes one 23cm/9in pie

Oriental fruit salad

125ml/½ cup clear honey
75ml/⅓ cup kirsch
10 dried figs, coarsely chopped
20 dried or fresh dates, halved and pitted
50g/½ cup whole unblanched hazel nuts
50g/½ cup whole unblanched almonds
1 medium honeydew melon

Mix together the honey and kirsch in a shallow dish. Add the figs, dates and nuts and stir well. Leave to soak for 4 hours, stirring occasionally.

Halve the melon and scoop out the seeds. Cut away the rind and cut the flesh into cubes. Stir the melon cubes into the mixture and pour into a serving dish. Chill for at least 1 hour before serving.

Serves 6

serving plate and fill the center with the remaining orange segments.

Serves 4

Lemon and orange meringue cake

5 egg whites
300g/1¼ cups sugar
2 tsp grated lemon rind
½ tsp lemon flavoring
FILLING
6 Tbsp unsalted butter, softened
375g/2 cups confectioners' sugar
2 egg yolks
2 drops orange food coloring
grated rind of ½ orange
1 Tbsp orange-flavored liqueur (optional)
2 Tbsp heavy cream
4 oranges, peel and pith removed and sliced

Draw a 23cm/9in circle on a piece of non-stick silicone paper. Put the paper on a baking sheet.

Beat the egg whites until they will hold a stiff peak. Beat in 60g/¼ cup of the sugar, a teaspoon at a time, and continue beating for 1 minute or until the mixture is very stiff and glossy. Carefully fold in the remaining sugar, the grated lemon rind and lemon flavoring.

Spoon or pipe one-third of the meringue

Home Baking

Quick bread

½ cake compressed yeast
300ml/1¼ cups lukewarm water
375g/3 cups flour
125g/1 cup wholewheat flour
1 tsp salt
1 Tbsp cracked wheat

Mash the yeast and 1 tablespoon of the water together to make a smooth paste. Leave in a warm, draft-free place for 15 minutes or until frothy. Sift the flour into a mixing bowl and add the wholewheat flour and salt. Make a well in the center and add the yeast mixture and remaining water. Gradually draw the flour into the liquid, mixing to a dough.

Turn the dough out of the bowl and knead for 3 minutes. Shape into a loaf and place in a greased small loaf pan. Cover the pan and leave to rise in a warm, draft-free place for 1 to 1½ hours or until risen to the top of the pan.

Sprinkle the top of the loaf with the cracked wheat and bake in a very hot oven (220°C/425°F) for 15 minutes. Reduce the oven temperature to fairly hot (190°C/375°F) and bake for a further 25 to 30 minutes. Cover top of loaf with foil if it is browning too fast. To test if the loaf is cooked, tip it out of the pan and rap the bottom with your knuckles. It should sound hollow.

Cool on a wire rack.
Makes one 500g/1lb loaf

Wholewheat bread

1 cake compressed yeast
925ml/3¾ cups lukewarm water
1.5kg/3lb wholewheat flour
1 Tbsp salt
2 Tbsp honey
1 Tbsp vegetable oil

Mash the yeast and 1½ tablespoons of the water together to make a smooth paste. Leave in a warm, draft-free place for 15 minutes or until frothy. Put the flour and salt into a mixing bowl and make a well in the center. Add the yeast mixture, honey, remaining lukewarm water and oil. Gradually draw the flour into the liquid, mixing to a dough.

Turn the dough out of the bowl and knead for 10 minutes or until elastic and smooth. Return to the bowl and sprinkle the dough with a little flour. Cover and let rise in a warm, draft-free place for 1 to 1½ hours or until almost doubled in bulk.

Punch down and knead the dough again for about 10 minutes. Cut it into four pieces and shape each piece into a loaf. Put into four greased small loaf pans.

Quick Bread can be made when you are short of time since it requires only one rising and little kneading.

Alternatively, put the dough into well-greased flower pots for an unusual shape. Cover and let rise in a warm place for 30 to 45 minutes or until risen to the tops of the pans.

Bake in a very hot oven (240°C/475°F) for 15 minutes. Reduce the oven temperature to hot (220°C/425°F) and bake for a further 25 to 30 minutes. To test if the loaves are cooked, tip them out of the pans and rap the bottoms with your knuckles. They should sound hollow.

Cool on a wire rack.
Makes four 500g/1lb loaves

Streusel kuchen

½ cake compressed yeast
1 Tbsp lukewarm water
250g/2 cups flour
½ tsp salt
¼ tsp ground ginger
½ tsp grated lemon rind
2 Tbsp sugar
150ml/⅔ cup lukewarm milk
60g/¼ cup butter, melted
1 egg, lightly beaten
TOPPING
60g/¾ cup graham crackers, crushed
2 Tbsp sugar
1 tsp ground cinnamon
60g/¼ cup butter, softened

Streusel-Kuchen, a yeast cake from Germany, is ideal buttered for a mid-morning or afternoon snack.

Mash the yeast and water together to make a smooth paste. Leave in a warm, draft-free place for 15 minutes or until frothy. Sift the flour into a mixing bowl with the salt and ginger. Add the lemon rind and sugar and make a well in the center. Pour in the yeast mixture, the milk, melted butter and egg. Gradually draw the flour into the liquid, mixing to a dough.

Turn the dough out of the bowl and knead for 3 minutes or until it is smooth and elastic. Return to the bowl, cover and let rise in a warm place for 1 to 1½ hours or until almost doubled in bulk.

Punch down and knead the dough again for about 3 minutes. Let it rest for 10 minutes, then roll it out to a square about 2.5cm/1in thick. With your hands, shape the dough into a rectangle about 5cm/2in thick. Place it in a greased large loaf pan.

Mix together all the ingredients for the topping, using your fingers, until the mixture resembles breadcrumbs. Sprinkle the topping over the dough and let rise in a warm place for about 30 minutes or until the dough has risen to the top of the pan.

Bake in a moderate oven (180°C/350°F) for 40 to 45 minutes or until the kuchen is risen and the topping is golden brown.

Remove from the pan and cool on a wire rack.
Makes one 1kg/2lb loaf

Orange yeast buns

½ cake compressed yeast
2 Tbsp lukewarm water
125ml/½ cup milk
150g/⅔ cup butter
500g/1lb (4 cups) flour
1 tsp salt
125g/½ cup sugar
2 eggs, lightly beaten
2 Tbsp butter, melted
90g/½ cup currants
grated rind of 2 large oranges
1 Tbsp mixed candied peel
chopped
¼ tsp ground cinnamon
ICING
250g/1⅓ cups confectioners' sugar
2 Tbsp orange juice

Mash the yeast and water together to make a smooth paste. Leave in a warm, draft-free place for 15 minutes or until frothy.

Meanwhile, scald the milk in a saucepan. Remove from the heat and add the butter. When the butter has melted, leave to cool to lukewarm.

Sift the flour, salt and half the sugar into a mixing bowl. Make a well in the center and add the yeast mixture, the milk and

butter mixture and the eggs. Gradually draw the flour into the liquid, mixing to a dough.

Turn the dough out of the bowl and knead for about 10 minutes or until elastic and smooth. Return to the bowl, cover and let rise in a warm place for 1 to 1½ hours or until doubled in bulk.

Punch down and knead the dough again for about 2 minutes. Roll out the dough into a square. Brush with the melted butter, then sprinkle over the remaining sugar, the currants, orange rind, candied peel and cinnamon. Roll up like a jelly roll. Cut the roll into 4cm/1½in thick slices and place these on a greased baking sheet. Leave a little space between the slices to allow for expansion. Let rise in a warm place for 20 minutes or until the slices are touching each other.

Bake in a fairly hot oven (190°C/375°F) for 30 to 35 minutes or until the rolls are golden brown. Remove from the oven and leave to cool slightly.

Meanwhile, mix together the confectioners' sugar and orange juice. Brush over the warm rolls, then, when they are cool enough to handle, transfer them to a wire rack to cool completely.

Makes 10-15 rolls

Orange Yeast Rolls may be cut in half and spread with butter and jam. Serve with freshly percolated coffee for a real treat.

Summer

The irony of Summer is that when food is at its most abundant, we don't always feel like cooking, or eating for that matter! So we've included a large selection of cold soups, ice creams and salads for crisp, cool meals that are quick to prepare and tempting to eat, plus some long, cool drinks to refresh you while you're making them. Eating outdoors, however, is such a popular pastime that even the most undomesticated of guests will be volunteering to cook food on a barbecue; and the aroma and flavor of meat cooked over charcoal is enough to tempt the most jaded palate.

Summer is the time for making not only hay, but also jam, while the sun shines, and capturing the flavor of fresh fruits in delicious homemade preserves. With these recipes and some for those inevitably not-so-warm evenings, you can make the most of what Summer has to offer and have time to enjoy it.

What's best in season

Fruit:			
Apples	Grapes	Melons	Peaches
Apricots	Grapefruit	Mulberries	Plums
Bananas	Lemons	Nectarines	Pears
Blackberries	Limes	Oranges	Pineapples
Blueberries	Loganberries	Passionfruit	Raspberries
Cherries	Guavas	Pawpaws	Rhubarb
Figs	Mangoes	Papayas	Strawberries
Gooseberries			

Vegetables:			
Asparagus	Celery	Lettuces	Pumpkin
Avocados	Cucumbers	Lima beans	Radishes
Beets	Eggplant	Mushrooms	Spinach
Cabbages	Fennel	Onions	String beans
Calabrese	Globe artichokes	Peas	Tomatoes
Corn	Green beans	Peppers	Watercress
Carrots	Kohlrabi	Potatoes	Zucchini

Herbs:			
Basil	Coriander	Marjoram	Sage
Bay	Dill	Mint	Summer savory
Chervil	Fennel	Parsley	Tarragon
Chives	Lemon balm	Rosemary	Thyme

Nuts:
Almonds

Fish:			
Bass	Haddock	Oysters	Sardine
Carp	Hake	Perch	Shrimp
Cod	Halibut	Pike	Sole
Crab	Herring	Porgy	Trout
Crayfish	Lobster	Prawns	Tuna
Eeel	Mackerel	Red snapper	Turbot
Flounder	Mullet	Salmon	Whiting
Grouper			

Poultry:

Available fresh or frozen
all year round

Game:			
Grouse	Pigeon	Rabbit	Venison
Hare	Quail	Snipe	

Meat and variety meats

Available fresh or frozen
all year round

Appetizers

Spinach salad

250g/8oz spinach, coarsely chopped
8 bacon slices, broiled until crisp and
crumbled
2 large avocados, peeled, halved,
seeded and chopped
DRESSING
6 Tbsp olive oil
salt and black pepper
½ tsp dry mustard
1 garlic clove, crushed
2 Tbsp white wine vinegar
1 Tbsp lemon juice

Put all the dressing ingredients in a
screwtop jar and shake well.

Mix together the spinach, bacon and
avocados in a salad bowl. Add the dressing
and toss well until the salad ingredients are
coated with the dressing. Serve immediately.
Serves 4

Mackerel fillets with mustard sauce

2 large mackerels, cleaned
1 Tbsp lemon juice
6 Tbsp butter
1½ Tbsp French mustard
2 egg yolks
1 Tbsp cider vinegar
salt and black pepper
2 Tbsp mixed herbs, freshly chopped

Lay each mackerel on a piece of greased
aluminum foil. Sprinkle with the lemon
juice and wrap the fish loosely, envelope-
style, so they are completely enclosed.
Place the packages on a baking sheet and
bake in a moderate oven (180°C/350°F)
for 20 minutes or until the mackerel is
cooked.

Meanwhile, prepare the sauce. Cream
the butter until it is soft and fluffy. Beat
together the mustard, egg yolks, vinegar
and salt and pepper to taste. Gradually
beat the mustard mixture into the butter.
Mix in the herbs. Spoon the sauce into a
serving bowl and chill.

When the mackerel is cooked, remove it
from the oven and open the foil. Pour any
cooking juices into a bowl and reserve.
Gently scrape off the skin and cut each
fish into four fillets, removing the bones.
Arrange the fillets in a shallow serving dish
and strain over the reserved cooking juices.
Allow to cool, then chill for a least 2 hours.

Serve cold with the mustard sauce.
Serves 4

Eggs in tomato shells

6 large tomatoes, peeled
salt and black pepper
2 Tbsp olive oil
1 small onion, finely chopped
2 tsp basil, freshly chopped
1 Tbsp tomato paste
6 eggs, hard-cooked
4 Tbsp mayonnaise
watercress

Cut a circle from the stalk end of each
tomato so there is a hole big enough to
insert an egg. Scoop out the pulp and
seeds, reserving them with the lids. Season
the insides of the tomato shells with salt
and pepper.

Heat the oil in a saucepan. Add the
onion and fry until it is soft but not brown.
Add the reserved tomato pulp and seeds,
the tomato lids, basil, tomato paste and salt
and pepper to taste. Cover and simmer for
15 to 20 minutes.

Remove from the heat and allow to cool.
Strain to extract seeds.

Place a hard-cooked egg in each tomato
shell and arrange on a serving dish. Chill
for 20 minutes.

Stir the mayonnaise into the tomato
mixture. Spoon over the eggs and garnish
the dish with watercress. Serve with brown
bread and butter.
Serves 6

*The rich, distinctive flavor of
Mackerel Fillets served with Mustard
Sauce makes a really tasty first
course.*

Eels in herb sauce

6 Tbsp butter
250g/8oz spinach, chopped
1 tsp tarragon, freshly chopped
3 Tbsp parsley, freshly chopped
1 tsp sage, freshly chopped
2 x 500g/1lb eels, skinned, cleaned and
cut into 8cm/3in pieces
salt and black pepper
300ml/1¼ cups white wine
3 egg yolks
1 Tbsp lemon juice

Melt the butter in a frying pan. Add the spinach, tarragon, parsley and sage and fry lightly. Add the eel pieces and mix together well. Add salt and pepper to taste with the wine and bring to a boil. Cover and simmer for 10 to 15 minutes or until the eel pieces are tender. Remove from the heat.

Beat the egg yolks until well mixed, then beat in 4 tablespoons of the hot liquid. Stir the egg mixture into the frying pan and add the lemon juice.

Turn into a serving dish and allow to cool. Chill for at least 2 hours before serving.
Serves 6-8

Tomato aspic

375ml/1½ cups hot chicken stock
375ml/1½ cups tomato juice
2 Tbsp tomato paste
½ tsp sugar
1 egg shell, crushed
1 egg white, lightly beaten
salt and white pepper
2 envelopes unflavored gelatin
watercress

Line a large strainer with a scalded piece of cheesecloth and place it over a large mixing bowl.

Put 300ml/1¼ cups of the chicken stock and the tomato juice in a saucepan. Stir in the tomato paste, sugar, egg shell, egg white and salt and pepper to taste. Bring to a boil, beating constantly. Remove from the heat.

Dissolve the gelatin in the remaining chicken stock. Strain it into the mixture in the saucepan and stir well. Pour the mixture through the cheesecloth lined strainer. If it is not absolutely clear, strain it again into another bowl.

Pour into a decorative mold and allow to cool, then chill for at least 2 hours or until completely set.

Unmold onto a serving dish and garnish with watercress.
Serves 4

Crab and avocado mousse

3 large avocados
2 Tbsp mayonnaise
1 tsp lemon juice
2 eggs, hard-cooked and chopped
salt and white pepper
4 scallions, chopped
2 envelopes unflavored gelatin
4 Tbsp hot water
125g/⅔ cup crabmeat, flaked
125ml/½ cup heavy cream
½ tsp curry powder
watercress

Halve the avocados and remove the seeds. Peel off the skin and cut the flesh into cubes. Place in the goblet of an electric blender with the mayonnaise, lemon juice, eggs, salt and pepper to taste and the scallions. Blend to a smooth purée.

Dissolve one envelope of the gelatin in half the hot water and strain into the avocado mixture. Stir well.

Pour half the avocado mixture into a greased 625ml/2½ cup capacity mold and smooth the top. Chill for 15 minutes.

Dissolve the remaining gelatin in the remaining water and mix with the crabmeat, cream and curry powder. Spoon over the avocado mixture in the mold, and top with the remaining avocado mixture. Smooth the top and chill for 4 hours or until completely set.

Unmold onto a serving dish and garnish with watercress.
Serves 4-6

Guacamole ring

3 large avocados
3 Tbsp mayonnaise
juice of 1 lemon
1 tsp prepared French mustard
2 tsp Worcestershire sauce
2 Tbsp tomato paste
¼ tsp cayenne pepper
salt and black pepper
300ml/1¼ cups heavy cream, stiffly
whipped
2 envelopes unflavored gelatin
4 Tbsp warm water
FILLING
500g/2⅔ cups shrimp (shelled),
deveined
1 medium green pepper, pith and
seeds removed and thinly sliced
2 small red peppers, pith and seeds
removed and thinly sliced
2 Tbsp lemon juice
3 Tbsp chives, freshly chopped

Halve the avocados and remove the seeds. Scoop out the flesh into a mixing bowl and

Crab and Avocado Mousse makes a luxurious fish course for a summer dinner party.

Simple and inexpensive, Marinated Mushrooms may also be served on cocktail sticks.

mash in the mayonnaise, lemon juice, mustard, Worcestershire sauce, tomato paste, cayenne and salt and pepper to taste. Fold in the cream.

Dissolve the gelatin in the water, then strain into the avocado mixture. Mix well. Turn into a greased 23cm/9in ring mold. Chill for at least 4 hours or until the mixture is firm to the touch.

Mix together the shrimp, green and red pepper slices and lemon juice with salt and pepper to taste.

Turn out the avocado ring onto a serving dish and fill the center with the pepper mixture. Arrange the remainder around the ring.

Sprinkle with the chives and serve.
Serves 8-10

Marinated mushrooms

500g/1lb small button mushrooms,
stalks removed
MARINADE
1 tsp salt
3 black peppercorns, coarsely crushed
2 tsp dill, freshly chopped
4 Tbsp tarragon vinegar
1 Tbsp lemon juice
4 Tbsp olive juice

Mix together the marinade ingredients in a shallow dish. Add the mushrooms and stir well. Cover and leave to marinate for 2 hours, stirring occasionally.

Drain the mushrooms, discarding the marinade, and pile in a serving dish. Serve lightly chilled.
Serves 4

Shrimp in tomato sauce

500g/2⅔ cups shrimp (shelled), deveined
salt
¼ tsp ground ginger
1½ tsp cornstarch
75ml/⅓ cup vegetable oil
SAUCE
1½ Tbsp butter
3 medium tomatoes, peeled and
quartered
2½ Tbsp soy sauce
2 Tbsp tomato paste
2 tsp cornstarch
75ml/⅓ cup chicken or beef stock
2 Tbsp sherry
1 tsp sugar

Put the shrimp in a shallow dish. Sprinkle with salt, the ginger and cornstarch and rub into the shellfish with your fingertips. Heat the oil in a frying pan and add the fish. Fry, stirring constantly, for 2 minutes. Remove from the pan with a slotted spoon. Keep hot.

Pour off the oil from the pan and add the butter. When it has melted add the tomato quarters. Fry for 2 minutes. Stir in the soy sauce and tomato paste and cook, stirring, for a further 30 seconds.

Mix together the cornstarch, stock, sherry and sugar and pour into the frying pan. Cook, stirring, until the mixture thickens slightly.

Return the shrimp to the pan and stir to coat them with the sauce. Cook for 1 to 2 minutes to heat them through, then serve, with boiled rice.
Serves 4

Soups

Gazpacho

3 slices brown bread,
cut into 2.5cm/1in cubes
300ml/1¼ cups tomato juice
2 garlic cloves, finely chopped
½ cucumber, peeled and finely chopped
1 green pepper, pith and seeds
removed and finely chopped
1 red pepper, pith and seeds
removed and finely chopped
1 large onion, finely chopped
750g/1½lb tomatoes, peeled, seeded
and finely chopped
75ml/⅓ cup olive oil
2 Tbsp red wine vinegar
salt and black pepper
1 tsp marjoram, freshly chopped
1 tsp basil, freshly chopped
ice cubes

Put the bread cubes in a mixing bowl and pour over the tomato juice. Leave to soak for 5 minutes, then mash to be sure they are completely saturated. Put the bread cubes and some of the tomato juice in a blender container and add the garlic, cucumber, peppers, onion and tomatoes. Blend to a smooth purée. Alternatively, purée the ingredients in a food mill.

Pour the mixture into the mixing bowl with the remaining tomato juice and add the oil, vinegar, salt and pepper to taste and the herbs. Mix well. The soup should be the consistency of light cream, so add more tomato juice if necessary.

Pour into a serving bowl or soup tureen and chill for at least 1 hour. Just before serving, stir the soup well and drop in a few ice cubes. Serve with small bowls of croûtons, chopped hard-cooked egg, chopped cucumber, onion and olives.
Serves 4

Cucumber and beer soup

125ml/½ cup sour cream
350ml/1½ cups beer
1 medium cucumber, peeled and chopped
salt
1 garlic clove, crushed
½ tsp sugar
1 tsp paprika

Mix together the sour cream and beer in a mixing bowl. Add the cucumber, salt to taste, the garlic and sugar. Mix well. Pour into a serving bowl and chill for at least 1 hour. Just before serving, sprinkle with the paprika.
Serves 6

Iced carrot and orange soup

2 Tbsp butter
1 large onion, thinly sliced
3 Tbsp flour
900ml/3½ cups chicken stock
625ml/2½ cups fresh orange juice
2 Tbsp chives, freshly chopped
salt and black pepper
pinch grated nutmeg
pinch ground allspice
500g/1lb carrots, scraped and cut into
2.5cm/1in pieces

Melt the butter in a saucepan. Add the onion and fry until it is soft but not brown. Remove from the heat and stir in the flour. Gradually stir in the stock, then the orange juice. Return to the heat and simmer, stirring, until thickened and smooth. Stir in the chives, salt and pepper to taste, the nutmeg, allspice and carrots.

Cover and simmer for 1 hour, stirring occasionally. Allow to cool.

Purée the soup in an electric blender or food mill, or push through a strainer. Chill for at least 2 hours before serving.
Serves 6

Cucumber and Beer Soup is a refreshing summer soup with an unusual flavor.

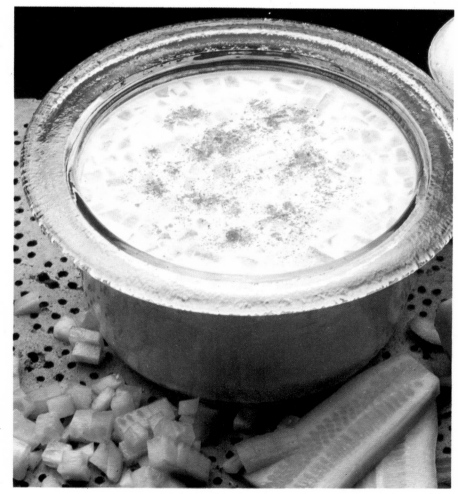

Lobster bisque

2 x 750g/1½lb lobsters, body shell split
and claws cracked
7 Tbsp unsalted butter
2 celery stalks, finely chopped
1 carrot, scraped and finely chopped
½ onion, finely chopped
1 tsp thyme, freshly chopped
pinch cayenne pepper
salt and white pepper
3 Tbsp brandy
250ml/1 cup dry white wine
625ml/2½ cups fish stock
1 Tbsp sherry
625ml/2½ cups milk
60g/½ cup flour
4 Tbsp heavy cream

Discard the stomach and intestinal vein from the lobster. If there is any coral (red roe), reserve it. Remove the meat from the body shells and claws and cut it into very small pieces. Reserve the shells.

Melt 3 tablespoons of the butter in a saucepan. Add the celery, carrot, onion, thyme, cayenne and salt and pepper to taste. Cook until the vegetables are soft but not brown.

Heat 2 tablespoons of the brandy in a ladle and set alight. Pour into the saucepan. When the flames have died away, add the wine and stock. Bring to a boil, then cover and simmer for 20 minutes.

Purée the vegetable and wine mixture by pushing it through a strainer or using an electric blender or food mill. Return to the saucepan. Crush the lobster shells using a pestle and mortar or an electric blender. Add to the saucepan and simmer for 25 minutes.

Meanwhile, mix the lobster meat with the coral, if any, and the sherry.

Melt the remaining butter in a saucepan. Add the flour and mix to a smooth paste. Remove from the heat and gradually stir in the milk. Return to the heat and cook, stirring, until the mixture is thickened and smooth. Strain the wine and lobster shell mixture and add the strained liquid to the milk mixture. Stir well, cover and simmer for 30 minutes.

Stir in the lobster and sherry mixture and remaining brandy. Taste and adjust the seasoning if necessary. Reheat gently and stir in the cream.

Serve hot.

Serves 4-6

Rich and creamy, Lobster Bisque is a perfect hors d'oeuvre for a formal dinner party.

Main Dishes

Flounder fillets in asparagus and mushroom sauce

8 flounder fillets, skinned
salt and black pepper
300ml/1¼ cups dry white wine
125g/1 cup flour
2 eggs, lightly beaten
90g/1 cup dry white breadcrumbs
60g/¼ cup butter
parsley sprigs and lemon wedges,
to serve
SAUCE
125g/1 cup mushrooms, thinly sliced
1 Tbsp water
1 Tbsp lemon juice
2 Tbsp butter
1½ Tbsp flour
250ml/1 cup light cream
salt and white pepper
15 thin asparagus tips, cooked

Fold four of the fish fillets in half and place in a greased shallow baking dish. Sprinkle with salt and pepper and pour over the wine. Cover the dish and poach in a moderate oven (180°C/350°F) for 25 to 30 minutes. Test with a fork: the flesh should flake easily.

Meanwhile, cut the remaining fillets into three, lengthwise. Coat the pieces with the flour, then with egg and then with breadcrumbs. Melt the butter in a frying pan. Place the fillets in the pan and fry for 2 to 3 minutes on each side or until golden brown. Remove from the heat and keep warm.

Remove the dish from the oven. Strain off the liquid and reserve it. Arrange the poached fillets in the center of a warmed serving dish. Surround with the fried fillets. Keep hot.

To make the sauce, put the mushrooms, water and lemon juice in a saucepan. Simmer for 4 to 5 minutes. Remove the mushrooms from the pan with a slotted spoon. Discard the cooking liquid. Melt the butter in the saucepan and stir in the flour. Cook, stirring, for 1 minute. Remove from the heat and gradually stir in the reserved poaching liquid and cream. Return to the heat and cook, stirring, until the sauce is thickened and smooth. Add salt and pepper to taste with the asparagus tips and mushrooms. Cook gently until the asparagus is heated through, then pour the sauce over the fish. Garnish with the parsley sprigs and lemon wedges and serve.
Serves 4-6

Porgy with bananas

1 × 1kg/2lb porgy, cleaned and gutted
2 Tbsp olive oil
salt and black pepper
1 tsp ground ginger
300ml/1¼ cups dry white wine
juice of 1 lemon
1 large bay leaf
1 small onion, finely chopped
60g/¼ cup butter
5 large bananas
4 Tbsp flour
chervil sprigs and lemon wedges, to serve

Rub the fish with the oil and sprinkle with salt and pepper and the ginger. Place it in a greased baking dish and leave in a cool place for 20 minutes.

Mix together the wine, lemon juice, bay leaf and onion. Pour this over the fish. Bake in a moderate oven (180°C/350°F) for 30 to 40 minutes. Test with a fork: the flesh should flake easily.

Ten minutes before the fish is cooked, melt 2 tablespoons of the butter in a frying pan. Add the bananas and fry for 6 minutes, turning frequently to brown evenly. Drain on paper towels and keep hot.

Transfer the fish to a warmed serving dish and surround with the bananas.

Strain the fish cooking liquid into a saucepan. Mix the remaining butter and the flour to make a smooth paste (beurre manié). Add this in small pieces to the cooking liquid and simmer, stirring, until the sauce is thickened and smooth. Pour the sauce over the fish and garnish with the chervil sprigs and lemon wedges.
Serves 4

Herrings in butter sauce

6 Tbsp flour
salt and black pepper
6 herrings, filleted
6 Tbsp butter
2 tsp lemon juice
1 Tbsp parsley, freshly chopped

Mix together the flour with salt and pepper on a plate. Dip the herrings in this seasoned flour to coat on both sides.

Melt the butter in a frying pan. Add the herring, in batches, and fry for 3 minutes on each side or until lightly browned and cooked. Test with a fork: the flesh should flake easily.

Transfer the herrings to a warmed serving dish. Spoon over the lemon juice and then the pan juices. Sprinkle with the parsley and serve.
Serves 4

Fresh asparagus, served either on their own or incorporated with other foods, is one of the delights of summer.

Lobster with whiskey and cream

2 × 1kg/2lb cooked lobsters, shells
split, claws cracked and stomach and
intestinal vein removed
60g/¼ cup butter
1 small onion, finely chopped
salt and black pepper
4 Tbsp whiskey
125ml/½ cup heavy cream
1 Tbsp parsley, freshly chopped

Remove the lobster meat from the shells and cut it into 2.5cm/1in pieces. Reserve the shells.

Melt the butter in a frying pan. Add the onion and fry until it is soft but not brown. Stir in the lobster and seasoning.

Warm the whiskey in a small pan. Remove from the heat and pour into the frying pan. Ignite. When the flames have died, cover and cook for 5 minutes.

Stir in the cream and heat through gently. Spoon the lobster mixture into the reserved shells and sprinkle over the parsley. Serve immediately.

Serves 4

Salmon with sauce verte

1 × 4kg/8lb salmon, cleaned
salt and black pepper
4 Tbsp olive oil
1 Tbsp grated lemon rind
2 bay leaves, crumbled
1 Tbsp parsley, freshly chopped
2 tsp thyme, freshly chopped
4 Tbsp dry white wine
SAUCE
2 Tbsp watercress, freshly chopped
4 Tbsp spinach, freshly chopped
2 Tbsp parsley, freshly chopped
500ml/1 pint mayonnaise
4 Tbsp heavy cream
1 Tbsp lemon juice
salt and black pepper

Rub the inside of the salmon with salt and pepper. Grease a sheet of aluminum foil large enough to enclose the salmon with 2 tablespoons of the oil. Place the salmon on the greased foil and sprinkle over the lemon rind, bay leaves, parsley and thyme. Fold up the two ends of the foil and pour the remaining oil and the wine over the fish. Fold the foil over the top so that the fish is securely enclosed. Place on a baking sheet and bake in a warm oven (170°C/325°F) for 1¼ to 1½ hours or until cooked. Test with a fork: the flesh should flake easily.

Unwrap the salmon and carefully transfer it to a flat working surface. Discard the foil and cooking juices. Gently skin the salmon, being careful not to break up the flesh. Leave to cool completely, then place on a serving platter.

Meanwhile, make the sauce. Wash the watercress, spinach and parsley and place in a saucepan. Cook in the water clinging to the leaves, stirring, for 6 minutes. Place in the goblet of a blender. Blend to a purée and cool.

Mix together the mayonnaise, cream, lemon juice and salt and pepper to taste. Add the puréed green mixture and mix well. Pour the sauce into a sauceboat and serve with the salmon.

Serves 12

Ocean rolls

4 white fish fillets, skinned
1 Tbsp lemon juice
2 Tbsp butter
1 scallion, finely chopped
125g/⅔ cup shrimp (shelled), deveined
125g/⅔ cup crabmeat, flaked
4 Tbsp corn kernels
1 tsp dill, freshly chopped
salt and black pepper
4 Tbsp heavy cream
375ml/1½ cups dry white wine
1 bay leaf
1 small onion, sliced
2 Tbsp flour

Lay the fillets on a flat working surface and sprinkle with the lemon juice. Melt half the butter in a frying pan. Add the scallion and fry for 2 minutes. Stir in the shrimp, crabmeat, corn, dill, salt and pepper to taste and the cream. Cook gently, stirring constantly, for 3 minutes.

Remove from the heat. Spoon equal amounts of the shrimp mixture onto each fish fillet, pressing it on with your fingertips. Roll up each fillet like a jelly roll and tie with string.

Bring the wine to a boil in a saucepan. Add the bay leaf and onion, then place the fish rolls in the liquid, in one layer. Simmer for 10 minutes. Turn the rolls over carefully and simmer for a further 10 minutes.

Transfer the rolls to a warmed serving dish and remove the string. Keep hot.

Strain the cooking liquid and return to the pan. Boil until reduced to one-third of the original quantity. Mix the remaining butter and the flour to a smooth paste (beurre manié) and add in small pieces to the cooking liquid, stirring constantly. Simmer, stirring, until thickened and smooth. Pour this sauce over the fish and serve.

Serves 4

Sole Véronique

500g/1lb Dover sole fillets, skinned and
halved
salt and black pepper
1 large onion, thinly sliced
1 bay leaf, crumbled
250ml/1 cup dry white wine
4 Tbsp water
2 Tbsp butter
30g/¼ cup flour
125ml/½ cup milk
4 Tbsp heavy cream
250g/8oz green grapes, peeled, halved
and seeded

Rub the fish pieces with salt and pepper and arrange in a greased baking dish. Sprinkle over the onion and bay leaf and pour over the wine and water. Bake in a moderate oven (180°C/350°F) for 15 to 20 minutes or until cooked. Test with a fork: the flesh should flake easily.

Transfer the fish to a warmed serving dish. Keep hot while you make the sauce. Strain the cooking liquid and reserve 125ml/½ cup.

Melt the butter in a saucepan. Add the flour and cook, stirring, for 1 minute. Remove from the heat and gradually stir in the milk and reserved cooking liquid. Return to the heat and simmer, stirring, until thickened and smooth. Stir in the cream and heat through gently.

Pour the sauce over the fish and arrange the grapes around the edge of the dish. Serve immediately.
Serves 4

Salmon with Sauce Verte – an extravagant but splendid main course for a summer day.

Red mullet with tomato sauce

4 Tbsp olive oil
1kg/2lb tomatoes, peeled, seeded and
coarsely chopped
2 garlic cloves, crushed
1 Tbsp thyme, freshly chopped
1 bay leaf
salt and black pepper
250g/1⅓ cups black olives, pitted
2 lemons, cut into 12 slices
12 small red mullet, cleaned and
scaled with heads left on

Heat the oil in a large frying pan. Add the tomatoes, garlic, thyme, bay leaf, and salt and pepper to taste. Simmer for 15 to 20 minutes or until the mixture is very thick.

Stir in the olives and lemon slices. Spoon half the sauce into another large frying pan. Place six fish in each pan and turn them over in the sauce until they are well coated.

Cover the pans and cook, turning the fish occasionally, for 15 to 20 minutes or until cooked. Test with a fork: the flesh should flake easily.

Discard the bay leaf, transfer to a warmed serving dish and serve hot.
Serves 6

Turbot with orange

4 turbot steaks
salt and black pepper
grated rind and juice of 2 oranges
grated rind and juice of 1 lemon
60g/¼ cup butter
1 orange, thinly sliced

Put the turbot steaks, in one layer, in a shallow flameproof casserole. Sprinkle over salt and pepper, the orange rind and juice and the lemon rind and juice. Leave to marinate for 1 hour.

Cut the butter into small pieces and dot over the dish. Broil for 5 to 8 minutes on each side or until cooked. Test with a fork: the flesh should flake easily.

Transfer the turbot steaks to a warmed serving dish and pour over the juices in the casserole. Garnish with the orange slices and serve.
Serves 4

Enjoy a summertime taste of the sea with Red Mullet with Tomato Sauce.

Provençale beef stew

1.5kg/3lb lean chuck steak, cut into
5cm/2in cubes
250g/8oz bacon, cut into 2.5cm/1in strips
125g/1 cup flour
250g/2 cups mushrooms, sliced
750g/1½lb tomatoes, peeled, seeded and
chopped
1 garlic clove, crushed
1 tsp grated orange rind
1 Tbsp parsley, finely chopped
1 bouquet garni
185ml/¾ cup beef stock
10 black olives, pitted and halved
MARINADE
300ml/1¼ cups dry white wine
4 Tbsp brandy
salt
6 black peppercorns
1 tsp thyme, freshly chopped
1 bay leaf
1 garlic clove, crushed
4 medium onions, thinly sliced
4 medium carrots, scraped and thinly
sliced

Mix together the marinade ingredients in a large bowl. Add the beef cubes and baste them thoroughly. Cover and marinate in the refrigerator for at least 12 hours,
basting occasionally.

Blanch the bacon strips in boiling water for 10 minutes. Drain well and pat dry with paper towels.

Remove the beef cubes from the marinade and pat dry with kitchen paper towels. Strain the marinade, reserving the vegetables but discarding the peppercorns and bay leaf.

Put the flour in a plastic bag and add the beef cubes. Shake so they are all coated with flour. Put two or three bacon strips on the bottom of a flameproof casserole. Spoon in some of the marinated vegetables, mushrooms and tomatoes. Cover with a layer of beef and sprinkle with the garlic, orange rind and parsley. Add the bouquet garni. Continue making layers of bacon, vegetables and beef cubes, ending with a layer of bacon. Pour in the reserved marinating liquid and stock and scatter over the olives.

Bring to a boil on top of the stove, then transfer to a warm oven (170°C/325°F). Cook for 4 hours or until the meat is very tender.

Remove from the oven and skim any fat from the surface. Taste and adjust the seasoning. Discard the bouquet garni and serve hot.

Serves 6-8

Provençal Beef Stew needs only to be accompanied by a crisp, green salad for a light but sustaining meal.

Veal Scallops with Lemon Sauce is a light summer dish originating from Italy.

Veal scallops with lemon sauce

4 veal scallops, pounded thin
4 Tbsp lemon juice
salt and black pepper
5 Tbsp butter
185ml/¾ cup dry white wine or chicken stock
1 Tbsp flour
1 large lemon, thinly sliced

Put the scallops in a shallow dish and sprinkle with 2 tablespoons of the lemon juice. Leave to marinate for 30 minutes, then pat dry with kitchen paper towels. Rub the scallops with salt and pepper.

Melt 4 tablespoons of the butter in a frying pan. Add the scallops and fry for 3 to 4 minutes on each side or until lightly browned. Remove the scallops from the pan.

Add the remaining lemon juice to the pan with the wine or stock and bring to a boil. Boil for 5 minutes. Return the scallops to the pan and cook for 1 minute. Mix the remaining butter with the flour to make a smooth paste. Add this in small pieces to the pan, stirring constantly, and simmer until the sauce is thickened and smooth.

Transfer the veal and sauce to a warmed serving dish and garnish with the lemon slices.

Serve hot.
Serves 4

Sukiyaki

1kg/2lb boneless loin steak, cut across the grain into very thin slices
250g/8oz can shirataki noodles, drained
125g/1 cup small spinach leaves, blanched
500g/1lb flat mushrooms, stalks removed and halved
1 large carrot, scraped and cut into 5cm/2in strips
12 scallions, cut into 5cm/2in pieces
1 canned bamboo shoot, drained, halved and thinly sliced
250ml/1 cup dashi or chicken stock
125ml/½ cup sake or dry sherry
4 eggs
2 Tbsp beef suet or chilled shortening
185ml/¾ cup soy sauce
60g/⅓ cup brown sugar

Arrange the steak, noodles, spinach,

mushrooms, carrot, scallions and bamboo shoot on a serving dish.

Pour the stock and sake or sherry into a small bowl. Break an egg into each of four individual serving bowls and beat lightly with a fork.

Heat a chafing dish or fondue pot over a burner at the table. When the dish or pot is hot, rub the bottom with the suet or shortening until lightly coated. Discard any extra fat.

Place about one-quarter of the meat and vegetables in the dish or pot and add about one-quarter of the stock and sake mixture and soy sauce. Sprinkle over one-quarter of the sugar. Fry for 5 to 6 minutes, stirring and turning constantly, until the meat and vegetables are tender.

Transfer the meat and vegetables to individual warmed serving dishes and serve with the egg, while the remaining meat and vegetables are cooked in the same way. The food must be served in batches because it would be overcooked if kept warm while the remainder is being cooked.

The liquid in the pan should always be simmering, and the flavor will become more concentrated as each subsequent batch of meat and vegetables is cooked. You may wish to reduce the quantities of soy sauce and sugar toward the end.
Serves 4

Stuffed veal rolls

8 veal scallops, pounded thin
8 slices proscuitto
4 Tbsp parsley, freshly chopped
2 Tbsp blanched almonds, slivered
2 Tbsp raisins
3 Tbsp grated Parmesan cheese
salt and black pepper
60g/¼ cup butter
185ml/¾ cup Marsala

Place the scallops flat on a working surface. Put a slice of proscuitto on each one.

Mix together the parsley, almonds, raisins, cheese and salt and pepper to taste in a mixing bowl. Divide this mixture between the scallops. Roll up the scallops and tie with string.

Melt the butter in a frying pan. Add the veal rolls and brown on all sides. Pour in the Marsala and bring to a boil. Cover and simmer for 20 minutes or until the veal is tender.

Remove the veal rolls from the pan and discard the string. Place the rolls on a serving dish and pour over the wine sauce in the pan.

Serve hot, with rice.
Serves 4

Vitello tonnato

1 × 1.5kg/3lb leg or loin of veal (boned weight)
1 garlic clove, cut into slivers
salt and pepper
4 Tbsp olive oil
SAUCE
200g/7oz can tuna fish, drained and flaked
125ml/½ cup mayonnaise
1 Tbsp lemon juice
GARNISH
2 tsp capers
2 Tbsp parsley, freshly chopped

Make incisions in the veal and insert the slivers of garlic. Tie into shape, if necessary, and rub with salt and pepper. Place in a roasting pan and pour over the oil. Roast in a fairly hot oven (200°C/400°F) for 20 minutes, then reduce the temperature to warm (170°C/325°F). Continue roasting for a further 1½ hours or until cooked.

Remove from the roasting pan and allow to cool. Skim the fat off the surface of the cooking juices and strain into a bowl.

When the veal is cold, slice it thinly and arrange the slices in a large shallow dish. Mash the tuna fish, mayonnaise and lemon juice together to make a smooth sauce. Thin to a pouring consistency with some of the veal cooking juices and adjust the seasoning. Pour the sauce over the veal slices and cover the dish. Leave to marinate in a cool place for 4-6 hours. Sprinkle over the capers and parsley and serve.
Serves 6-8

Planter's pork chops

2 Tbsp butter
1 Tbsp vegetable oil
1 garlic clove, crushed
4 pork chops
4 Tbsp lemon juice
2 tsp brown sugar
salt and black pepper
150ml/⅔ cup dry white wine
1 banana
4 pineapple rings
4 orange slices
4 watercress sprigs

Melt the butter with the oil in a frying pan. Add the garlic and fry for 1 minute. Add the chops and fry for 4 minutes on each side or until evenly browned. Transfer the chops to a baking dish, arranging them in one layer.

Pour off the cooking liquid from the pan. Add 3 tablespoons of the lemon juice, the sugar, salt and pepper to taste and the wine. Bring to a boil, then pour over the

Used here in the recipe for Sukiyaki, scallions are equally delicious chopped over summer salads.

Right: A superb dish, Orange and Pork Casserole is flavored with vermouth and makes a splendid dinner party main course.
Above: Pork has an affinity to fruit, and the succulent, summer plum is no exception.

chops. Bake in a moderate oven (180°C/350°F) for 25 minutes.

Meanwhile, cut the banana in half lengthwise, then across to make four pieces. Sprinkle with the remaining lemon juice to prevent discoloration.

Place a pineapple ring, orange slice and piece of banana on each chop. Continue baking for 5 minutes or until the chops are cooked.

Transfer the chops and fruit to individual warmed dishes and garnish with the watercress. Serve hot.
Serves 4

Pork chops with plums

500g/1lb plums, pitted
4 Tbsp sugar
¼ tsp ground cinnamon
250ml/1 cup red wine
4 thick pork chops, trimmed of excess fat
salt and black pepper

Put the plums, sugar, cinnamon and wine in a saucepan and cook for 10 to 15 minutes or until the plums are very soft.

Meanwhile, rub the chops with salt and pepper. Broil for 3 minutes on each side or until lightly browned. Transfer the chops to a baking dish, arranging them in one layer. Pour over the plum mixture and bake in a moderate oven (180°C/350°F) for 1 hour.

Serve hot.
Serves 4

Orange pork casserole

1 × 1.5kg/3lb loin of pork (boned weight), trimmed of excess fat
1 garlic clove, halved
salt and black pepper
½ tsp ground allspice
grated rind of 1 small orange
1 Tbsp rosemary, freshly chopped
4 large juicy oranges
2 Tbsp butter
300ml/1¼ cups sweet vermouth
1 Tbsp cornstarch
1 Tbsp orange juice

Rub the pork all over with the garlic halves, then discard the garlic. Rub with salt and pepper. Lay the pork on a flat working surface and sprinkle over the allspice, orange rind and rosemary. Roll up the meat and tie with string at 2.5cm/1in intervals.

Peel the oranges, removing all the pith, and slice the flesh thinly.

Melt the butter in a flameproof casserole. Put the pork in the pot and brown on all sides. Add the vermouth and bring to a boil. Cover the meat with the orange slices, cover the pot and simmer for 2½ hours or until the pork is cooked through and very tender.

Transfer the meat to a warmed serving dish. Remove and discard the string. Arrange the orange slices around the meat. Keep hot.

Skim the fat off the surface of the cooking liquid and strain into a saucepan. Dissolve the cornstarch in the orange juice. Stir in a little of the hot liquid. Add to the strained cooking liquid. Simmer, stirring, until the sauce is thickened and smooth. Pour the sauce into a sauceboat and serve with the meat.

Serves 6

Meatballs with hot Mexican sauce

MEATBALLS

1kg/2lb ground pork
1 large onion, finely grated
2 garlic cloves, crushed
60g/½ cup ground almonds
60g/⅔ cup fresh breadcrumbs
1 egg, lightly beaten
1 Tbsp parsley, freshly chopped
¾ tsp ground cinnamon
salt and black pepper
3 Tbsp medium dry sherry
1 Tbsp butter
2 Tbsp olive oil

SAUCE

1 large onion, finely chopped
1 garlic clove, crushed
½ Tbsp brown sugar
6 medium tomatoes, peeled, seeded and chopped
1 medium green pepper, pith and seeds removed and thinly sliced
1 medium red pepper, pith and seeds removed and thinly sliced
1 green chili pepper, finely chopped
¼ tsp cayenne pepper
1 tsp paprika
1 Tbsp parsley, freshly chopped
150ml/⅔ cup beef stock
salt and black pepper
2 tsp cornstarch
4 Tbsp medium dry sherry

Mix together all the ingredients for the meatballs except the butter and oil, adding salt and pepper to taste. Knead well with your hands, then form the mixture into about 36 walnut-sized balls.

Melt the butter with the oil in a frying pan. Add the meatballs, in batches, and fry for 6 to 8 minutes or until they are evenly browned.

Remove the meatballs from the pan and keep warm while you make the sauce. Add the onion, garlic and brown sugar to the frying pan and fry until the onion is soft and golden brown. Stir in the tomatoes, peppers, chili pepper, cayenne, paprika and parsley and simmer for a further 3 minutes.

Add the stock with salt and pepper to taste and bring to a boil. Dissolve the cornstarch in the sherry. Stir a little of the hot sauce into the mixture, then stir into the sauce. Add the meatballs, cover the pan and simmer for 20 to 25 minutes or until the meatballs are completely cooked through.

Transfer to a warmed serving dish and serve immediately, with noodles or steamed rice.

Serves 4-6

Fresh red and green pepers add flavor and texture to Meatballs with Hot Mexican Sauce.

Canary Island Chicken – even its name suggests a taste of sunshine and color.

Grilled lamb chops with rosemary

4 Tbsp olive oil
2 Tbsp lemon juice
salt and black pepper
2 Tbsp rosemary, freshly chopped
1 garlic clove, crushed
8 thick lamb chops

Mix together the oil, lemon juice, salt and pepper to taste, the rosemary and garlic in a shallow dish. Add the chops and turn to coat them on all sides. Leave to marinate for 2 hours.

Broil the chops for 8 to 10 minutes on each side, basting with the marinade frequently. Transfer to a warmed serving dish and spoon over any remaining marinade. Serve hot.
Serves 4

Lamb with tomatoes

60g/¼ cup butter
2 Tbsp vegetable oil
1 × 1kg/2lb shoulder of lamb
(boned weight), cut into 4cm/1½in cubes
salt and black pepper
500g small/1lb small tomatoes,
peeled and seeded
1 Tbsp flour
125ml/½ cup white wine
250ml/1 cup veal or chicken stock
1 garlic clove, crushed
2 Tbsp parsley, freshly chopped

Melt 2 tablespoons of the butter with the oil in a frying pan. Add the lamb cubes and sprinkle with salt and pepper. Fry until the cubes are lightly browned and tender. Transfer to a warmed serving dish, using a slotted spoon. Keep hot.

Melt the remaining butter in another pan. Add the tomatoes and fry gently for 5 minutes. Remove the tomatoes from the pan with a slotted spoon and arrange around the lamb cubes. Keep hot.

Stir the flour into the fat remaining in the pan in which the lamb was cooked. Cook, stirring, until the flour is lightly browned. Gradually stir in the wine and stock with the garlic and simmer, stirring, until the liquid has reduced to half the original quantity. Pour this sauce over the lamb and sprinkle with the parsley. Serve hot.
Serves 4

Canary Island chicken

90g/¾ cup flour
salt and black pepper
1 × 2kg/4lb chicken, cut into
eight serving pieces
6 Tbsp butter
4 Tbsp olive oil
2 garlic cloves, crushed
2 medium onions, chopped
300ml/1¼ cups dry white wine
300ml/1¼ cups chicken stock
1 bouquet garni
1 tsp saffron powder
1 Tbsp hot water
60g/½ cup blanched almonds, shredded
hard-cooked and
2 eggs, finely chopped
1 Tbsp parsley, freshly chopped

Mix 60g/½ cup of the flour with salt and pepper on a plate. Coat the chicken pieces in this seasoned flour. Melt 60g/½ cup of the butter with the oil in a flameproof casserole. Add the garlic and onions and fry until the onions are soft but not brown. Add the chicken pieces and brown lightly on all sides.

Pour in the wine and chicken stock and add the bouquet garni. Bring to a boil, then cover and simmer for 45 minutes.

Dissolve the saffron in the hot water. Add to the casserole with the almonds. Simmer, uncovered, for a further 15 minutes.

Transfer the chicken pieces to a warmed serving dish. Discard the bouquet garni from the casserole. Mix the remaining butter and remaining flour to a paste and add in small pieces to the casserole liquid. Simmer, stirring, until thickened.

Pour the sauce over the chicken and garnish with the egg and parsley. Serve hot.
Serves 4

Chicken with peach sauce

salt and black pepper
1 × 2kg/4lb chicken, skinned and cut
into 6 serving pieces
4 Tbsp vegetable oil
1 small onion, finely chopped
1 garlic clove, crushed
¼ tsp red pepper flakes
¼ tsp ground ginger
250ml/1 cup chicken stock
4 Tbsp lime juice
4 Tbsp lemon juice
25g/1oz butter
4 peaches, peeled, halved, pitted and
sliced

Rub salt and pepper into the chicken pieces. Heat the oil in a frying pan. Add the chicken pieces, in batches, and brown on all sides. Remove from the pan and place in a baking dish.

Add the onion and garlic to the frying pan and fry until the onion is soft but not brown. Stir in the red pepper flakes, ginger and stock and bring to a boil. Remove from the heat and stir in the lime and lemon juices. Pour over the chicken pieces.

Melt the butter in a clean frying pan. Add the peach slices and fry for 6 minutes or until they are beginning to pulp. Add to the baking dish with the chicken. Cover and bake in a moderate oven (180°C/350°F) for 1 hour or until the chicken is tender.

Serve the chicken and peach sauce on a bed of boiled rice.
Serves 4

Chicken Florentine

125g/1 cup Parmesan cheese, grated
125g/2 cups dry white breadcrumbs
3 Tbsp flour
salt and black pepper
1 egg
1 Tbsp water
6 chicken breasts, boned and skinned
185g/¾ cup butter
2.5kg/5lb spinach
1½ Tbsp lemon juice
750g/1½lb mushrooms, sliced
1 lemon, sliced

Mix together the cheese and breadcrumbs. Season the flour well with salt and pepper. Beat the egg and water together until well mixed. Dip the chicken breasts first in the seasoned flour, then in the beaten egg and finally in the cheese mixture, coating well with each. Chill for 1 hour.

Melt 125g/½ cup of the butter in a frying pan. Add the chicken breasts and brown on all sides. Cover and cook gently for

about 25 to 30 minutes or until the chicken is tender.

Meanwhile, put the spinach in a saucepan. Do not add any water as there should be enough left on the leaves after washing. Cook for about 7 minutes or until tender, then drain well, pressing out all excess moisture. Chop the spinach coarsely and arrange on a warmed serving dish. Sprinkle with the lemon juice and keep hot.

Melt half the remaining butter in a saucepan. Add the mushrooms and fry quickly for 2 to 3 minutes. Using a slotted spoon, transfer the mushrooms to the serving dish, arranging them around the spinach. Place the chicken breasts on top. Keep hot.

Add the remaining butter to the pan in which the mushrooms were cooked. Melt it and cook until it is brown. Pour over the chicken and garnish with the lemon slices.
Serves 6

Andalusian chicken

1 × 2kg/4lb chicken
60g/¼ cup butter
1 Tbsp olive oil
1 large onion, halved
1 bouquet garni
1 Tbsp flour
125ml/½ cup white wine
2 Tbsp tomato paste
STUFFING
125g/½ cup long-grain rice, cooked
125g/½ cup cooked ham, diced
2 tsp paprika
salt and black pepper
GARNISH
2 Tbsp oil
1 large onion, sliced, in rings
2 large green peppers, pith and seeds
removed and sliced into rings
500g/1lb tomatoes, peeled and chopped
salt and black pepper

Mix together the ingredients for the stuffing, with salt and pepper to taste. Use to stuff the chicken and close with a skewer or trussing thread.

Melt the butter with the oil in a flameproof casserole. Add the chicken and brown on all sides. Add the onion and bouquet garni, cover and cook gently for about 1½ hours or until the chicken is tender.

Meanwhile, make the garnish. Heat the oil in a frying pan. Add the onion and fry until it is soft but not brown. Add the peppers and tomatoes with salt and pepper to taste and continue to cook until the vegetables are just tender. Remove from heat and keep hot.

Transfer the chicken to a warmed serving

Don't reserve summer peaches exclusively for desserts; in Chicken with Peach Sauce they add flavor and color.

dish. Remove the skewer or trussing thread. Surround with the garnish.

Discard the onion and bouquet garni from the casserole and sprinkle in the flour. Stir well, then stir in the wine and tomato paste. Bring to a boil and simmer until thickened. Pour over the chicken and serve.
Serves 4

Mango chicken

1 × 2kg/4lb chicken, cut into serving pieces
salt and black pepper
2 Tbsp butter
2 Tbsp vegetable oil
1 large onion, thinly sliced
1 mango, peeled, pitted and sliced
1 tsp grated lemon rind
¼ tsp ground coriander
¼ tsp ground cinnamon
250ml/1 cup chicken stock
250ml/1 cup light cream
2 tsp flour
1 Tbsp lemon juice
1 Tbsp water
2 lemons, thinly sliced

Luscious mangoes cooked with chicken, cream and spices, Mango Chicken may be garnished with lemon slices.

Rub the chicken pieces with salt and pepper. Melt the butter with the oil in a frying pan. Add the chicken pieces and brown on all sides. Transfer to a flameproof casserole.

Add the onion to the pan and fry until it is soft but not brown. Transfer the onion to the casserole, using a slotted spoon.

Add the mango slices to the pan and fry, turning once, for 4 minutes. Stir in the lemon rind, coriander, cinnamon and chicken stock and bring to a boil. Pour into the casserole.

Cover the casserole and bake in a fairly hot oven (190°C/375°F) for 1¼ hours or until the chicken is tender.

Transfer the chicken pieces to a warmed serving dish. Keep hot. Bring the liquid in the casserole to a boil on top of the stove. Reduce the heat to low and stir in the cream. Mix together the flour, lemon juice and water. Add a little of the hot liquid then stir into the casserole. Heat, stirring, until well mixed and thickened. Pour the sauce over the chicken and garnish with the lemon slices. Serve hot.
Serves 4

Barbecue Food

Hamburgers

1.5kg/3lb lean ground beef
60g/⅔ cup fresh breadcrumbs
salt and black pepper
1½ tsp thyme, freshly chopped
1 egg, lightly beaten
ACCOMPANIMENTS
3 medium tomatoes, thinly sliced
1 large onion, thinly sliced and pushed
out into rings
6 large lettuce leaves
6 hamburger buns
relishes, tomato ketchup, mustard, etc.

Mix together the beef, breadcrumbs, salt and pepper to taste, the thyme and egg. Knead with your hands, then form into six patties.

Arrange the tomatoes, onion rings and lettuce on a serving dish. Halve the buns.

Barbecue the hamburgers for about 5 to 7 minutes on each side. This will produce rare hamburgers. If you prefer them well-done, increase the cooking time accordingly. When the hamburgers are nearly ready, place the buns on the grid to heat through.

Place a hamburger on each bun bottom and add the tops. Serve hot, with the accompaniments.
Serves 6

Barbecued spiced duck

1 Tbsp ground coriander
2 tsp ground fenugreek
2 tsp ground cumin
1 tsp ground turmeric
1 tsp ground cinnamon
½ tsp ground cardamom
¼ tsp ground cloves
¼ tsp grated nutmeg
1 tsp mild chili powder
salt and black pepper
1cm/½in piece green ginger, peeled and
finely chopped
juice of 1 lemon
2 small onions, minced
2 garlic cloves, crushed
125g/1⅓ cups shredded coconut
185ml/¾ cup boiling water
1 × 2.5kg/5lb duck, split open through
the breastbone, ribs broken at the
backbone

Mix together the spices, salt and pepper to taste, the ginger, lemon juice, onions and garlic. Soak the coconut in the water for 5 minutes, then add to the spice mixture. Stir well to form a thick paste.

Tie the wings and legs of the duck together so that the cavity is spread open. Cover the duck with some of the spice paste. Place it, cavity side up, on the barbecue grilling surface and cook for about 20 minutes. Turn the duck over and cook for a further 20 minutes. Baste with the spice paste from time to time. Continue cooking and turning until the duck is cooked through and the juices run clear when the thigh is pierced. Serve hot.
Serves 4

Lamb kebabs marinated in yogurt

1 × 1kg/2lb leg of lamb (boned weight),
cut into 2.5cm/1in cubes
150ml/⅔ cup plain yogurt
1 Tbsp ground coriander
1 tsp ground turmeric
½ tsp chili powder
1 tsp salt
2 garlic cloves, crushed
2.5cm/1in piece green ginger, grated or
finely chopped
1 Tbsp coriander leaves, freshly chopped
2 lemons, cut into wedges

Put the lamb cubes in a bowl. Mix together the yogurt, coriander, turmeric, chili powder, salt, garlic and ginger. Pour over the lamb cubes and mix well to coat each cube. Cover and leave to marinate for at least 6 hours or overnight.

Stir the meat and marinade well, then thread the meat cubes onto skewers. Barbecue for about 8 minutes, turning and basting with any remaining marinade.

Slide the lamb cubes onto a warmed serving dish and sprinkle with the coriander leaves. Garnish with the lemon and serve.
Serves 4

Frankfurter and bacon kebabs

8 frankfurters, each cut into 4 pieces
1 large pineapple, peeled, cored and
cut into chunks
8 bacon slices, rolled
8 small onions
2 green peppers, pith and seeds removed
and cut into pieces
60g/¼ cup butter, melted

Thread the frankfurter pieces onto eight skewers, alternating with pineapple chunks, bacon slice rolls, onions and pieces of green pepper. Brush with melted butter and barbecue for about 15 minutes, turning frequently and basting with the melted butter. Serve hot.
Serves 4

Chicken with Orange and Figs makes an elegant kebab dish for a summer barbecue.

Prawn, pepper and mushroom kebabs

16 king prawns, shelled and deveined
2 small green peppers, pith and seeds
removed and cut into 16 pieces
16 medium mushrooms, stalks removed
16 sage leaves
2 lemons, quartered and each quarter
cut across in half
MARINADE
4 Tbsp olive oil
2 Tbsp lemon juice
3 garlic cloves, crushed
salt and black pepper

Mix together the marinade ingredients, with salt and pepper to task, in a shallow dish. Add the prawns and stir to coat them with the marinade. Leave to marinate for 1 hour, turning occasionally.

Remove the prawns from the marinade and pat dry with paper towels. Reserve the marinade.

Thread a prawn onto a skewer, then add a piece of pepper, a mushroom, a sage leaf and a piece of lemon. Continue filling the skewer in this order, allowing four of each ingredient to each of four skewers.

Barbecue the kebabs for about 10 minutes, turning and basting with the reserved marinade.

Serve hot.
Serves 4

Chicken with orange and figs

16 chicken portions
60g/¼ cup butter, melted
salt and black pepper
3 large oranges, each cut into 6 portions
16 figs, fresh or dried

Brush the chicken portions with the butter and sprinkle with salt and pepper. Barbecue for about 8 minutes on each side. Remove the chicken portions from the barbecue and thread onto skewers with the orange portions and figs. (The chicken may be put on skewers from the beginning of the cooking, if desired, but it will not be evenly browned.) Brush with the butter again and continue to barbecue for a further 10 to 15 minutes. Baste with the butter and turn frequently.

Serve hot.
Serves 8

Vegetables

Tomatoes baked with basil

60g/¼ cup butter
2 large onions, thinly sliced and pushed
out into rings
2 large tomatoes, thinly sliced
2 Tbsp basil, freshly chopped
salt and black pepper
1 tsp sugar
90g/1 cup fresh breadcrumbs

Melt half the butter in a frying pan. Add the onions and fry until they are soft but not brown. Remove from the heat and place half the onion rings in a greased baking dish. Cover with half the tomato slices and sprinkle with half the basil, salt and pepper and a little sugar. Make another layer of onion rings and tomato slices, chopped basil, salt and pepper to taste and sugar.

Cover the top with the breadcrumbs. Cut the remaining butter into small pieces and dot over the top. Bake in a fairly hot oven (190°C/375°F) for 30 minutes. Remove the dish from the oven and serve at once, straight from the dish.
Serves 4

Asparagus with orange sauce

500g/1lb asparagus
125g/½ cup butter
Juice of 1 orange
1 tsp finely grated orange rind

Scrape and trim the asparagus stalks and tie in a bundle. Place in a pan of boiling salted water, keeping the tips above the water level, and cover partially. Cook for 15 to 20 minutes or until tender. Drain well and arrange on a warmed serving dish. Keep hot.

Melt the butter in a saucepan. Stir in the orange juice and rind and cook for 2 minutes or until the sauce is hot. Pour over the asparagus and serve immediately.
Serves 4

Lima beans with mushrooms

750g/3 cups lima beans (shelled)
60g/¼ cup butter
250g/8oz button mushrooms
2 Tbsp flour
225ml/⅞ cup chicken stock
250ml/1 cup light cream
salt and black pepper
2 Tbsp Parmesan cheese, grated

Cook the lima beans in boiling salted water for 8 to 10 minutes or until they are just tender. Drain well, then refresh under cold running water. Drain again.

Melt half the butter in a frying pan. Add the mushrooms and fry for 4 minutes. Remove from the heat and set aside.

Melt the remaining butter in a saucepan. Stir in the flour and cook, stirring, for 1 minute. Remove the pan from the heat and gradually stir in the chicken stock. Return to the heat and simmer, stirring, until thickened and smooth.

Stir in the cream, salt and pepper to taste and the Parmesan, then fold in the mushrooms and lima beans. Cook gently for 3 to 4 minutes, or until the vegetables are heated through. Serve hot.
Serves 4

Basil Baked Tomatoes is an unusual and fragrant accompaniment to pork, lamb or chicken.

Zucchini with lemon and parsley

750g/1½lb zucchini, cut into 1cm/½in
thick slices
6 Tbsp butter
2 Tbsp olive oil
2 Tbsp lemon juice
salt and black pepper
3 Tbsp parsley, freshly chopped

Blanch the zucchini slices in boiling water for 3 minutes. Remove the pan from the heat and drain well.

Melt two-thirds of the butter with the oil in a frying pan. Add the zucchini slices and fry for 8-10 minutes. Sprinkle over the lemon juice with salt and pepper to taste, then add the remaining butter and the parsley.

Turn over the slices to coat well and serve hot.

Serves 4

Corn fritters

250g/1½ cups corn kernels
60g/½ cup flour
2 Tbsp sugar
salt and black pepper
2 eggs lightly beaten
2 Tbsp grated Parmesan cheese
vegetable oil for deep-frying

Mix together the corn, flour, sugar, salt and pepper to taste, the eggs and cheese. Heat the oil in a deep fat fryer until it reaches 185°C/360°F or until a small cube of stale bread dropped into the oil turns golden in 50 seconds.

Drop a few tablespoonfuls of the corn mixture into the oil. Fry for 3 to 4 minutes or until the fritters are golden brown. Remove from the pan with a slotted spoon and drain on kitchen paper towels. Keep hot while you fry the remaining fritters.

Serves 4

Corn Fritters – the Spanish way to cook and serve corn.

Side Salads

Apricot salad

1kg/2lb apricots
4 Tbsp sour cream
3 Tbsp tarragon vinegar
1 Tbsp sugar
salt and black pepper
2 Tbsp tarragon, freshly chopped

Blanch and peel the apricots, then halve and remove the pits. Arrange the apricots in a glass serving dish. Crack the pits and remove the kernels. Chop the kernels.

Mix together the sour cream, vinegar, sugar and salt and pepper to taste. Spoon this dressing over the apricots and sprinkle with the tarragon and chopped apricot kernels.
Serves 4

Fennel and cucumber salad

1 cucumber, peeled and thinly sliced
1 head Florence fennel, cut into thin strips
4 radishes, thinly sliced
3 scallions, finely chopped
3 Tbsp olive oil
1 Tbsp lemon juice
1 garlic clove, chrushed
salt and black pepper
2 tsp parsley, freshly chopped

Put the cucumber, fennel, radishes and scallions in a serving dish. Put the remaining ingredients except parsley, with salt and pepper to taste, in a screwtop jar and shake well to mix. Pour this dressing over the salad ingredients and toss well to coat. Chill for at least 30 minutes. Sprinkle with parsley just before serving.
Serves 4

Green bean and bacon salad

6 bacon slices
500g/1lb green beans
6 medium tomatoes, peeled, seeded and chopped
1 egg, hard-cooked and finely chopped
DRESSING
6 Tbsp olive oil
3 Tbsp lemon juice
pinch sugar
salt and black pepper
1 Tbsp basil, freshly chopped (optional)

Broil the bacon until it is crisp. Meanwhile, cook the beans in boiling salted water for about 10 minutes or until they are just tender.

Drain the bacon on paper towels, cool and crumble. Allow to cool. Drain the beans and refresh under cold running water. Drain again.

Put all the dressing ingredients, with salt and pepper to taste, in a screwtop jar. Shake well to mix.

Put the bacon, beans and tomatoes in a shallow serving dish. Pour over the dressing and toss well to coat all the ingredients. Chill for 30 minutes. Just before serving, sprinkle the egg on top.
Serves 6

Greek Salad

1 head romaine lettuce, torn into pieces
10 radishes, sliced
250g/8oz feta cheese, cut into cubes
2 Tbsp marjoram, freshly chopped
4 tomatoes, peeled and sliced
6 anchovies, finely chopped
6 black olives, halved and pitted
1 Tbsp parsley, freshly chopped
DRESSING
4 Tbsp olive oil
1½ Tbsp white wine vinegar
1 tsp chives, freshly chopped
2 tsp lemon thyme, freshly chopped
4 scallions, finely chopped
1 tsp sugar
salt and black pepper

Arrange the lettuce pieces in a large salad bowl. Scatter over the radishes and pile the cheese cubes in the center. Sprinkle with the marjoram. Arrange the tomato slices in a ring around the edge, overlapping them, and top with the anchovies and olives.

Put all the dressing ingredients in a screwtop jar, with salt and pepper to taste, and shake well to mix. Pour this dressing over the salad and sprinkle over the parsley. Serve immediately.
Serves 4-6

Yogurt and cucumber salad

625ml/2½ cups plain yogurt
½ cucumber, diced
4 scallions, finely chopped
salt and black pepper
1 green chili pepper, finely chopped
¼ tsp paprika

Mix together the yogurt, cucumber, scallions and salt and pepper to taste. Pour into a serving dish, cover and chill for 1 hour.

Sprinkle over the chili pepper and paprika just before serving.
Serves 4-6

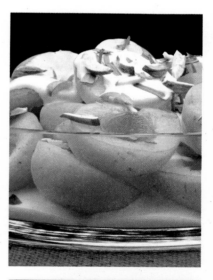

Below: Apricot Salad is a different and colorful accompaniment for hot or cold ham.
Bottom: Fennel, with its delicate, aniseed-like flavor, makes an excellent side salad – especially with fish dishes.

Salads

Lobster and pineapple salad

MARINADE
2 garlic cloves, crushed
salt and black pepper
½ tsp prepared mustard
¼ tsp sugar
1 Tbsp red wine vinegar
3 Tbsp olive oil
SALAD
1 × 1kg/2lb lobster, cooked
2 Tbsp mayonnaise
½ tsp soy sauce
½ tsp cayenne pepper
salt and black pepper
½ pineapple, peeled, cored and diced
2 celery stalks, chopped
6 lettuce leaves
1 lemon, thinly sliced

Mix together the marinade ingredients, with salt and pepper to taste, in a shallow dish.

Cut the soft undershell from the lobster body with scissors. Remove the meat and cut it into thin slices. Reserve the body shell. Crack the claws and remove the meat. Slice it thinly. Add the lobster meat to the marinade and toss well to coat. Cover and marinate in the refrigerator for 45 minutes.

Drain the lobster meat, discarding any remaining marinade. Beat together the mayonnaise, soy sauce, cayenne and salt and pepper to taste in a mixing bowl. Add the lobster meat, pineapple and celery and mix well. Pile into the reserved lobster shell.

Arrange the lettuce leaves on a serving plate. Place the filled lobster on the lettuce and garnish with the lemon slices. Serve immediately.
Serves 2

Chicken and avocado salad with Russian dressing

1 × 2kg/4lb chicken, roasted and cooled
2 avocados
10 black olives, halved and pitted
DRESSING
300ml/1¼ cups mayonnaise
pinch cayenne pepper
1 tsp chili sauce
1 egg, hard-cooked and finely chopped
1 scallion, finely chopped
1 tsp parsley, freshly chopped
salt and black pepper

First make the dressing. Mix all the ingredients together well and adjust the seasoning, if necessary. Chill for 15 minutes.

Skin the chicken and remove the meat from the bones. Cut the meat into bite-size pieces and place in a serving dish. Halve the avocados and remove the seeds, then peel and dice the flesh. Add to the chicken with the olives.

Pour the dressing over the salad ingredients and toss well to coat. Serve immediately.
Serves 4-6

Lobster and Pineapple Salad – an exotic summer dish which may be served as part of a cold buffet or as an appetizer.

Crab Louis

1 romaine or iceberg lettuce, separated
into leaves
500g/1lb crabmeat, flaked
2 tomatoes, thinly sliced
½ cucumber, thinly sliced
4 eggs, hard-cooked and thinly sliced
1 Tbsp capers
DRESSING
250ml/1 cup mayonnaise
3 Tbsp olive oil
1 Tbsp lemon juice
2 Tbsp tomato ketchup
1 tsp Worcestershire sauce
1 Tbsp chives, freshly chopped
1 Tbsp parsley, freshly chopped
salt and black pepper
75ml/⅓ cup heavy cream

First make the dressing. Mix all the
ingredients together, with salt and pepper
to taste, in a bowl. Chill for 30 minutes.
    Line a salad bowl or serving dish with the
lettuce leaves. Pile the crabmeat in the
center and spoon over the dressing.
Arrange the tomato, cucumber and egg
slices around the crabmeat and garnish
with the capers. Serve immediately.
Serves 4

Florida salad

125g/½ cup cream cheese
4 Tbsp light cream
2 Tbsp lemon juice
pinch cayenne pepper
salt and black pepper
1 medium green pepper, pith and seeds
removed and shredded
1 large eating apple, cored and diced
1 small pineapple, peeled, cored and
diced
3 large celery stalks, sliced
1 large orange, peeled and thinly sliced
1 banana, sliced
6 large lettuce leaves
4 radishes, thinly sliced
1 Tbsp chives, freshly chopped

Beat together the cream cheese, cream,
lemon juice, cayenne and salt and pepper
to taste. Put the green pepper, apple,
pineapple, celery, orange and banana in a
mixing bowl and pour over the cream
cheese mixture. Toss well to coat all the
fruit and vegetables. Chill for at least 30
minutes.
    Line a glass salad bowl with the lettuce
leaves and pile the fruit and vegetable
mixture on top. Arrange the radish slices
around the edge and sprinkle over the
chives. Serve immediately.
Serves 4

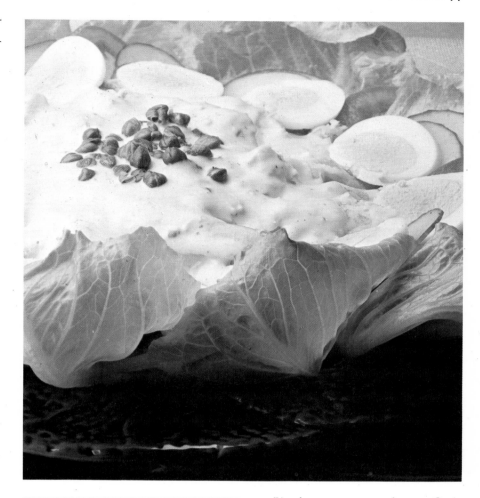

Pineapple cheese salad

½ pineapple, peeled, cored and chopped
175g/6oz mild white cheese, such as
Monterey Jack cut into 6mm/¼in cubes
1 pear, peeled, cored and chopped
12 small radishes
2 celery stalks, cut into 6mm/¼in thick
slices
1 head French or Belgian endive, cut
into 1cm/½in thick slices
8 watercress sprigs
DRESSING
4 Tbsp olive oil
salt and black pepper
½ tsp sugar
2 Tbsp light cream
1½ Tbsp lemon juice
1 Tbsp tarragon, freshly chopped

Mix together the pineapple, cheese, pear,
radishes, celery and endive in a mixing
bowl. Put all the dressing ingredients,
with salt and pepper to taste, in a screwtop
jar and shake well to mix. Pour this dressing
over the salad ingredients and toss well.
Pile into a serving dish or individual
dishes and garnish with the watercress
sprigs. Serve immediately.
Serves 4

*Simple to prepare, superb to eat, Crab
Louis is ideal for a very special
occasion.*

Crisp, crunchy corn is delicious added to summer salads or on its own.

Light Dishes

Seafood crêpes

BATTER
250g/2 cups flour
½ tsp salt
2 eggs
25g/6 cup butter, melted
475ml/2 cups milk
2 Tbsp vegetable oil
FILLING
6 Tbsp butter
2 Tbsp vegetable oil
2 Tbsp bean sprouts
4 small scallions, finely chopped
75ml/⅓ cup dry white wine
2 Tbsp parsley, freshly chopped
1 Tbsp chervil, freshly chopped
175g/1 cup clams, fresh (shucked) *or*
canned and drained
175g/1 cup crabmeat, flaked
175g/1 cup shrimp (shelled), deveined
salt and white pepper
2 Tbsp flour
300ml/1¼ cups milk

Sift the flour and salt into a mixing bowl. Make a well in the center and add the eggs, melted butter and half the milk. Mix to a smooth cream, gradually drawing the flour into the liquids. Beat in the rest of the milk. Alternatively, make the batter in an electric blender.

Lightly grease a frying pan or crêpe pan with a little of the oil. Heat the pan, then pour about 4 tablespoons of the batter into the center. Tip the pan so it is coated with the batter. Cook for just over 1 minute, then turn the crêpe over and cook the other side for about 30 seconds.

Slide the crêpe out of the pan. Keep hot on a plate over a pan of hot water while you cook the remaining crêpes in the same way. Stack them up, interleaving with wax paper. Keep hot while you make the filling.

Melt two-thirds of the butter with the oil in a saucepan. Add the bean sprouts and scallions and fry for 1 minute, stirring constantly. Stir in the wine and bring to a boil. Boil to reduce to about half the original quantity.

Remove the pan from the heat. Add half the parsley, the chervil, clams, crabmeat, shrimp and salt and pepper to taste. Return to a gentle heat and warm the mixture until it is hot.

Melt the remaining butter in another saucepan. Stir in the flour and cook, stirring, for 1 minute. Remove from the heat and simmer, stirring, until thickened and smooth. Carefully stir in the seafood mixture.

Lay the crêpes out flat and put about 2 tablespoons of the filling in the center of each. Roll up the crêpes and place on a hot serving dish.

Sprinkle with the remaining parsley and serve.
Serves 4-6

Corn and shrimp savory

60g/¼ cup butter
500g/1lb corn kernels
1 green pepper, pith and seeds removed
and finely chopped
375g/2 cups shrimp (shelled), deveined
125ml/½ cup heavy cream
salt and black pepper
6 slices hot buttered toast
pinch cayenne pepper

Melt the butter in a frying pan. Add the corn and green pepper and cook for 5 minutes. Stir in the shrimp and cream and cook gently for a further 4 minutes or until heated through. Add salt and pepper to taste.

Arrange the toast on individual warmed serving plates and spoon over the corn mixture.

Sprinkle with cayenne and serve.
Serves 3-6

Omelette nicoise

1 Tbsp olive oil
1 small onion, thinly sliced
1 garlic clove, crushed
2 large tomatoes, peeled, seeded and
chopped
3 anchovies, chopped
8 black olives, pitted and chopped
6 eggs
salt and black pepper
2 Tbsp cold water
1 Tbsp butter

Heat the oil in a frying pan. Add the onion and garlic and fry until the onion is soft but not brown. Stir in the tomatoes, anchovies, and olives and cook for a further 3 minutes or until the tomatoes are tender but still firm. Remove from the heat and keep hot.

Beat together the eggs, salt and pepper to taste and the water. Melt the butter in a frying pan or omelet pan. Pour in the egg mixture and cook until set, lifting the set edges to let the uncooked egg mixture run onto the pan. Spoon over the anchovy mixture. Fold over the omelet and slide onto a warmed serving dish. Cut into two or three and serve.
Serves 2-3

Above: Corn and Shrimp Savory, served on toast, makes an easily prepared lunch or supper snack. Left: Filled with a tempting assortment of seafood, Seafood Crêpes makes an excellent supper dish.

Zucchini risotto

125g/½ cup butter
2 garlic cloves, crushed
500g/1lb zucchini, thinly sliced
salt and black pepper
500g/1lb tomatoes, peeled and chopped
150ml/⅔ cup dry white wine
500g/1lb Italian rice, such as avorio
900ml/3½ cups chicken stock, boiling
60g/½ cup Parmesan cheese, grated

Melt three-quarters of the butter in a saucepan. Add the garlic and fry for 1 minute. Add the zucchini slices and fry for 10 to 12 minutes or until lightly browned. Stir in salt and pepper to taste, the tomatoes and wine. Bring to a boil.

Add the rice and simmer for 5 minutes. Stir in about one-third of the stock. Regulate the heat so that the rice is bubbling all the time. When the rice swells and the liquid is absorbed, add another third of the stock. Add the final third when that has been absorbed.

Stir in the remaining butter and the Parmesan and simmer for a further one minute.

Serve immediately.
Serves 4-6

Stuffed green peppers with yogurt and tomato sauce

4 large green peppers
150ml/⅔ cup plain yogurt
4 tsp parsley, freshly chopped
FILLING
2 Tbsp oil
2 onions, finely chopped
2 celery stalks, finely chopped
185g/1 cup long-grain rice, cooked
2 Tbsp, parsley, freshly chopped
1 tsp basil, freshly chopped
2 tsp marjoram, freshly chopped
salt and black pepper
1 egg, lightly beaten
SAUCE
3 Tbsp butter
1 onion, finely chopped
1 Tbsp flour
250ml/1 cup chicken stock
375g/12oz tomatoes, peeled and chopped
salt and black pepper
½ tsp sugar
1 Tbsp tomato paste

Cut the tops off the peppers and scoop out the seeds and white pith.

Heat the oil for the filling in a saucepan. Add the onions and celery and fry until the onions are soft but not brown. Stir in the rice, parsley, basil, marjoram and salt and pepper to taste. Remove from the heat and cool slightly, then beat in the egg. Stuff the peppers with this mixture, pressing it down well.

To make the sauce, melt the butter in a flameproof casserole. Add the onion and fry until it is soft but not brown. Stir in the flour and cook, stirring, for 1 minute. Remove from the heat and gradually stir in the stock. Return to the heat and simmer, stirring, until thickened. Stir in the tomatoes, salt and pepper to taste, the sugar and tomato paste.

Place the stuffed peppers in the sauce, upright. Cover and transfer to a moderate oven (180°C/350°F). Bake for 35 to 40 minutes or until the peppers are tender.

Remove the lid and spoon the yogurt on top of each pepper. Sprinkle with the parsley and serve, straight from the casserole.

Serves 4

Stuffed Green Peppers with Yogurt and Tomato Sauce – a taste of the Mediterranean that is ideal for a light summer meal.

Desserts

Summer pudding

1kg/2lb raspberries, or other berries
125g/½ cup sugar
125ml/½ cup milk
8 slices stale white bread, crusts
removed
300ml/1¼ cups heavy cream

Put the raspberries in a mixing bowl and sprinkle over the sugar. Sprinkle the milk over the bread slices to moisten them. Line a greased deep baking dish or mold with the bread slices, reserving two slices for the top. Pour the raspberries into the dish and place the reserved bread slices over them.

Cover the dish with a sheet of wax paper and place a plate and heavy weight on top of the bread. Chill for at least 8 hours.

Whip the cream until it is thick. Pile into a serving dish. Turn out the pudding onto a plate and serve with the cream.

Serves 4-6

Damson soufflé

500g/1lb damsons, pitted and chopped
500ml (1 pint) plus 1 Tbsp water
250g/1 cup plus 1 tsp sugar
1 Tbsp cornstarch
2 Tbsp butter
4 eggs, separated
1 Tbsp rum

Put the damsons in a saucepan with all but 1 tablespoon of the water. Simmer gently, covered, for 15 to 20 minutes or until the fruit is soft. Remove from the heat and cool slightly, then purée in an electric blender or food mill. Alternatively, push the fruit mixture through a strainer.

Return the damson purée to the saucepan and stir in all but 1 teaspoon of the sugar. Stir over a gentle heat to dissolve the sugar, then remove from the heat.

Dissolve the cornstarch in the remaining water. Add to the damson mixture and stir well. Return to the heat and cook, stirring, until thickened and smooth. Stir in the butter. When it has melted, remove from the heat. Allow to cool.

Lightly beat the egg yolks and rum together. Stir into the damson mixture. Beat the egg whites until they will hold a stiff peak. Fold into the damson mixture. Spoon into a greased soufflé dish and sprinkle over the remaining sugar. Bake in a fairly hot oven (200°C/400°F) for 30 to 35 minutes or until well risen and lightly browned. Serve immediately.

Serves 6

Raspberry bombe with melba sauce

6 large macaroons
300ml/1¼ cups heavy cream
3 Tbsp brandy
2 Tbsp sugar
2 egg whites
500g/1lb raspberries
1 Tbsp confectioners' sugar

Crumble the macaroons into a mixing bowl. Whip the cream until it is thick. Add the brandy and 1 tablespoon of the sugar and continue whipping until stiff. Beat the egg whites until they will hold a stiff peak. Fold the egg whites into the whipped cream. Fold in the crumbled macaroons.

Spoon into a chilled 2¼ pint capacity mold. Cover the top with foil and freeze for at least 2 hours.

Meanwhile, prepare the sauce. Push the raspberries through a strainer into a mixing bowl and stir in the confectioners' sugar. Chill the sauce.

Unmold the bombe onto a serving dish. Pour over the raspberry sauce and serve.

Serves 10-12

Hazelnut cookie cake

150g/1¼ cups flour
60g/¼ cup sugar
90g/¾ cup hazelnuts, chopped
and toasted
125g/½ cup butter, softened
1 egg yolk
250ml/1 cup heavy cream
250g/1½ cups strawberries or
raspberries, hulled
1 Tbsp confectioners' sugar

Sift the flour and sugar into a mixing bowl. Stir in the hazelnuts. Make a well in the center and add the butter and egg yolk. Work the butter and egg yolk together, then incorporate the flour and sugar to make a soft dough. Chill for 30 minutes.

Divide the dough into three and roll each portion into a ball. Roll out each ball to a 20cm/8in circle. Place the circles on three greased baking sheets and bake in a moderate oven (180°C/350°F) for 15 minutes or until the undersides are pale golden brown. Do not let the tops of the cookies color. Cool on the baking sheets for 5 minutes, then carefully transfer to wire racks. Allow to cool completely. Whip the cream until thick. Slice the fruit.

Sandwich together the three cookies with the cream and fruit. Sift the confectioners' sugar over the top.

Serves 6-8

Top: Soft white bread enclosing fresh juicy raspberries, Summer Pudding is a traditional British favorite. Above: Fresh damsons turn a sweet soufflé into a special treat.

Redcurrant Cheesecake – a midsummer dream – tastes just as good as it looks!

Redcurrant cheesecake

250g/3 cups graham crackers, crushed
125g/½ cup butter, melted
1 tsp ground cinnamon
500g/1lb (2 cups) cream cheese
60g/¼ cup sugar
125ml/½ cup light cream
625g/5 cups redcurrants
2 envelopes unflavored gelatin
2 Tbsp water
500ml/1 pint heavy cream
1 egg white

Mix together the crushed crackers, melted butter and cinnamon. Press into the bottom of a greased loose-bottomed 23cm/9in cake pan. Smooth the surface.

Beat the cream cheese and sugar together until well mixed. Stir in the light cream and 500g/4 cups of the redcurrants. Dissolve the gelatin in the water and strain into the redcurrant mixture. Stir well and spoon into the cake pan. Chill for at least 30 minutes or until it is completely set.

Meanwhile, whip the heavy cream until it is thick. Beat the egg white until it will hold a stiff peak. Fold the egg white into the whipped cream.

Remove the sides from the cake pan and slide the cheesecake onto a serving plate. Spoon over the cream mixture and top with the remaining redcurrants.
Serves 6

Figs and peaches with sour cream

8 figs, sliced
4 large peaches, peeled, pitted and sliced
300ml/1¼ cups sour cream
2 Tbsp brown sugar

Put the fig and peach slices in a shallow serving dish. Stir in the sour cream. Sprinkle the brown sugar over the top. Chill for 30 minutes before serving.
Serves 4

Fruit salad with Madeira sauce

250g/1½ cups raspberries
1 eating apple, peeled, cored and diced
125g/1 cup purple grapes, halved and seeded
2 Tbsp chopped walnuts
1 pear, peeled, cored and sliced
125g/1 cup cherries, pitted
1 banana, thinly sliced
SAUCE
2 eggs
3 egg yolks
60g/¼ cup sugar
2 Tbsp Madeira

Put the fruit and nuts in a serving dish and chill for 1 hour.

Mix together the eggs, egg yolks, sugar and Madeira in a heatproof mixing bowl. Place over a pan of simmering water and beat until the mixture is thick and pale and will make a ribbon trail on itself when the beater is lifted. Do not let the bowl become too hot or the mixture will curdle. Remove from the heat and pour over the fruit. *Serves 4*

Brandy meringue frozen pudding

MERINGUE
2 egg whites
125g/½ cup sugar
PUDDING
3 eggs, separated
¼ tsp vanilla extract
75ml/⅓ cup brandy
250ml/1 cup heavy cream
75g/⅓ cup sugar

Line a baking sheet with non-stick silicone paper. Beat the egg whites until they will form a stiff peak. Add 2 teaspoons of the sugar and continue beating for 1 minute. Fold in the remaining sugar. Drop tablespoonfuls of the meringue mixture onto the

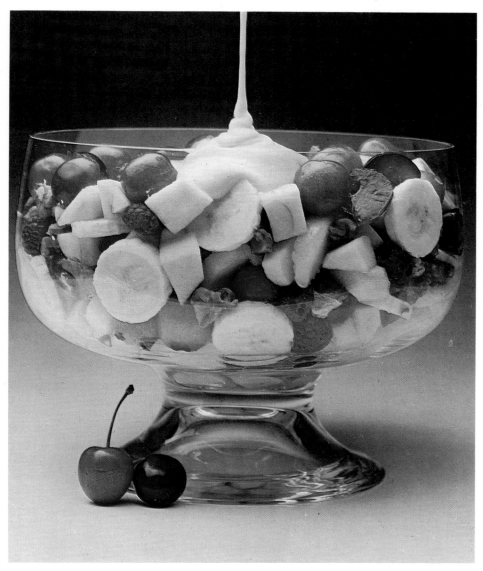

A cool summer treat, Fruit Salad with Madeira Sauce is deliciously refreshing.

baking sheet. Bake in a cool oven (150°C/300°F) for 2½ hours or until they are pale golden brown and crisp. Remove from the oven and allow to cool.

Meanwhile, beat the egg yolks, vanilla and brandy together. Whip the cream until it is thick. Beat the egg whites until they will hold a stiff peak. Add 2 teaspoons of the sugar and continue beating for 1 minute. Fold in the remaining sugar. Fold the cream into the egg yolk and brandy mixture, then fold in the egg white mixture. Spoon into a 1.5l/2½ pint capacity freezer-proof mold. Freeze for 1 hour.

Crumble the meringues. Fold into the pudding mixture and return to the freezer. Freeze for a further 1 hour or until hard and set. To serve, unmold onto a serving dish.
Serves 6

Lemon and lime chiffon

4 eggs, separated
125g/½ cup sugar
1 tsp grated lemon rind
5 Tbsp lemon juice
1 envelope unflavored gelatin
2 Tbsp lime juice, warmed
4 Tbsp heavy cream

Put the egg yolks and sugar in a heatproof mixing bowl. Place the bowl over a pan of hot water and beat until the mixture is pale and thick and leaves a ribbon trail when the beater is lifted. Alternatively, use an electric mixer without heat.

Remove from the heat and beat in the lemon rind and juice. Dissolve the gelatin in the lime juice and strain into the lemon mixture. Stir well. Allow to cool.

Whip the cream until it is thick, then beat into the lemon and lime mixture. Beat the egg whites until they will hold a stiff peak. Fold into the lemon and lime mixture. Spoon into a serving bowl or individual dishes and chill for at least 3 hours or until set.
Serves 4

Pistachio ice cream

250ml/1 cup light cream
125g/1 cup pistachio nuts, shelled,
blanched and chopped
250ml/1 cup heavy cream
½ tsp almond extract
3 eggs, separated
60g/¼ cup sugar
75ml/⅓ cup water

Put the light cream and nuts in the goblet of an electric blender and blend to a purée. Pour into a saucepan and stir in the heavy cream. Heat gently, then cover and remove from the heat. Allow to cool.

Pour the pistachio mixture into a mixing bowl and stir in the almond extract. Beat the egg yolks until well mixed. Put the sugar and water in a saucepan and dissolve the sugar over gentle heat. Bring to a boil and boil until the syrup reaches 110°C/220°F on a sugar thermometer. Remove from the heat and allow to cool for 1 minute.

Pour the syrup onto the egg yolks in a steady stream, beating constantly. Continue beating until the mixture is thick and fluffy. Stir in the pistachio mixture. Beat the egg whites until they will hold a stiff peak and fold into the pistachio mixture with a metal spoon.

Pour the mixture into an ice-cream container equipped with paddles (a sorbetiere) or into a hand-propelled ice-cream churn, and freeze. Alternatively, freeze, remove from freezer, beat and freeze again.
Makes 625ml/2½ cups

Apricot mousse with blackberries

500g/1lb apricots
4 Tbsp water
1 tsp lemon juice
60g/¼ cup sugar
4 egg whites
250g/1½ cups blackberries
4 Tbsp confectioners' sugar

Halve and pit the apricots. Put them in a saucepan with the water, lemon juice and sugar, and poach until they are very soft. If necessary, add a little more water to the pan if the mixture becomes too dry. Remove from the heat and allow to cool.

Purée the apricots in an electric blender or food mill. Alternatively, push them through a strainer. Return the purée to the saucepan and stir in the sugar. Stir over gentle heat to dissolve the sugar. Remove from the heat and cool.

Beat the egg whites until they will hold a stiff peak. Fold them into the apricot purée. Spoon into a serving dish or individual dishes and chill for at least 2 hours.

Mix together the blackberries and confectioners' sugar.

Just before serving, top each portion of mousse with a heaping spoonful of blackberries.
Serves 6
Note: this may also be made successfully with dried apricots. Use 350g/2 cups and simmer them in enough water to cover for 10 to 15 minutes or until very tender. Continue as above.

Rich and deliciously flavored, serve Nectarine Cream Mold as a summertime treat.

Peach tart

TART SHELL
185g/1½ cups flour
pinch salt
3 Tbsp butter
3 Tbsp shortening
2-3 Tbsp iced water
FILLING
4 large peaches, peeled, pitted and sliced
1 Tbsp peach brandy (optional)
TOPPING
2 Tbsp ground almonds
1 Tbsp chopped almonds
1 Tbsp chopped walnuts
3 Tbsp brown sugar
1 tsp grated orange rind
1 Tbsp butter, cut into small pieces

To make the tart shell, sift the flour and salt into a mixing bowl. Add the butter and shortening and cut into small pieces. Rub fat into the flour until the mixture resembles breadcrumbs. Stir in enough water to bind the mixture and knead to a dough. Chill for 30 minutes.

Roll out the dough and use to line a 23cm/9in tart pan. Bake in a fairly hot oven (200°C/400°F) for 15 minutes. Allow to cool before serving.

Arrange the peach slices in the tart shell and sprinkle with the peach brandy, if using. Mix together the ground and chopped almonds, walnuts, sugar and orange rind. Sprinkle over the peaches and dot the butter over the top. Broil until the topping is crisp and bubbling.

Serve hot or cold, with cream.
Serves 4-6

Nectarine cream mold

6 medium nectarines, peeled, pitted
and finely chopped
pinch ground allspice
90g/½ cup confectioners' sugar
2 Tbsp brandy
1 envelope unflavored gelatin
4 Tbsp hot water
300ml/1¼ cups heavy cream

Mix together the nectarines, allspice, confectioners' sugar and brandy. Dissolve the gelatin in the hot water and strain into the nectarine mixture. Stir well. Whip the cream until it is thick and fold into the nectarine mixture. Spoon into a greased 1.2l/2½ pint capacity mold. Chill for 2 hours or until set. Serve, unmolded.
Serves 4

Drinks

Badminton cup

½ cucumber, peeled and sliced
125g/⅔ cup confectioners' sugar
juice of 1 lemon
pinch grated nutmeg
5 Tbsp orange-flavored liqueur
1 bottle claret or other dry red wine
175ml/¾ cup soda water, chilled
2 borage sprigs (optional)

Put the cucumber, sugar, lemon juice, nutmeg, liqueur and wine in a punch bowl. Stir to dissolve the sugar. Stir in the soda water and add some ice cubes. Float borage sprigs on top, if using. Serve immediately.
Makes about 1 liter/2 pints

Tea punch

2 Tbsp tea leaves
1.2l/2½ pints boiling water
Finely pared rind of 1 large lemon
185g/1 cup brown sugar
250ml/1 cup dark rum
250ml/1 cup brandy
625ml/2½ cups soda water (optional)

Place the tea leaves in a teapot or heatproof container and pour over the boiling water. Cover and leave to infuse for 5 minutes.

Put the lemon rind and sugar in a mixing bowl and crush them together with a wooden spoon or pestle to release the zest from the rind. Pour the tea onto the sugar mixture and stir to dissolve the sugar. Allow to cool.

Strain the tea mixture into a punch bowl. Discard the lemon rind and tea leaves. Stir the rum and brandy into the strained tea. Serve chilled, adding the soda water, if used, just before serving.
Makes about 2 liters/4 pints

Don't reserve mint for sauce alone. Mint Ale is a deliciously refreshing drink.

Vermouth punch

1 bottle dry vermouth, chilled
125ml/½ cup orange-flavored liqueur
125ml/½ cup brandy
3 drops orange bitters
400ml/1¾ cups soda water, chilled
1 orange, thinly sliced
1 lemon, thinly sliced

Put some crushed ice in a chilled punch bowl. Pour over the vermouth, liqueur, brandy, orange bitters and soda water and stir well. Float the orange and lemon slices on the surface and serve.
Makes about 1.5 liters/3 pints

Ginger beer

1 lemon
250g/1 cup sugar
50g/2oz green ginger, bruised
1 Tbsp cream of tartar
3l/6 pints boiling water
¼ cake compressed yeast

Peel the lemon and set the rind aside. Squeeze the juice into a container and reserve.

Mix together the lemon rind, sugar, green ginger, cream of tartar and boiling water in a bowl. Stir well to dissolve the sugar. Set aside and allow to cool to lukewarm.

Mash the yeast and 2 tablespoons of the ginger liquid to a paste. Add to the remaining ginger liquid and stir well. Leave in a warm, draft-free place for at least 1-2 days, or until the yeast has stopped frothing.

Strain the mixture into a large jug or pitcher, discarding the lemon rind and ginger. Stir in the lemon juice. Pour the ginger beer into bottles and cover. Serve cold.
Makes about 3.75 liters/7½ pints

Lemonade

grated rind and juice of 6 lemons
250g/1 cup sugar
1.2l/2½ pints boiling water

Put the lemon rind and sugar in a tall jug or heatproof pitcher. Pour in the boiling water and stir to dissolve the sugar. Set aside and allow to cool, then chill for 2 hours.

Stir in the lemon juice and strain the lemonade into another pitcher. Serve chilled.
Makes 1.5 liters/2½ pints

Mint ale

6 large mint sprigs, roughly chopped
250g/1⅓ cups confectioners' sugar
3 Tbsp water
juice of 12 lemons, chilled
900ml/3½ cups dry ginger ale, chilled
3 mint sprigs (optional)

Mix together the chopped mint, sugar and water in a mixing bowl. Pound with a wooden spoon or pestle until the sugar has dissolved. Set aside for 2 hours.

Strain the mint mixture into a pitcher. Stir in the lemon juice and ginger ale. Garnish with the mint sprigs if you are using them and serve.
Makes about 1.2 liters/2½ pints

Lemonade and Ginger Beer – two fresh thirst-quenchers for those long summer days.

Preserves

Jam

Jam-making is one of the best ways of preserving the lush fruits of summer. The jams' bright colors and fresh tastes will recapture the warmth of the summer sun when fall and winter skies threaten rain or snow.

Fruit for jam-making should be dry, fresh, in good condition and just ripe. Those which make an easily set jam, being rich in pectin, are black- and redcurrants, gooseberries, damsons, crab apples, apples, cranberries, quinces and some plums. Fruits with a moderate setting quality are apricots, gage plums, blackberries, loganberries and raspberries. Finally, those which will not produce a good set without some help are black and red cherries, strawberries, pears, figs, grapes and pineapple.

To add pectin, the natural jellying substance present in most unripe fruit, to pectin-poor fruit, mix it with fruit rich in pectin. A popular combination is blackberry and apple. Alternatively, the pectin-rich fruit can be added in the form of juice (called pectin stock). Try redcurrant, apple or gooseberry. Or use a commercial liquid or powder pectin, available from most good drug stores.

The first stage in jam making is to soften the fruit by cooking it with a little water if it is not sufficiently juicy. This cooking releases the pectin. If the fruit is deficient in acid, lemon juice, tartaric or citric acid, redcurrant or gooseberry juice may be added. Next, the sugar is stirred in with a wooden spoon until it is completely dissolved.

The jam is brought to a boil and boiled until setting point is reached. The simplest test for setting point is to spoon a little of the jam onto a saucer. When it has cooled, push it with your finger: it should set and crinkle. If you prefer, use a sugar thermometer which should register 105°C/220°F if the jam has reached setting point and is ready.

Before canning jam containing whole fruit, allow it to cool until a skin forms on the top. Spoon the jam into clean, dry jars, filling right to the top. Cover with a well-fitting lid of wax paper, pressing it down to exclude any air. Cover the jars with cellophane or plastic covers and secure with rubber bands. Alternatively, use canning jars.

When the jam is cold, label the jars and store in a cool, dark place until you are ready to use.

Preserve the warmth and color of summer fruits to cheer you in the colder seasons.

Strawberry jam

2.5kg/5lb strawberries, hulled
125ml/½ cup lemon juice
2kg/4lb (8 cups) sugar

Put the strawberries and lemon juice in an aluminum or stainless steel pan. Simmer, stirring frequently, until the fruit is very soft. Stir in the sugar and continue stirring until it has dissolved.

Bring to a boil and boil rapidly until setting point is reached. Remove from the heat and allow to cool for 10 minutes before canning.
Makes about 3.25kg/7lb

Peach jam

1 medium cooking apple, chopped
thinly pared rind of 2 lemons
2 whole cloves
1.5kg/3lb peaches, pitted and sliced
300ml/1¼ cups water
1 tsp ground allspice
1.5kg/3lb (6 cups) sugar

Tie the apple, lemon rind and cloves in a piece of cheesecloth. Put the peaches, water and cheesecloth bag in an aluminum or stainless steel pan. Bring to a boil, stirring constantly, then simmer until the peaches are soft.

Remove the cheesecloth bag, pressing it against the side of the pan to extract all the liquid. Stir the allspice and sugar into the peaches and continue stirring until the sugar has completely dissolved. Bring to a boil and boil rapidly until setting point is reached.

Remove from the heat and allow to cool for 10 minutes before canning.
Makes about 2.25kg/5lb

Plum and apple jam

750g/1½lb plums, halved and pitted
750g/1½lb cooking apples, peeled,
cored and sliced
1 Tbsp lemon juice
300ml/1¼ cups water
1.5kg/3lb (6 cups) sugar

Put the plums, apples, lemon juice and water in an aluminum or stainless steel pan. Bring to a boil, stirring constantly, then simmer gently until the fruit is soft and tender.

Stir in the sugar and continue stirring until the sugar has dissolved. Bring to a boil and boil rapidly until setting point is reached.

Remove from the heat and can.
Makes about 2.25kg/5lb

Autumn

As the leaves turn to gold and the evenings draw in, so our appetites tend to increase. Fortunately, this coincides with the maturing of the fruits on trees and hedges, heralded by the Spring blossoms, and the opening of the game season. Use the fresh root vegetables to help fill out warming casseroles, and the tree fruits to make chutneys and relishes to add bite to cold meats. Satisfy the family's hunger with fruit breads and buttered muffins spread with jam made in the Summer. Autumn is the time for gathering field mushrooms, eating by a bonfire, baking cakes and meats, and sitting down to enjoy freshly harvested and prepared food.

What's best in season

Fruit:

Apples	Dates	Oranges	Plums
Bananas	Figs	Papayas	Pomegranates
Blackberries	Grapes	Pawpaws	Pumpkin
Blueberries	Grapefruit	Peaches	Quinces
Crabapples	Lemons	Pears	Strawberries
Cranberries	Limes	Persimmons	Tangerines
Damsons	Melons	Pineapples	

Vegetables:

Avocados	Corn	Leeks	Rutabaga
Beets	Cucumbers	Lettuces	Shallots
Broccoli	Curly endive	Mushrooms	Spinach
Brussels sprouts	Eggplant	Onions	Squashes
Cabbages	Fennel	Oyster plant	Stick beans
Calabrese	French or Belgian endive	Parsnips	Tomatoes
Carrots	Green beans	Peppers	Turnips
Cauliflowers	Jerusalem artichokes	Potatoes	Watercress
Celeriac	Kale	Pumpkin	Zucchini
Celery	Kohlrabi	Radishes	

Herbs:

Bay	Lemon balm	Rosemary	Tarragon
Chives	Marjoram	Sage	Thyme
Coriander	Mint	Summer and winter	
Dill	Parsley	savory	
Fennel			

Nuts:

Almonds	Brazil nuts	Chestnuts	Hazelnuts

Fish:

Bass	Grouper	Mussels	Shrimp
Carp	Haddock	Oysters	Sole
Clam	Hake	Perch	Sprat
Cockles	Halibut	Pike	Trout
Cod	Herring	Prawns	Tuna
Crab	Mackerel	Red snapper	Turbot
Eel	Mullet	Scallop	Whiting
Flounder			

Poultry:

Available fresh or frozen
all year round

Game:

Bear	Muskrat	Quail	Venison
Beaver	Opossum	Rabbit	Wild ducks
Grouse	Partridge	Snipe	Woodcock
Hare	Pheasant	Squirrel	Other small game birds
Hazelhen	Pigeon		

Meat and offal:

Available fresh or frozen
all year round

Appetizers

Ham custard molds

60g/¼ cup butter
125g/1 cup button mushrooms, sliced
1 medium onion, finely chopped
30g/1 cup fresh breadcrumbs
1 Tbsp milk
250g/1 cup cooked ham, finely chopped
or ground
250ml/1 cup white or bechamel sauce
60g/½ cup Cheddar cheese, grated
1 Tbsp tomato paste
1 Tbsp parsley, freshly chopped
¼ tsp Worcestershire sauce
1 tsp marjoram, freshly chopped
3 eggs, separated

Melt 1 tablespoon of the butter in a frying pan. Add the mushrooms and cook until they are just tender. Remove the mushrooms from the pan with a slotted spoon and chop them very finely.

Add the remaining butter to the pan and when it has melted add the onion. Fry until it is soft but not brown. Meanwhile, sprinkle the breadcrumbs with the milk and press to moisten them.

Add the onions to the mushrooms with the breadcrumbs, ham, sauce, cheese, tomato paste, parsley, Worcestershire sauce, marjoram and egg yolks. Mix together well.

Beat the egg whites until they will hold a stiff peak. Fold them into the ham mixture. Spoon into eight small greased molds and place the molds in a roasting pan. Add enough boiling water to the pan to come halfway up the sides of the molds. Bake in a warm oven (170°C/325°F) for 40 minutes or until lightly set.

Turn the individual custards out of the molds and serve hot.
Serves 8

Zucchini stuffed with almonds

4 large or 8 small zucchini
3 Tbsp olive oil
1 medium onion, finely chopped
90g/¾ cup ground almonds
125ml/½ cup heavy cream
90g/¾ cup dry breadcrumbs
90g/¾ cup Gruyère cheese, grated
salt and pepper
1 tsp marjoram, freshly chopped
1 tsp chervil, freshly chopped
1 egg, lightly beaten
60g/¼ cup butter, melted

Blanch the zucchini in boiling salted water

for 5 minutes. Drain and refresh under cold running water, then drain again. Cut the zucchini in half lengthwise and carefully hollow out the flesh, leaving boat-shaped shells of skin. Chop the flesh. Press it with a wooden spoon to extract as much liquid as possible and drain away the liquid.

Heat the oil in a frying pan. Add the onion and fry until soft but not brown. Stir in the zucchini flesh and cook for a further 5 minutes. Turn into a mixing bowl and stir in the almonds, cream and half of the breadcrumbs. Add two-thirds of the cheese, salt and pepper to taste, the herbs and egg and mix well. If the mixture is not thick and firm, add more breadcrumbs until it is.

Arrange the zucchini shells in a greased baking dish and fill with the almond-cheese mixture. Mix together the remaining cheese and breadcrumbs and sprinkle over the tops. Sprinkle with the melted butter. Bake in a fairly hot oven (200°C/400°F) for 15 to 20 minutes or until bubbling and brown.

Serve hot.
Serves 4

These molded Ham Custards make unusual and attractive savory appetizers.

Below: Moules Marinières – an impressive yet simple dish to prepare which originated from France's Atlantic coast.
Bottom: Mussels must be purchased fresh. Discard any with open shells.

Moules marinières

4 dozen mussels
60g/¼ cup butter
1 small onion, finely chopped
1 garlic clove, crushed
1 celery stalk, finely chopped
1 bouquet garni
500ml/2 cups dry white wine
salt and black pepper
2 Tbsp parsley, freshly chopped

Scrub the mussels and scrape off the beards. Discard any mussels that are not tightly shut or any that seem too heavy as they may be full of sand. Leave to soak in cold water for 2 hours, then wash and drain again.

Melt the butter in a saucepan. Add the onion and garlic and fry until the onion is soft but not brown. Add the celery, bouquet garni, wine and salt and pepper to taste and bring to a boil. Add the mussels to the pan and cook gently, shaking the pan occasionally, for 5 to 10 minutes or until the mussels open.

Transfer the mussels to a warmed serving dish with a slotted spoon. Discard the empty shell halves. Set the mussels aside and keep them hot for the moment.

Strain the cooking liquid and return to the heat. Bring to a boil and boil for 2 minutes. Pour over the mussels and sprinkle with the parsley.

Serve hot.
Serves 4

Eggplant slices

1 large eggplant, peeled and cut into 1cm/½in thick slices
salt
3 Tbsp butter, melted
6 Tbsp dry breadcrumbs
1 Tbsp oregano, freshly chopped
60g/½ cup Parmesan cheese, grated
TOMATO SAUCE
2 Tbsp olive oil
1 small onion, finely chopped
1 garlic clove, crushed
500g/1lb tomatoes, peeled and chopped
salt and black pepper
1 Tbsp oregano, freshly chopped

First make the tomato sauce. Heat the oil in a saucepan. Add the onion and garlic and fry until the onion is soft but not brown. Stir in the tomatoes with salt and pepper to taste and the oregano and simmer gently for 20 minutes or until the sauce is very thick.

Meanwhile, place the eggplant slices in a colander, sprinkle with salt and leave for 20 minutes. Rinse and pat dry with paper towels.

Dip each eggplant slice in the melted butter and then in the breadcrumbs to coat well. Place on a greased baking sheet. Bake in a very hot oven (230°C/450°F) for 15 minutes or until the slices are tender and lightly browned.

Top each slice with a spoonful of tomato sauce and sprinkle with the oregano and cheese. Return to the oven and bake for a further 10 minutes or until the topping is lightly browned.

Serve hot.
Serves 6-8

Cold marinated oysters

16 oysters, shucked
MARINADE
185ml/¾ cup dry white wine
4 Tbsp olive oil
4 Tbsp lemon juice
salt and black pepper
1 tsp thyme, freshly chopped
1 tsp chervil, freshly chopped
1 tsp parsley, freshly chopped
1 garlic clove, crushed

Mix together all the marinade ingredients,

with salt and pepper to taste, in a saucepan. Leave for 15 minutes.

Add the oysters to the saucepan and bring to a boil. Remove from the heat and pour the oysters and marinade into a shallow serving dish. Allow to cool, then chill well. Serve cold.

Serves 4

Pears stuffed with blue cheese

2 large dessert pears, peeled, halved and cored
1 tsp lemon juice
3 Tbsp unsalted butter, softened
90g/1 cup blue cheese, such as Roquefort, crumbled
4 large lettuce leaves

Brush the pears all over with the lemon juice to prevent discoloration.

Mix together the butter and blue cheese, mashing with a fork. Form into four balls.

Place a lettuce leaf on each of four small plates. Place a pear half on each, cut side up, and top with a cheese ball. Chill for 30 minutes before serving.

Serves 4

Mushroom and bacon pots

250g/8oz bacon, coarsely chopped
2 Tbsp butter
500g/1lb button mushrooms
salt and black pepper
2 Tbsp brandy
4 Tbsp heavy cream
4 Tbsp Gruyère cheese, grated
4 parsley sprigs

Fry the bacon in a frying pan until it is crisp and has rendered most of its fat. Add the butter and when it has melted add the mushrooms with salt and pepper to taste. Cook for 3 to 4 minutes or until the mushrooms are just tender.

Warm the brandy in a ladle. Pour over the mushroom mixture and set alight. When the flames have died down, stir in the cream. Remove from the heat and spoon into four individual flameproof dishes. Sprinkle a tablespoon of Gruyere cheese over each.

Broil for 4 minutes or until the cheese has melted and is lightly browned. Remove from the heat, garnish with the parsley sprigs and serve.

Serves 4

A delectable combination of oysters, white wine and herbs, Marinated Oysters make an exquisite first course.

Soups

Pumpkin soup

2 Tbsp butter
2 small onions, thinly sliced and
pushed out into rings
500g/4 cups pumpkin flesh, chopped
1.2l/2½ pints chicken stock
salt
1 celery stalk, chopped
1 large potato, peeled and chopped
1 Tbsp lemon juice
few drops Tabasco sauce
1 tsp paprika
250ml/1 cup heavy cream
croûtons, to serve

Melt the butter in a saucepan. Add the onions and pumpkin and fry until the onions are soft but not brown. Stir in the stock, salt to taste, the celery, potato, lemon juice, Tabasco and paprika. Bring to a boil, then cover and simmer for 30 to 35 minutes or until the vegetables are tender.

Purée the soup in an electric blender, then strain it back into the saucepan. Alternatively, push the soup through a strainer. Stir the cream into the puréed soup and reheat gently without boiling.

Serve hot, garnished with croûtons.
Serves 4-6

Game soup

2 Tbsp butter
1 Tbsp vegetable oil
1 pheasant or partridge carcass, broken
into several pieces
250g/1 cup cooked game meat, cut into
small cubes
1 large onion, sliced
1 large carrot, scraped and sliced
1 small turnip, peeled and chopped
1 Tbsp flour
900ml/3⅔ cups beef stock
60g/¼ cup cooked ham, chopped
1 bouquet garni
salt and black pepper
150ml/⅔ cup Madeira

Melt the butter with the oil in a saucepan. Add the carcass, meat, onion, carrot and turnip and fry until the vegetables are lightly browned. Sprinkle over the flour and cook, stirring, for 1 minute. Remove from the heat and gradually stir in the

Warming and colorful, Pumpkin Soup may be served with tiny croûtons for an invigorating start to an autumn meal.

stock with a wooden spoon.

Return to the heat and bring to a boil. Simmer, stirring, until the liquid has thickened. Add the ham, bouquet garni and salt and pepper to taste. Cover and simmer gently for 2 hours.

Remove and discard the carcass pieces and bouquet garni. Stir in the Madeira. Simmer, uncovered, for a further 10 minutes and serve.

Serves 4-6

Corn chowder

2 Tbsp butter
1 medium onion, finely chopped
1 Tbsp flour
250ml/1 cup chicken stock
300ml/1¼ cups milk
2 medium potatoes, peeled, parboiled
for 10 minutes, drained and
finely chopped
500g/3 cups corn kernels
salt and pepper
250ml/1 cup heavy cream
2 Tbsp chopped pimiento

Melt the butter in a saucepan. Add the onion and fry until it is soft but not brown. Sprinkle over the flour and cook, stirring, for 1 minute. Remove from the heat and gradually stir in the stock and milk. Return to the heat and bring to the boil. Simmer, stirring, until thickened and smooth.

Stir in the potatoes, corn and salt and pepper to taste, cover and cook gently for 20 minutes.

Stir in the cream and heat through gently without boiling. Stir in the pimiento and serve.

Serves 4-6

Donegal mussel soup

3 dozen mussels
3 Tbsp butter
2 shallots, finely chopped
1 Tbsp parsley, freshly chopped
1 tsp thyme, freshly chopped
1 bay leaf
salt and black pepper
185ml/¾ cup hard cider
1 large leek, thinly sliced
1 celery stalk, chopped
4 Tbsp flour
625ml/2½ cups milk, scalded
625ml/2½ cups fish stock, warmed
3 fennel sprigs, freshly chopped
½ tsp grated nutmeg
150ml/⅔ cup heavy cream

Scrub the mussels and scrape off the beards. Discard any mussels that are not

tightly shut or any that seem too heavy as they may be full of sand. Leave to soak in cold water for 2 hours, then wash and drain again.

Grease a large saucepan with 1 tablespoon of the butter. Sprinkle the shallots over the bottom and add the parsley, thyme and bay leaf. Arrange the mussels on top and season with pepper. Pour in the cider. Bring to a boil, cover and cook for 10 minutes, shaking the pan occasionally.

Remove from the heat. Take the mussels out of the pan, discarding any which are still closed. Remove the meat from the shells, discarding the shells. Strain the cooking liquid and reserve.

Melt the remaining butter in the cleaned-out saucepan. Add the leek and celery and fry until lightly browned. Sprinkle over the flour and cook, stirring, for 1 minute. Remove from the heat and stir in the milk and fish stock. Return to the heat and simmer, stirring, until thickened. Simmer for 15 minutes.

Remove from the heat and strain the liquid into another saucepan. Stir in the reserved mussel cooking liquid, the fennel, nutmeg and salt and pepper to taste. Add the mussels and cream and stir well. Heat through gently without boiling. Serve hot.

Serves 4

Cucumber, potato and dill soup

2 Tbsp butter
2 shallots, finely chopped
2 small potatoes, peeled and diced
1 Tbsp flour
1l/2 pints chicken stock
1 Tbsp lemon juice
salt and black pepper
1 bay leaf
1 Tbsp dill, freshly chopped
2 medium cucumbers, peeled and
thickly sliced
250ml/1 cup sour cream

Melt the butter in a saucepan. Add the shallots and fry until they are soft but not brown. Add the potatoes and fry for a further 4 minutes. Sprinkle over the flour and stir well. Gradually stir in the stock, then stir in the lemon juice, salt and pepper to taste, the bay leaf, dill and cucumbers. Bring to a boil, stirring, then cover and simmer for 30 minutes.

Remove from the heat. Discard the bay leaf and purée the soup in an electric blender or by pushing it through a strainer. Return the puréed soup to the saucepan and stir in the sour cream. Heat through gently without boiling. Serve hot.

Serves 6

Delicately flavored with fennel and nutmeg, Donegal Mussel Soup makes a rich, creamy first course.

Main Dishes

Grey mullet Martigues

4 small gray mullets, cleaned
salt and black pepper
2 medium onions, thinly sliced
3 tomatoes, peeled and sliced
1 carrot, scraped and cut into strips
4 Tbsp olive oil
250ml/1 cup dry white wine
1 tsp oregano, freshly chopped
1 tsp marjoram, freshly chopped
1 lemon, thinly sliced

Sprinkle the fish with salt. Make three parallel diagonal cuts across each fish. Place half the onions in a greased shallow baking dish. Top with the tomato slices and carrot strips, then the remaining onions. Place the fish on top, in one layer, and pour over the olive oil and wine. Sprinkle with salt and pepper, the oregano and marjoram and top with the lemon slices.

Cover the dish with foil and bake in a moderate oven (180°C/350°F) for 35 minutes. Remove the foil and continue baking for 15 minutes or until the fish are cooked. Test with a fork: the flesh should flake easily.

Serve hot.

Serves 4

Porgy with fennel and white wine

1 × 1kg/2lb porgy, cleaned
2 sprigs fennel
2 sprigs thyme
2 Tbsp butter
salt and black pepper
150ml/⅔ cup dry white wine
1 Tbsp olive oil
1 bulb Florence fennel, sliced
2 tomatoes, sliced
1 lemon, thinly sliced

Make two deep incisions along the back of the fish. Insert the fennel sprigs in the incisions. Place the thyme sprigs and butter inside the fish and sprinkle with salt and pepper. Place the fish on a rack in a roasting pan. Pour over the wine and olive oil and arrange the fennel, tomato and lemon slices over the top.

Bake in a moderate oven (180°C/350°F) for 30 minutes or until the fish is cooked. Test with a fork: the flesh should flake easily.

Transfer the fish to a warmed serving dish and serve hot.

Serves 4

Haddock with cider

250ml/1 cup hard cider
2 medium onions, thinly sliced
1 green pepper, pith and seeds removed and chopped
750g/1½lb haddock fillets, skinned
3 tomatoes, peeled and chopped
1 tsp marjoram, freshly chopped
pinch cayenne pepper
salt and white pepper
3 Tbsp fresh white breadcrumbs
30g/¼ cup Parmesan cheese, grated

Bring the cider to a boil in a saucepan. Add the onions and green pepper and simmer for 5 minutes or until the cider has reduced by about one-quarter. Remove from the heat.

Cut the fish into 10cm/4in pieces and put them into a flameproof casserole. Add the cider mixture and tomatoes and mix well. Stir in the marjoram, cayenne and salt and pepper to taste. Cover the casserole and bake in a warm oven (170°C/325°F) for 30 minutes or until the fish is cooked. Test with a fork: the flesh should flake easily.

Mix together the breadcrumbs and cheese. Uncover the casserole and sprinkle the breadcrumb and cheese mixture over the top. Broil until the topping is lightly browned. Serve hot.

Serves 4

Cod provençal

4 Tbsp olive oil
1 small onion, thinly sliced
1 garlic clove, chopped
1 green pepper, pith and seeds removed and thinly sliced
60g/2oz can anchovies, drained and chopped
60g/⅓ cup black olives, pitted
pinch fennel seeds
8 × 125g/4oz cod steaks
3 small tomatoes, thinly sliced
salt and black pepper
3 Tbsp tomato paste
125ml/½ cup dry red wine

Heat half the oil in a frying pan. Add the onion, garlic and green pepper and fry until the onion is soft but not brown. Remove from the heat and stir in the anchovies, olives and fennel seeds.

Place four cod steaks in a greased shallow baking dish. Top each with one-quarter of the anchovy mixture. Place the remaining cod steaks on top and arrange the tomato slices over these. Brush the tomatoes with the remaining oil and sprinkle with salt and pepper.

Mix together the tomato paste and wine. Pour into the baking dish around the fish. Bake in a fairly hot oven (200°C/400°F) for 30 minutes. Baste the fish with the cooking liquid in the dish at least twice during baking.

Serve hot.

Serves 4

Seafood casserole

250g/8oz crabmeat, flaked
1 egg, lightly beaten
2 Tbsp parsley, freshly chopped
salt and black pepper
4 sole fillets, skinned and halved
16 king prawns (shelled),
deveined
250g/1⅔ cups shrimp (shelled),
deveined
250g/8oz scallops, quartered
125ml/½ cup fish stock
125ml/½ cup dry white wine
4 Tbsp lemon juice

150ml/⅔ cup heavy cream
1 lemon, cut into wedges

Mash the crabmeat, egg, parsley and salt and pepper to taste together to make a paste. Spread thickly over one side of each half fillet of sole and roll up like jelly rolls. Place in a flameproof casserole. Add the prawns, shrimp, scallops, stock, wine and lemon juice. Bring the liquid to a boil, then cover and transfer to a moderate oven (180°C/350°F). Cook for 20 minutes or until the sole is tender.

Transfer the fish rolls and shellfish to a warmed serving dish. Set the seafood aside and keep hot.

Strain the cooking liquid into a saucepan. Bring to a boil and boil until the liquid has reduced to about half the original quantity. Stir in the cream and heat through gently without boiling. Pour this sauce over the seafood and serve immediately, garnished with the lemon wedges.

Serves 8

Cod Provençal is an attractive dish of cod steaks with anchovies, olives and green peppers in a delicious red wine and tomato sauce.

A simple, unassuming dish of Mackerel in White Wine Sauce makes a pleasant lunch or dinner.

Mackerel in white wine sauce

4 mackerel, cleaned and filleted
salt and black pepper
3 Tbsp butter
185ml/¾ cup fish stock
185ml/¾ cup white wine
2 Tbsp dry sherry
½ tsp fennel seed
1 tsp grated lemon rind

Place the mackerel fillets in a greased shallow baking dish. Sprinkle with salt and pepper and dot with the butter, cut into small pieces.

Bring the stock, wine, sherry, fennel seed and lemon rind to a boil in a saucepan. Boil for 10 minutes or until reduced to half the original quantity. Pour over the fillets and bake in a fairly hot oven (190°C/375°F) for 10 to 15 minutes or until the fish is cooked. Test with a fork: the flesh should flake easily.

Transfer the fish and cooking liquid to a warmed serving dish and serve.
Serves 4

Eel stew

500g/1lb fish heads and trimmings
1.2l/2½ pints plus 1 Tbsp water
1 bouquet garni
salt and black pepper
4 peppercorns
1 celery stalk, chopped
1 carrot, scraped and chopped
3 Tbsp olive oil
60g/½ cup blanched almonds, chopped
1 large red pepper, pith and seeds removed and sliced
1 large onion, halved and sliced
3 garlic cloves, crushed
1 tsp thyme, freshly chopped
1 tsp paprika
½ tsp cayenne pepper
1kg/2lb eels, skinned and cut into serving pieces
1 tsp cornstarch

Put the fish heads and trimmings, all but 1 tablespoon water, the bouquet garni, 1 teaspoon salt, the peppercorns, celery and carrot in a saucepan. Bring to a boil, then cover and simmer for 30 minutes. Strain this court bouillon and set aside.

Heat the oil in a flameproof casserole. Add the almonds, red pepper, onion and garlic. Fry until the almonds are golden and the onion soft but not brown. Stir in the thyme, paprika, cayenne and black pepper to taste. Cook for a further 2 minutes. Add the eel pieces and fry, stirring, for 5 minutes.

Stir in the court bouillon and bring to a boil. Cover and simmer for 30 minutes. Dissolve the cornstarch in the remaining tablespoon of water and stir in a little of the hot liquid. Stir into the stew. Cook for a further 2 to 3 minutes, stirring, or until the stew has thickened slightly. Serve hot.
Serves 4

Scallops with vermouth sauce

500g/1lb Jerusalem artichokes, peeled
16 scallops, halved
juice of 1 lemon
90g/¾ cup flour
salt and black pepper
60g/¼ cup butter
4 shallots, finely chopped
2 garlic cloves, crushed
125g/1 cup mushrooms, sliced
1 Tbsp tarragon, freshly chopped
1 Tbsp parsley, freshly chopped
75ml/⅓ cup dry vermouth
250ml/1 cup light cream

Cook the artichokes in boiling salted water to which you have added a squeeze of lemon juice and salt, for 30 minutes, or until they are tender. Drain well and slice.

Sprinkle the scallops with the lemon juice and leave to marinate for 5 minutes. Mix together the flour with salt and pepper and use to coat the scallops.

Melt the butter in a frying pan. Add the scallops and fry until lightly browned. Add the shallots, garlic, artichoke slices, mushrooms, tarragon, parsley and salt and pepper to taste. Stir well and cook for 5 minutes.

Meanwhile, heat the vermouth in a small saucepan. Ignite it and, when the flames die down, stir in the cream. Heat through gently without boiling, then stir into the scallop mixture.

Transfer to a warmed serving dish and serve immediately.
Serves 4

Carpetbag steak

1kg/2lb sirloin steak, in one piece,
about 5cm/2in thick
12 oysters, shucked
salt and black pepper
¼ tsp cayenne pepper
1 Tbsp butter, melted
watercress, to garnish

Slit the steak lengthwise to form a pocket. Fill the pocket with the oysters and sprinkle the oysters with salt and pepper and the cayenne. Sew up the opening with a trussing needle and thread or string.

Brush the steak with the melted butter

A sensational dish for a dinner party, Carpetbag Steak is a famous Australian recipe of sirloin steak stuffed with oysters.

and broil for 5 to 6 minutes on each side, using a fierce heat to seal the meat. Reduce the heat, or increase the distance from the heat, and broil for a further 10 minutes on each side, depending on how well-done you like your steak.

Remove the string or thread and place the steak on a warmed serving dish. Garnish with the watercress and serve.

Serves 4

Veal stroganoff

6 veal scallops, pounded thin
60g/¼ cup butter
2 Tbsp olive oil
2 medium onions, thinly sliced
350g/12oz button mushrooms
375ml/1½ cups sour cream
1 tsp prepared French mustard
1 Tbsp tomato paste
salt and black pepper
1 Tbsp parsley, freshly chopped

Cut the scallops into strips 5cm/2in long and 6mm/¼in wide. Melt the butter with the oil in a frying pan. Add the veal strips and fry until they are lightly browned. Remove from the pan and keep hot.

Add the onions to the pan and fry until they are soft but not brown. Add the mushrooms and fry until they are just tender.

Mix together the sour cream, mustard, tomato paste and salt and pepper to taste. Stir into the onion and mushroom mixture and cook, stirring, for 1 minute. Return the veal strips to the pan and cook for a further 2 minutes to reheat.

Transfer the Stroganoff to a warmed serving dish and sprinkle with the parsley. Serve hot.

Serves 6

Breast of veal with piquant lemon stuffing

1 × 2kg/4lb breast of veal (boned weight)
60g/¼ cup butter
½ small onion, finely chopped
3 bacon slices, chopped
125g/1 cup fresh white breadcrumbs
1 Tbsp parsley, freshly chopped
grated rind and juice of ½ lemon
1 small cooking apple, peeled, cored and grated
salt and pepper
1 egg, beaten
1 green eating apple, cored and sliced to garnish

Melt the butter in a frying pan. Add the onion and bacon and fry until the onion is soft but not brown and the bacon crisp. Transfer to a mixing bowl with a slotted spoon. Stir in the breadcrumbs, parsley, lemon rind and juice, grated apple, salt and pepper to taste and the beaten egg. Mix well.

Lay the veal flat on a work surface and cover with the stuffing. Roll up like a jelly roll and tie at approximately 1 inch intervals with string or thread.

Wrap the veal roll in foil and place in a roasting pan. Roast in a moderate oven (180°C/350°F) for 2 hours. Remove the foil and roast for a further 30 minutes or until the veal is cooked through. During the final 30 minutes of cooking time, baste frequently with a bulb baster, with the juices collected in the foil.

Transfer veal roll to a warmed serving dish and remove the string. Garnish the veal with the apple slices and serve immediately.

Serves 6

Beef with corn and tomatoes

1kg/2lb top round, cut into 5cm/2in cubes
4 Tbsp paprika
2 Tbsp flour
60g/¼ cup butter
2 medium onions, chopped
2 garlic cloves, chopped
250g/8oz tomatoes, peeled and chopped
1 Tbsp thyme, freshly chopped
1 bay leaf
salt and black pepper
2 carrots, scraped and sliced
250ml/1 cup dry white wine
500g/3 cups corn kernels
150ml/⅔ cup light cream
75ml/⅓ cup brandy

Mix together the paprika and flour. Place in a plastic bag. Toss the beef cubes in the seasoned flour. Melt the butter in a flameproof casserole. Add the onions and garlic and fry until the onions are soft but not brown. Add the meat cubes, in batches, and brown them on all sides. Stir in the tomatoes, thyme, bay leaf, salt and pepper to taste and the carrots. Cover the casserole and cook gently for 20 minutes, stirring occasionally.

Stir in the wine, re-cover and simmer for a further 45 minutes. Add the corn, stir well and re-cover. Simmer for a further 20 minutes or until the meat is cooked through and very tender.

Mix together the cream and brandy. Stir into the casserole and simmer gently, uncovered, for 15 minutes. Serve hot, from the casserole.

Serves 4

Below: Breast of Veal with Piquant Lemon Stuffing makes a meal with a fruity tang.
Opposite: A substantial, autumn-colored dish, Beef with Corn and Tomatoes is best served straight from the casserole.

Beef Stew with Dumplings served with sour cream is a hearty, satisfying main dish.

Beef stew with dumplings

30g/¼ cup flour
salt and black pepper
chunk steak, cut into 2.5cm/1in
1kg/2lb cubes
2 tbsp butter
1 Tbsp vegetable oil
1 large onion, finely chopped
2 Tbsp brandy, warmed (optional)
1 bay leaf
1.2l/2½ pints beef stock, boiling
175g small/6oz small mushrooms
150ml/⅔ cup sour cream
DUMPLINGS
250g/4 cups fresh breadcrumbs
4 Tbsp water
3 eggs, lightly beaten
salt and black pepper
1½ Tbsp parsley, freshly chopped
1 medium onion, finely chopped
½ tsp ground mace

Mix together the flour with salt and pepper in a plastic bag. Add the beef cubes and shake to coat them all with the flour. Melt the butter with the oil in a frying pan. Add the onion and fry until it is soft but not brown. Transfer the onion to a casserole.

Add the beef cubes to the pan, in batches, and fry until they are browned on all sides. Transfer to the casserole.

If you are using the brandy, set it alight and pour it over the beef cubes in the casserole. When the flames have died down, add the bay leaf and stock. Cover the casserole and bake in a warm oven (170°C/325°F) for 2 hours.

Meanwhile, make the dumplings. Put the breadcrumbs in a mixing bowl and sprinkle with the water. Toss lightly with a fork, then mix in the remaining ingredients with salt and pepper to taste. Form the mixture into walnut-sized balls.

Add the dumplings and mushrooms to the casserole, re-cover and continue to cook for 30 minutes.

Spoon the sour cream over the top and serve hot, from the casserole.
Serves 4

Brewer's pot roast

1 × 2kg/4lb top round
salt and black pepper
4 Tbsp vegetable oil
4 medium leeks, thinly sliced
6 medium parsnips, peeled and sliced
900ml/3⅔ cups beef stock
1 bouquet garni
250ml/1 cup light beer
1 tsp butter
2 tsp flour
parsley sprigs, to garnish

Rub the meat with salt and pepper. Heat the oil in a flameproof casserole. Put the beef in the pot and brown on all sides. Add half the sliced leeks and parsnips and cook for 8 minutes. Pour in the stock and bring to a boil. Add the bouquet garni. Cover and simmer gently for 2½ to 3 hours or until the meat is very tender.

Transfer the meat to a warmed dish and keep hot.

Skim any fat from the surface of the liquid in the casserole. Strain into a saucepan and add the remaining leeks and parsnips. Bring to a boil and boil for 20 to 25 minutes or until the liquid is reduced to about half the original quantity.

Stir in the beer and bring back to a boil. Blend the butter and flour together to make a smooth paste (beurre manié). Add in small pieces to the beer mixture and simmer, stirring, until thickened. Taste and adjust the seasoning, if necessary.

Carve the meat into thick slices and arrange on a warmed serving dish. Pour over the sauce and garnish with parsley sprigs. Serve hot.
Serves 6

Sautéed steak with shallot and wine sauce

1kg/2lb filet mignon or porterhouse
steak
2 Tbsp butter
1 Tbsp vegetable oil
SAUCE
2 Tbsp flour
3 Tbsp butter
1 Tbsp vegetable oil
2 shallots, finely chopped
1 garlic clove, crushed
300ml/1¼ cups red wine
300ml/1¼ cups beef stock
1 bay leaf
1 tsp thyme, freshly chopped
salt and black pepper

Cut the steak into pieces about 5cm/2in square and 1cm/½in thick. Melt the butter with the oil in a frying pan. Add the steak

Brewer's Pot-Roast makes a delicious family meal. Serve it with potatoes baked in their jackets and a glass of beer.

pieces and sauté until the outside is browned but the inside is still pink – about 2 to 3 minutes on each side. Transfer the meat to a warmed serving dish and keep hot while you make the sauce.

Mix together the flour and 1 tablespoon of the butter to make a paste (beurre manié). Melt the remaining butter with the oil in the cleaned-out frying pan. Add the shallots and garlic and fry until the shallots are soft, but not brown. Stir in the wine, stock, bay leaf, thyme and salt and pepper to taste. Bring to a boil and boil until the liquid has reduced to half the original quantity.

Add the beurre manié in small pieces, stirring, and continue simmering, stirring, until the sauce thickens. Remove the bay leaf and pour the sauce over the steak. Serve immediately.
Serves 6

Danish pork

1 × 1kg/2lb loin of pork (boned
weight) rolled and tied
2 cooking apples, peeled, cored and
sliced
salt and black pepper
2 Tbsp butter
1 medium onion, chopped
300ml/1¼ cups water
2 Tbsp flour
1 tsp prepared mustard
125ml/½ cup sour cream

A subtle yet remarkably tasty dish, Danish Pork is surprisingly quick and easy to prepare.

Make about 10 long slits in the pork on both sides. Insert half the apple slices in the slits. Rub the pork with salt and pepper. Melt the butter in a flameproof casserole. Add the pork, onion and remaining apple slices. Brown the pork on all sides.

Pour in the water and cover the casserole. Simmer gently for 1¼ hours.

Transfer to a warmed serving dish.

Mix together the flour and mustard. Add a little water and mix into a paste. Stir in a little hot liquid from the casserole and then stir the liquid into the casserole. Cook, stirring, for 3 minutes. Remove from the heat and stir in the sour cream. Spoon some of this sauce over the pork and serve the remainder in a sauceboat.
Serves 4

Marinated pork scallops

1kg/2lb pork tenderloin
2 garlic cloves, crushed
1cm/½in piece green ginger, peeled and
finely chopped
1 tsp rosemary, freshly chopped
salt and black pepper
6 juniper berries, bruised
1 Tbsp clear honey
2 Tbsp lemon juice
125ml/½ cup dry sherry
3 Tbsp butter
250g/2 cups button mushrooms, sliced
3 Tbsp tomato paste
2 tsp cornstarch
3 Tbsp water

Ask the butcher to partly slit the tenderloin and bash them to make scallops. Cut into manageable pieces and lay in a shallow dish.

Mix together the garlic, ginger, rosemary, salt and pepper to taste, the juniper berries, honey, lemon juice and half the sherry. Pour this marinade over the pork. Cover the dish and leave to marinate in the refrigerator for 6 hours, turning the pieces of pork occasionally.

Remove the pork pieces from the marinade and pat dry with paper towels. Reserve the marinade.

Melt the butter in a frying pan. Add the pork pieces and fry until lightly browned on all sides. Transfer to a shallow baking dish.

Add the mushrooms to the frying pan and fry for 3 minutes. Add to the pork in the baking dish.

Put the reserved marinade in the frying pan and stir in the tomato paste and remaining sherry. Bring to a boil. Pour over the pork in the baking dish and bake in a moderate oven (180°C/350°F) for 30 minutes.

Dissolve the cornstarch in the water. Stir in a little of the hot liquid, then stir into the liquid in the dish and bake for a further 10 minutes. Serve hot.

Serves 4

Maple spareribs

150ml/⅔ cup maple syrup
¼ tsp cayenne pepper
salt and black pepper
2 garlic cloves, crushed
2 Tbsp tomato paste
1 Tbsp prepared mustard
2 Tbsp lemon juice
2kg/4lb pork spareribs, cut into 2-rib
serving pieces

Mix together the maple syrup, cayenne pepper, salt and pepper to taste, the garlic, tomato paste, prepared mustard and lemon juice.

Put the spareribs in a roasting pan. Roast in a fairly hot oven (200°C/400°F) for 30 minutes.

Remove the spareribs from the pan and pour off the fat. Return the ribs to the pan and pour over the maple syrup mixture. Return to the oven and reduce the temperature to moderate (180°C/350°F). Roast for a further 45 minutes, basting frequently with the maple syrup mixture.

Remove from the oven, transfer to a warmed dish and serve hot.

Serves 4

Aromatic Maple Spareribs is an unusual and delicious dish adapted from a New England recipe.

Junipered pork chops

4 large pork chops
2 garlic cloves, halved
salt and black pepper
20 juniper berries, crushed
4 Tbsp olive oil

Rub the chops with the cut sides of the garlic cloves. Discard the garlic. Rub the chops with salt and pepper, then press the juniper berries into the meat. Brush with the oil and broil the chops for about 10 minutes on each side. Serve hot.
Serves 4

Ham braised in white wine with mushroom sauce

7 Tbsp butter
2 Tbsp vegetable oil
1 medium onion, thinly sliced
1 large carrot, scraped and sliced
800ml/3¼ cups dry white wine
1 bouquet garni
1 × 4.5kg/10lb processed ham
2 scallions, thinly sliced
500g/1lb mushrooms, thinly sliced
salt and pepper
2 Tbsp flour
300ml/1¼ cups heavy cream

Melt 2 tablespoons of the butter with the oil in a flameproof casserole. Add the onion and carrot and fry until the onion is soft but not brown. Stir in the wine, then add the bouquet garni. Bring to a boil and simmer for 2 minutes. Remove from the heat.

Place the ham in the casserole and baste it with the pan liquids. Braise in a warm oven (170°C/325°F) for 2 hours. Baste the ham occasionally with the cooking liquid.

Meanwhile, make the sauce. Melt 4 tablespoons of the remaining butter in a saucepan. Add the scallions and fry until they are soft. Stir in the mushrooms and cook until they are lightly browned. Remove from the heat. Transfer the ham to a warmed dish or board. Keep hot.

Strain the cooking liquid from the casserole into a saucepan. Add the liquid from the pan of mushrooms. Bring to a boil and boil until the liquid has reduced to about half the original quantity.

Blend the remaining butter with the flour to make a smooth paste (beurre manié). Add this in small pieces to the cooking liquid. Simmer, stirring, until thickened and smooth. Stir in the mushroom mixture and the cream. Heat through gently without boiling. Pour the sauce into a sauceboat and serve with the ham.
Serves 12-14

Lamb chops in dried fruit sauce with saffron rice

60g/¼ cup butter
6 large lamb chops
250ml/1 cup water
salt and black pepper
¼ tsp ground cinnamon
½ tsp garam masala
90g/½ cup raisins
175g/1 cup dried apricots, soaked overnight and drained
RICE
175g/1 cup long-grain rice, soaked in cold water for 30 minutes and drained
500ml/2 cups water
salt
1 tsp ground saffron
60g/¼ cup butter, melted

Melt the butter in a frying pan. Add the chops, in batches, and brown on all sides. Pour the fat out of the pan and add the water, salt and pepper to taste, the cinnamon, garam masala, raisins and apricots. Bring to a boil, then cover and simmer for 20 minutes.

Meanwhile, prepare the rice. Put the rice and water in a saucepan. Stir in salt and the saffron. Bring to a boil, then cover and simmer for 15 minutes or until the rice is tender and all the liquid has been absorbed.

Transfer the rice to a warmed serving dish. Sprinkle over the melted butter and toss to coat. Top with the chops and fruit sauce. Serve hot.
Serves 6

Lamb roasted with gin

1 × 2kg/4lb leg of lamb
2 garlic cloves, cut into slivers
salt and black pepper
1 Tbsp rosemary sprigs
1 tsp ground ginger
60g/¼ cup butter
250g/1 cup beef stock
75ml/⅓ cup gin

Make incisions in the meat and insert the garlic slivers in the cuts. Rub the meat with salt, pepper and ginger.

Melt the butter in a roasting pan. Put the meat in the pan and brown it on all sides. Pour over the stock and gin. Carefully arrange the rosemary sprigs over the meat.

Transfer the pan to a fairly hot oven (200°C/400°F) and roast for 15 minutes. Reduce the temperature to moderate (180°C/350°F) and continue roasting for a further 1½ hours or until the juices run only faintly pink or almost clear when the

Roast lamb with a little difference –
Lamb Roasted with Gin.

meat is pierced through with a skewer.

Transfer the lamb to a warmed serving dish or carving board. Skim any fat from the surface of the cooking juices, then pour them over the meat.

Serve immediately.

Serves 4

Spicy lamb and eggplant stew

2 small eggplants, thinly sliced
salt and black pepper
125ml/½ cup olive oil
1kg/2lb boned shoulder of lamb, cut into 5cm/2in cubes
1 medium onion, thinly sliced
2 large tomatoes, peeled, seeded and chopped
2 Tbsp tomato paste
3 Tbsp lemon juice
½ tsp grated nutmeg
½ tsp curry powder
425ml/1¾ cups water

Sprinkle the eggplant slices with salt and leave for 30 minutes. Rinse and pat dry with paper towels.

Heat 2 tablespoons of the oil in a frying pan. Add the lamb cubes, in batches, and brown on all sides. Remove the meat from the pan and place it in a casserole.

Add the onion to the frying pan and fry until it is soft but not brown. Stir in the tomatoes, tomato paste, lemon juice, nutmeg, curry powder and salt and pepper to taste. Cook, stirring, for 6 minutes. Stir in the water and bring to a boil. Pour over the meat in the casserole.

Heat one-third of the remaining oil in the cleaned-out frying-pan. Add about one-third of the eggplant slices and fry until they are lightly browned on all sides. Drain on paper towels. Fry the remaining eggplant slices in the same way, then cut them into 1cm/½in strips. Add the eggplant strips to the casserole and mix well.

Place the casserole in a moderate oven (180°C/350°F) and bake for 1 hour or until the lamb cubes are tender. Serve hot, from the casserole.

Serves 4

Moussaka

500g/1lb eggplants, sliced
salt and black pepper
2 Tbsp butter
1 medium onion, finely chopped
1 garlic clove, crushed
500g/1lb lean lamb, ground
4 tomatoes, chopped
2 Tbsp tomato paste
2 tsp thyme, freshly chopped
3 Tbsp flour
125ml/½ cup vegetable oil
300ml/1¼ cups white *or* bechamel sauce
2 egg yolks
30g/¼ cup kefalotiri *or* Parmesan cheese, grated

Sprinkle the eggplant slices with salt and leave for 30 minutes. Meanwhile, melt the butter in a frying pan. Add the onion and garlic and fry until the onion is soft but not brown. Add the meat and fry until it is evenly browned. Stir in the tomatoes, tomato paste, thyme and salt and pepper to taste. Cook for 4 minutes. Remove from the heat.

Rinse the eggplant slices and dry with paper towels. Coat the slices with the flour. Heat half the oil in a frying pan. Add half the eggplant slices and fry until lightly browned on each side. Drain on paper towels and fry the remaining slices in the remaining oil.

Arrange half the eggplant slices in a baking dish. Spoon over the meat and tomato mixture and cover with the remaining eggplant slices. Mix together the sauce and egg yolks. Pour over the eggplant slices to cover them completely. Sprinkle

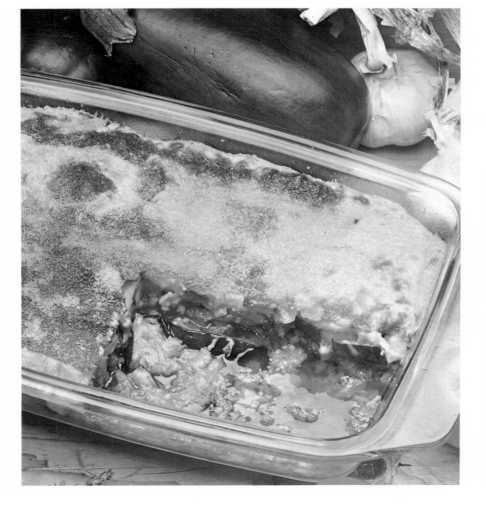

Moussaka – a favorite and filling dish from Greece.

over the top with the grated cheese.

Bake in a fairly hot oven (190°C/375°F) for 35 to 40 minutes or until the top is lightly browned. Serve hot, from the baking dish.

Serves 4

Chicken casserole

60g/½ cup flour
salt and black pepper
1 Tbsp dill, freshly chopped
1 × 2.5kg/5lb chicken, skinned and cut
into serving pieces
2 eggs, lightly beaten
60g/¼ cup butter
2 Tbsp vegetable oil
300ml/1¼ cups chicken stock
1 medium green pepper, pith and seeds
removed and cut into rings
2 tomatoes, peeled and sliced
125ml/½ cup heavy cream
60g/½ cup Samsoe or Cheddar cheese,
grated

Mix together the flour, salt and pepper and dill. Coat the chicken pieces with the beaten egg and then with the dill mixture. Melt the butter with the oil in a flameproof casserole. Add the chicken pieces, in batches, and brown on all sides. Pour in the chicken stock and bring to a boil. Cover and simmer gently for 40 minutes or until the chicken is tender.

Transfer the chicken pieces to a warmed flameproof serving dish. Keep hot.

Add the green pepper to the casserole and simmer for 4 minutes. Stir in the tomatoes and cook for a further 2 minutes. Remove the vegetables from the casserole with a slotted spoon and arrange around the chicken.

Stir the cream into the liquid in the casserole. Heat through gently without boiling, then pour this sauce over the chicken. Sprinkle over the cheese and broil until it has melted and browned. Serve hot.

Serves 4-6

Chicken Casserole, topped with cheese, is a tempting dish ideal for a family supper.

Chicken curry

2 tsp salt
1 Tbsp tumeric
1.5kg/3lb chicken pieces, skinned
4 Tbsp vegetable oil
1 large onion, finely chopped
2 garlic cloves, finely chopped
5cm/2in pieces green ginger, peeled and
finely chopped
1 green chili pepper, finely chopped
1 Tbsp ground coriander
1½ tsp ground cumin
1 Tbsp garam masala
1 tsp chili powder
500g/1lb tomatoes, peeled and strained
1cm/½in slice creamed coconut
1 Tbsp coriander leaves, freshly
chopped

Combine 1 teaspoon of salt and 2 teaspoons of tumeric and rub the chicken pieces with this mixture.

Heat the oil in a frying pan. Add the chicken pieces, in batches, and fry until lightly browned on all sides. Remove from the pan. Add the onion to the pan and fry until it is golden brown. Add the garlic, ginger and green chili pepper and fry for a further 4 minutes. Mix together the coriander, cumin, garam masala, chili powder, remaining teaspoon of turmeric and 2 tablespoons of water. Add this spice paste to the frying pan and fry, stirring, for 8 minutes. If the mixture becomes too dry, add 2 to 3 tablespoons of water.

Stir in the tomatoes and remaining teaspoon of salt. Return the chicken pieces to the pan, cover and simmer for 40 to 45 minutes or until the chicken is tender.

Add the creamed coconut and stir until it has dissolved into the sauce. Simmer for a further 10 minutes, uncovered. Taste and adjust the seasoning, if necessary. If you like, add a teaspoon of sugar. Stir in the coriander leaves and serve with boiled rice.
Serves 4

Yogurt chicken

1 × 2kg/4lb chicken, skinned
1 tsp salt
juice of ½ lemon
2 green chili peppers, very finely
chopped
250ml/1 cup plain yogurt
4 Tbsp coriander leaves, freshly chopped
5cm/2in piece green ginger, peeled and
finely chopped
4 garlic cloves, crushed
60g/¼ cup butter, melted
lemon and cucumber slices, to garnish

Prick the chicken all over with a fork. Rub with the salt, lemon juice and chili peppers. Leave to marinate for 30 minutes.

Mix together the yogurt, coriander, ginger and garlic. Rub this mixture over the chicken. Cover and marinate for 8 hours.

Put half the butter in a roasting pan. Put the chicken and marinade in the pan and roast in a fairly hot oven (200°C/400°F) for 20 minutes. Reduce the temperature to moderate (180°C/350°F) and roast for a further 30 minutes or until the chicken is tender. Baste frequently with the marinade in the pan and the remaining butter.

Transfer the chicken to a warmed serving dish. Keep hot. Boil the cooking juices for 3 to 5 minutes to reduce slightly. Pour over the chicken and serve.
Serves 4

Normandy duck

1 × 2½kg/5lb duck
250g/4 cups fresh white breadcrumbs
300ml/1¼ cups strong hard cider
60g/¼ cup butter
2 Tbsp olive oil
1kg/2lb cooking apples, peeled, cored
and sliced
3 celery stalks, finely chopped
1 tsp ground cinnamon or cloves
salt and black pepper
75ml/⅓ cup Calvados *or* applejack
185ml/¾ cup heavy cream

Prick the skin of the duck all over. Put the breadcrumbs in a mixing bowl and pour over 4 tablespoons of the cider. Squeeze with your hand so the breadcrumbs are completely moistened.

Melt the butter with the oil in a saucepan. Add the apples and celery and fry for about 10 minutes or until tender. Stir in the cinnamon or cloves and salt and pepper to taste. Remove from the heat and stir in the breadcrumbs. Spoon this stuffing into the cavity in the duck and truss.

Place the duck on a rack in a roasting pan and roast in a moderate oven (180°C/350°F) for 15 minutes. Pour over the remaining cider and continue roasting for 1¼ hours or until the juices run clear when the thigh is pierced with a fork.

Transfer the duck to a warmed serving dish. Untruss and keep hot.

Skim the fat from the surface of the liquid in the roasting pan. Pour the liquid into a saucepan and bring to a boil. Boil until reduced to half the original quantity. Stir in the Calvados or applejack and cream and heat through gently without boiling. Pour this sauce into a sauceboat and serve with the duck.
Serves 4

Cooked in a spicy yogurt sauce, Yogurt Chicken is first marinated then roasted to make a really scrumptious dish.

Duck with braised red cabbage

125g/½ cup butter
2 medium onions, finely chopped
1 garlic clove, finely chopped
1 large head red cabbage, shredded
2 medium cooking apples, peeled, cored
and coarsely chopped
1 small onion, studded with 4 cloves
1 tsp ground allspice
salt and black pepper
300ml/1¼ cups dry red wine
150ml/⅔ cup beef stock
1 × 2½kg/5lb duck

Melt half the butter in a flameproof casserole. Add the onions and garlic and fry until the onions are soft but not brown. Stir in the cabbage, apples, clove-studded onion, allspice and salt and pepper to taste. Simmer for 5 minutes, stirring occasionally to brown the cabbage evenly. Stir in the wine and stock and bring to a boil. Cover and braise in a warm oven (170°C/325°F) for 3½ hours.

After the cabbage has been cooking for 1½ hours, prepare the duck. Prick the skin all over and rub the cavity with salt and pepper. Truss the duck. Melt the remaining butter in a frying pan. Put the duck in the pan and brown on all sides. Transfer it to a rack in a roasting pan and place in the oven. Roast for 1¾ to 2 hours, or until the juices run clear when the thigh is pricked with a fork.

Transfer the duck to a warmed serving platter. Arrange the braised cabbage around it and serve.

Serves 4

Pheasant in red wine

2 young pheasants
salt and black pepper
2 medium onions, finely chopped
125g/½ cup butter
1 Tbsp vegetable oil
900ml/3⅔ cups dry red wine
1 bay leaf
125g/½ cup mushrooms, thinly sliced
4 bacon slices
30g/¼ cup flour
150ml/⅔ cup heavy cream

Rub the insides of the pheasants with salt and pepper. Put half the onions into the cavities in the birds. Truss.

Melt three-quarters of the butter with the oil in a frying pan. Add the pheasants

A splendid dish befitting autumn, Pheasant in Red Wine can be served with the season's juicy cranberries.

and brown on all sides. Transfer the pheasants to a flameproof casserole.

Add the remaining onions to the frying pan and fry until golden brown. Stir in the wine and bring to a boil. Add salt and pepper to taste with the bay leaf and mushrooms. Simmer for 5 minutes.

Place the bacon slices over the breasts of the pheasants. Pour the wine mixture around the birds. Cover the casserole and braise on top of the stove for 50 minutes to 1 hour or until the pheasants are tender.

Transfer the pheasants to a warmed serving dish. Discard the bacon and keep the birds hot.

Bring the liquid in the casserole back to a boil and boil until it has reduced to half the original quantity. Blend the remaining butter with the flour to make a smooth paste. Add this, in small pieces, to the liquid in the casserole. Simmer, stirring, until thickened and smooth. Stir in the cream and heat through without boiling. Pour this sauce into a sauceboat and serve with the pheasant.

Serves 4

Marinated venison stew

1kg/2lb lean venison, cut into 5cm/2in cubes
60g/¼ cup butter
salt and black pepper
1 Tbsp rosemary, freshly chopped
3 medium carrots, scraped and quartered
1 small turnip, peeled and chopped
250g/8oz small onions, peeled
3 medium potatoes, peeled and halved
400g/14oz can tomatoes
3 Tbsp tomato paste
MARINADE
375ml/1½ cups red wine
250ml/1 cup beef stock
3 Tbsp olive oil
1 large onion, thinly sliced
8 black peppercorns
3 garlic cloves, crushed
2 Tbsp parsley, freshly chopped
1 Tbsp rosemary, freshly chopped
1 bouquet garni

Mix together all the marinade ingredients

Full of flavor, Marinated Venison Stew makes a nourishing meal for the hunting season.

Because different varieties can be grown throughout the year, the patato is not a seasonal vegetable. It is used, however, in different ways at different times of the year. In spring, we enjoy the delicate flavor of new potatoes; in summer, mayonnaise and potato salads; and in winter and autumn, they taste particularly good mashed, baked or used to fill out warming stews and casseroles as in Marinated Venison Stew.

in a shallow dish. Add the venison cubes and leave to marinate for 12 hours.

Remove the meat from the marinade and pat dry with paper towels. Reserve the marinade, discarding the peppercorns. Melt the butter in a flameproof casserole. Add the venison cubes and brown on all sides. Stir in the reserved marinade, salt and pepper to taste and the rosemary. Bring to a boil, then cover and simmer for 1½ hours.

Add the carrots, turnip, onions, potatoes, tomatoes with the can juice and the tomato paste and stir well. Re-cover the casserole and continue to simmer for a further 1 hour or until the meat is very tender.

Discard the bouquet garni and serve.

Serves 4

Hare casseroled in wine and herb sauce

8 bacon slices
salt and black pepper
1 tsp thyme, freshly chopped
90g/¾ cup flour
2.5kg/5lb hare, skinned and cut into serving pieces
1 Tbsp butter
1 medium onion, finely chopped
2 garlic cloves, crushed
250ml/1 cup dry red wine
185ml/¾ cup chicken stock
2 Tbsp dry sherry
1 Tbsp cranberry sauce
1 tsp parsley, freshly chopped
1 tsp marjoram, freshly chopped
½ tsp tarragon, freshly chopped
grated rind of ½ lemon

Broil the bacon until crisp and golden brown. Drain on paper towels. Reserve the bacon fat in the broiler pan.

Mix together salt and pepper, half the thyme and the flour. Coat the hare pieces in this mixture.

Pour the bacon fat into a frying pan and add the butter. Melt it and add the hare pieces. Brown well on all sides. Transfer the hare pieces to a casserole. Add the onion and garlic to the frying pan and fry until the onion is soft. Transfer the onion and garlic to the casserole.

Discard the fat in the frying pan. Put the wine, stock and sherry in the pan and bring to a boil. Stir in the cranberry sauce, parsley, marjoram, tarragon, lemon rind and remaining thyme. Pour over the hare.

Crumble the bacon into the casserole. Cover and braise in a moderate oven (180°C/350°F) for 2½ hours or until the hare pieces are tender. Serve immediately, from the casserole.

Serves 4-6

Pigeon pie

PASTRY
350g/3 cups flour
1 tsp salt
150ml/⅔ cup water
125g/½ cup shortening
1 egg yolk, lightly beaten
1 egg, lightly beaten
FILLING
8 pigeon breasts, boned and sliced
125g/½ cup cooked ham, finely chopped
275g/1¼ cups pork sausage meat
175g/¾ cup button mushrooms, quartered
1 egg, hard-cooked and finely chopped
salt and black pepper
1 tsp grated lemon rind
pinch cayenne pepper
125ml/½ cup beef stock
4 Tbsp dry red wine

Sift the flour and salt into a mixing bowl. Bring the water and shortening to a boil in a saucepan. When the shortening has melted, remove from the heat. Make a well in the center of the flour and add the egg yolk and fat and water mixture. Gradually draw the flour into the liquid, mixing to a smooth dough. Knead until it is shiny.

Cut off one-third of the dough and set aside in a warm place. Roll out the remaining dough to a circle about 25cm/10in in diameter. Turn a deep 15cm/6in diameter cake pan or large coffee can upside-down and grease the outside. Cover the outside of the pan or can with the dough circle. Place a sheet of foil over the pan or can and turn it right side up. Wrap the paper around the dough-covered pan or can and tie with string. Chill for 20 to 30 minutes or until firm.

Mix together the pigeon meat, ham, sausage meat, mushrooms, egg, salt and pepper to taste, the lemon rind and cayenne.

Gently ease the pan or can out of the dough case. Place the dough case on a greased baking sheet. Fill with the pigeon mixture. Roll out the remaining piece of dough to a circle just larger than the top of the dough case. Place this lid on top and press the edges together to seal. Brush the pie all over with the beaten egg. Make a 5cm/2in slit in the center of the dough lid.

Bake in a fairly hot oven (200°C/400°F) for 1 hour. Reduce the temperature to moderate (180°C/350°F). Remove the foil.

Bring the stock and wine to a boil in a saucepan. Pour through the slit in the dough lid. Bake for a further 1 hour or until the meat is tender and the pastry well browned. Serve hot or cold.

Serves 4-6

Vegetables

Aniseed carrots

750g/1½lb carrots, scraped
1 Tbsp brown sugar
60g/¼ cup butter
1½ tsp aniseed
salt and black pepper

Put the sugar, butter, aniseed and salt and pepper to taste in a saucepan. Heat until the mixture starts to bubble, stirring to dissolve the sugar. Add the carrots, stir well to coat and cover the pan. Simmer for about 15 minutes or until the carrots are tender. Serve hot.
Serves 4

Cauliflower with Italian sauce

2 Tbsp butter
1 medium onion, chopped
3 large mushrooms, sliced
2 Tbsp cooked ham, shredded
1 Tbsp flour
75ml/⅓ cup white wine
185ml/¾ cup beef stock
2 tsp tomato paste
salt and black pepper
1 large cauliflower, broken into flowerets

Melt the butter in a saucepan. Add the onion, mushrooms and ham and fry, stirring, for 10 minutes. Sprinkle over the flour and cook, stirring, for 1 minute. Gradually stir in the wine and stock with the tomato paste and salt and pepper to taste. Bring to a boil and simmer, stirring, until thickened. Simmer gently for 20 minutes.

Meanwhile, cook the cauliflower in boiling salted water for 9 to 12 minutes or until the flowerets are just tender. Drain well and transfer to a warmed serving dish. Pour over the sauce and serve hot.
Serves 4

Corn bake

4 eggs
30g/¼ cup flour
375ml/1½ cups light cream
60g/¼ cup butter, melted
salt and black pepper
500g/3 cups corn kernels

Beat the eggs in a mixing bowl until they are frothy. Stir in the flour, cream and melted butter, then the remaining ingredients with salt and pepper to taste. Pour into a greased shallow baking dish. Bake in a moderate oven (180°C/350°F) for 1 to 1½ hours or until the top is golden brown and a skewer inserted in the center comes out clean. Serve hot.
Serves 4

Brussels sprouts with peppers and tomatoes

3 Tbsp butter
1 large onion, finely chopped
1 garlic clove, crushed
1 green pepper, pith and seeds removed and chopped
500g/1lb tomatoes, peeled and chopped
750g/1½lb Brussels sprouts
salt and black pepper
½ tsp dried basil

Melt the butter in a saucepan. Add the onion, garlic and green pepper and fry until the onion, garlic and green pepper and fry until the onion is soft but not brown. Stir in the tomatoes, sprouts, salt and pepper to taste and the basil. Cover and cook until the sprouts are tender.
Serves 4

Left: Aniseed Carrots is an unusual combination of flavors making a most attractive vegetable dish.
Below: Brussels sprouts, with their delicate, slightly nutty flavor are one of the treats of the colder months.

Red cabbage braised with red wine

2 Tbsp butter
1 medium head red cabbage,
coarsely chopped
250ml/2 cup dry red wine
4 Tbsp wine vinegar
2 Tbsp brown sugar
salt and black pepper
pinch grated nutmeg

Melt the butter in a flameproof casserole. Add the cabbage and cook for 10 minutes, stirring occasionally. Stir in the remaining ingredients, with salt and pepper to taste, and bring to a boil. Cover the casserole and transfer to a warm oven (170°C/325°F). Braise for 2 to 2½ hours or until the cabbage is tender. Serve hot.
Serves 6

Below: As lettuce becomes scarce and more expensive, try thinly-sliced cabbage as a substitute in salads. Bottom: Rutabaga puréed with apples, makes an ideal autumn vegetable dish.

Glazed turnips

2 Tbsp butter
1 Tbsp olive oil
750g/1½lb young turnips, peeled
and quartered
2 Tbsp brown sugar
185ml/¾ cup chicken stock

Melt the butter with the oil in a saucepan. Add the turnips and cook until they are golden brown. Sprinkle over the sugar and cook, stirring occasionally, for 5 minutes.

Add the chicken stock and bring to a boil. Cover and simmer gently for 30 minutes or until the turnips are tender but still firm and most of the stock has been absorbed. Serve hot.
Serves 4

Rutabaga and apple purée

5 medium rutabagas, peeled and chopped
3 large tart apples, peeled, cored
and chopped
60g/¼ cup butter, softened
1 tsp lemon juice
½ tsp ground allspice
salt and pepper

Cook the rutabaga in boiling salted water for 30 minutes or until they are tender. Meanwhile, put a 1cm/½in layer of water in another saucepan and add the apple slices. Cook gently until the apples are very soft. Mash the apples to a purée.

Drain the rutabaga and put in a mixing bowl. Add the apple purée and butter and mash with a fork or potato masher. Beat in the lemon juice and spice. Spoon into a warmed serving dish and serve.
Serves 6-8

Ratatouille

3 medium eggplants, thinly sliced
2 Tbsp butter
4 Tbsp olive oil
2 large onions, thinly sliced
3 garlic cloves, crushed
1 large green pepper, pith and seeds
removed and chopped
1 large red pepper, pith and seeds
removed and chopped
5 medium zucchini, sliced
500g/1lb tomatoes, peeled and chopped
1 tsp dried basil
1 Tbsp parsley, freshly chopped
salt and black pepper

Sprinkle the eggplant slices with salt and leave for 30 minutes. Rinse and pat dry.

Melt the butter with the oil in a frying pan. Add the onions and garlic and fry until the onions are soft but not brown. Add the remaining ingredients, with salt and pepper to taste, and cover the pan. Simmer for 40 to 45 minutes or until the vegetables are very tender. Serve hot or cold.
Serves 4-6

Breaded pumpkin slices with tomato sauce

1kg/2lb pumpkin, peeled and sliced
2 eggs, lightly beaten
60g/⅔ cup dry breadcrumbs
60g/¼ cup butter
30g/¼ cup Parmesan cheese, grated
SAUCE
2 Tbsp olive oil
1 onion, finely chopped
1 garlic clove, crushed
500g/2 cups tomatoes, peeled, seeded
and chopped
1 Tbsp tomato paste
1 tsp dried basil
1 Tbsp parsley, freshly chopped
1 tsp sugar
salt and black pepper

First make the sauce. Heat the oil in a saucepan. Add the onion and garlic and fry until the onion is soft but not brown. Stir in the remaining ingredients, with salt and pepper and simmer for 10 minutes.

Coat the pumpkin slices with the eggs, then with the breadcrumbs. Melt the butter in a frying pan. Add the pumpkin slices, in batches, and brown on all sides. Transfer to a greased baking dish.

Pour the tomato sauce over the pumpkin slices and sprinkle with the Parmesan. Bake in a moderate oven (180°C/350°F) for 30 minutes. Serve hot.
Serves 4

Salads

Cabbage and pepper salad

1 red pepper, pith and seeds removed
and thinly sliced
1 green pepper, pith and seeds removed
and thinly sliced
6-8 scallions finely chopped
1 cucumber, cut into 1cm/½in cubes
500g/1lb tomatoes, thinly sliced
½ white cabbage, thinly sliced
2 Tbsp clear honey
juice of 1 lemon
10 Tbsp oil
4 Tbsp vinegar
salt and black pepper

Mix together the peppers, scallions,
cucumber cubes, tomatoes and cabbage in
a large salad bowl. Put the remaining
ingredients, with salt and pepper to taste,
in a screwtop jar and shake well. Pour this
dressing over the salad and toss to coat.
Serve soon after dressing the salad.
Serves 8

Endive and tomato salad

3 heads French or Belgian endive,
thinly sliced
6 tomatoes, sliced
8 black olives, pitted
2 Tbsp red wine or cider vinegar
1 Tbsp clear honey
1 small onion, finely chopped
3 Tbsp olive oil
2 tsp lemon juice
salt and black pepper
½ tsp sugar

Put the endive, tomatoes and olives in a
salad bowl. Mix together the remaining
ingredients, with salt and pepper to taste,
in a screwtop jar. Shake well, then pour
this dressing over the vegetables. Toss to
coat and chill for 20 minutes before
serving.
Serves 4

Beet and dill salad

6 small beets, cooked and skinned
salt and black pepper
1 medium onion, thinly sliced and
pushed out into rings
75ml/⅓ cup wine vinegar
3 Tbsp olive oil
1½ tsp sugar
1 Tbsp dill, freshly chopped

Thinly slice the warmed beets and place

them in a bowl.

Sprinkle salt and pepper over the beet
slices, then add the remaining ingredients.
Toss gently to coat and transfer to a
serving dish.

Chill before serving.
Serves 6

Leek and sour cream salad

1kg/2lb leeks, washed, trimmed and
cut into 2.5cm/1in slices
150ml/⅔ cup sour cream
1 Tbsp lemon juice
1 tsp prepared German or French
mustard
½ tsp sugar
salt and black pepper

Cook the leeks in boiling salted water for 8
to 12 minutes or until they are just tender.

Remove from the heat, drain well and
allow to cool.

Put the leeks in a salad bowl. Mix together the remaining ingredients, with salt
and pepper to taste, and pour over.

Stir gently to mix, with a wooden spoon.
Chill before serving.
Serves 4-6

*Below: Endive is another salad
vegetable which comes into its own in
colder weather.*
*Bottom: A clean-tasting, crunchy
Cabbage and Pepper Salad makes a
pleasant change as an accompaniment
to roast meat.*

Light Dishes

Zucchini eggah

500g/1lb small zucchini, thinly sliced
¼ tsp grated nutmeg
300ml/1¼ cups milk
2 Tbsp olive oil
1 small onion, halved and thinly sliced
1 garlic clove, crushed
8 eggs
salt and black pepper
1 Tbsp chives, freshly chopped
60g/1 cup fresh white breadcrumbs
2 Tbsp butter

Lay the zucchini slices in a shallow dish. Sprinkle with the nutmeg and pour over the milk. Leave to soak for 30 minutes, then drain off the milk, reserving 2 tablespoons.

Heat the oil in a frying pan. Add the zucchini slices, onion and garlic and fry until the onion is soft but not brown. Remove from the heat.

Mix together the eggs, reserved milk, salt and pepper to taste and the chives. Stir in the zucchini mixture and bread-crumbs.

Melt the butter in the cleaned-out frying pan. Pour in the egg mixture and cook slowly for 30 minutes. Place the pan under the broiler and cook until the top is lightly browned. Serve hot, cut into wedges.
Serves 4

Stuffed eggplant

4 eggplants
2 Tbsp olive oil
2 small onions, chopped
2 garlic cloves, crushed
4 large tomatoes, peeled and chopped
12 green olives, pitted
salt and black pepper
60g/½ cup Parmesan cheese, grated
30g/⅓ cup dry breadcrumbs
2 Tbsp butter, cut into small pieces

Put the eggplants in a saucepan and cover with water. Bring to a boil, then cover and simmer for 15 minutes. Drain well and cut the eggplants in half, lengthwise. Scoop out the flesh, leaving shells 6mm/¼in thick. Reserve the shells. Chop the flesh.

Heat the oil in a frying pan. Add the onions and garlic and fry until the onions are soft but not brown. Stir in the tomatoes, olives, eggplant flesh and salt and pepper to taste. Simmer for 10 minutes.

Fill the eggplant shells with the tomato mixture and place in a baking dish. Sprinkle the cheese and breadcrumbs over

the tops and dot with the pieces of butter. Bake in a moderate oven (180°C/350°F) for 30 minutes. Serve hot.
Serves 4

Canelloni with spinach and meat

TOMATO SAUCE
2 Tbsp olive oil
1 small onion, finely chopped
400g/14oz can tomatoes
5 Tbsp tomato paste
½ tsp dried basil
1 tsp sugar
salt and black pepper
FILLING
1 Tbsp butter
1½ Tbsp olive oil
1 small onion, finely chopped
2 garlic cloves, finely chopped
250g/1 cup lean ground beef
30g/¼ cup Parmesan cheese, grated
1½ Tbsp heavy cream
1 egg
1 Tbsp oregano, freshly chopped
salt and black pepper
CREAM SAUCE
2 Tbsp butter
30g/¼ cup flour
150ml/⅔ cup milk
3 Tbsp heavy cream
salt and white pepper
PASTA
250g/8oz cannelloni rolls or sheets
90g/¾ cup Parmesan cheese, grated
1 Tbsp butter, cut into small pieces

First make the tomato sauce. Heat the oil in a saucepan. Add the onion and fry until it is soft but not brown. Stir in the remaining ingredients, with salt and pepper to taste, and cover the pan. Simmer for 40 minutes.

To make the filling, melt the butter with the oil in a frying pan. Add the onion and garlic and fry until the onion is soft but not brown. Meanwhile, cook the spinach for 5 to 7 minutes or until it is tender. (Do not add water: there should be enough left on the leaves after washing.) Drain the spinach well and chop finely.

Add the meat to the frying pan and fry until it is evenly browned. Stir in the spinach and cook, stirring, until the moisture has evaporated. Turn the mixture into a mixing bowl. Allow to cool slightly, then mix in all of the remaining ingredients, including salt and pepper to taste.

To make the cream sauce, melt the butter in a saucepan. Remove the pan from the heat and stir in the flour. Gradually stir in the milk and return to the heat. Simmer,

Canelloni with Spinach and Meat is popular, filling and reasonably economical – the perfect family meal.

stirring, until thickened and smooth. Remove from the heat and stir in the cream with salt and pepper to taste.

Cook the cannelloni in boiling salted water for 6 to 15 minutes or until it is just *al dente* (tender to the bite). Drain well. Fill the cannelloni rolls with the filling (or place a spoonful of filling on each cannelloni sheet and roll up).

Pour a thin layer of tomato sauce into a large shallow baking dish. Place the cannelloni on top, in one or two layers. Pour over the cream sauce, then the tomato sauce. Sprinkle with the Parmesan cheese and dot with the pieces of butter. Bake in a fairly hot oven (190°C/375°F) for 30 minutes or until the sauce is bubbling and the cheese is lightly browned. Serve hot, from the dish.

Serves 4

Neapolitan pizza

½ cake compressed yeast
125ml/½ cup plus 1 Tbsp lukewarm water
250g/2 cups flour
1 tsp salt
2 tsp olive oil
FILLING
2 Tbsp tomato paste
4 medium tomatoes, peeled, seeded and chopped
250g/8oz mozzarella cheese, sliced
8 anchovies, halved
black pepper
2 tsp oregano, freshly chopped

Mash the yeast and 1 tablespoon of the water together to make a smooth paste. Set aside in a warm, draft-free place until frothy. Sift the flour and salt into a mixing bowl. Make a well in the center and pour in the yeast mixture and remaining water. Gradually draw the flour into the liquids, mixing to a dough.

Turn the dough out of the bowl and knead for 10 minutes or until elastic and smooth. Return to the bowl, cover and leave in a warm, draft-free place for 45 minutes to 1 hour or until doubled in bulk.

Punch down and knead the dough again for 3 minutes. Cut it in half and roll out each half to a circle about 6mm/¼in thick. Place the dough circles on a greased baking sheet.

Cover the top of each dough circle with tomato paste, then arrange the tomatoes, cheese and anchovies on top. Sprinkle with the pepper and oregano, then with the oil. Bake in a very hot oven (230°C/450°F) for 15 to 20 minutes or until the pastry is crisp and the cheese melted.

Serve hot.

Serves 2-4

Three cheese quiche

PASTRY
175g/1½ cups flour
½ tsp salt
3 Tbsp butter
3 Tbsp shortening
2-3 Tbsp iced water
FILLING
90g/¾ cup Roquefort or other blue cheese, crumbled
90g/⅔ cup Camembert cheese, rind removed
90g/⅓ cup cream cheese
1 Tbsp butter, softened
1 shallot, finely chopped
4 Tbsp light cream
3 eggs
salt and white pepper
pinch cayenne pepper

Sift the flour and salt into a mixing bowl. Add the butter and shortening and cut into small pieces. Rub the fat into the flour until the mixture resembles breadcrumbs. Stir in enough water to bind, then knead to a dough. Chill for 20 minutes.

Roll out the dough and use to line a 23cm/9in tart pan. Pre-bake in a fairly hot oven (200°C/400°F) for 5 minutes.

Mash the cheeses and butter together in a mixing bowl. Beat in the shallot. Mix together the cream, eggs, salt and pepper to taste and the cayenne. Stir into the cheese mixture. Pour into the tart shell and place on a baking sheet. Bake in a fairly hot oven (200°C/400°F) for 30 to 35 minutes or until the pastry is golden brown.
Serves 4-6

Traditional Neapolitan Pizzas made with tomatoes, anchovies, Mozarella cheese and oregano should be served sizzling hot, with an Italian wine.

Squash soufflé

60g/¼ cup butter
1 small onion, finely minced
60g/½ cup flour
salt and black pepper
¼ tsp cayenne pepper
1 Tbsp chives, freshly chopped
300ml/1¼ cups milk
250g/2 cups autumn squash, peeled,
seeded and grated
2 Tbsp sour cream
4 egg yolks
5 egg whites

Melt the butter in a saucepan. Add the onion and fry until it is golden brown. Stir in the flour and cook, stirring, for 1 minute. Remove the pan from the heat and stir in salt and pepper to taste, the cayenne and chives. Gradually stir in the milk. Return to the heat and cook, stirring, until thickened and smooth. Remove from the heat.

Stir in the squash, sour cream and egg yolks. Allow to cool slightly.

Beat the egg whites until they will hold a stiff peak. Fold them into the squash mixture. Spoon into a greased 1.5⅓ pint capacity soufflé dish. Bake in a fairly hot oven (190°C/375°F) for 35 to 40 minutes or until well risen and golden brown. Serve at once.
Serves 4

Crab patties

500g/1lb crabmeat, flaked
90g/1½ cups fresh white breadcrumbs
1 egg yolk
2 Tbsp mayonnaise
12 scallions, finely chopped
1 egg, hard-cooked and finely chopped
½ tsp marjoram, freshly chopped
2 tsp lemon juice
salt and black pepper
pinch cayenne pepper
125ml/½ cup vegetable oil
watercress, to garnish

Mix together the crabmeat, breadcrumbs, egg yolk, mayonnaise, scallions, egg, marjoram, lemon juice, salt and pepper to taste and the cayenne. Form the mixture into 5cm/2in balls and flatten into patties.

Heat the oil in a frying pan. Add the patties, in batches, and fry for 3 to 5 minutes on each side or until deep golden brown. Drain on paper towels and keep hot while you fry the remaining patties.

Transfer the patties to a warmed serving dish and garnish with the watercress. Serve hot.
Serves 4-6

Home Baking

Parkin

500g/4 cups flour
1 tsp baking soda
1 tsp salt
2 tsp ground ginger
500g/5 cups rolled oats
250g/1 cup butter
250ml/1 cup molasses
250ml/1 cup light corn syrup
4 Tbsp clear honey
2 Tbsp brown sugar
375ml/1½ cups milk

Sift the flour, soda, salt and ginger into a mixing bowl. Stir in the rolled oats. Put the butter, molasses, syrup, honey and sugar in a saucepan and heat gently, stirring to dissolve the sugar and melt the butter. Remove from the heat and add to the flour mixture with the milk. Beat well to mix.

Pour the batter into two greased 25cm/10in square cake pans. Bake in a moderate oven (180°C/350°F) for 45 to 50 minutes or until the cakes are firm to the touch.

Cool in the pans for 15 minutes, then turn out onto a wire rack. Store the parkins in an airtight tin for at least 1 week before eating.
Makes two 25cm/10in cakes

German spice squares

350g/3 cups flour
½ tsp salt
1 tsp baking powder
½ tsp ground ginger
½ tsp ground cinnamon
¼ tsp grated nutmeg
½ tsp ground cloves
2 Tbsp cocoa powder
3 large eggs
125g/⅔ cup brown sugar
175ml/¾ cup clear honey

Sift the flour, salt, baking powder, spices and cocoa powder into a mixing bowl. Beat together the eggs and sugar. Warm the honey and add with the eggs and sugar to the flour mixture. Mix well together until the batter is smooth. Pour into a greased 30cm/12in square cake pan. Smooth the top.

Bake in a moderate oven (180°C/350°F) for 30 minutes or until a skewer inserted into the center of the cake comes out clean.

Allow to cool in the pan before cutting into squares.
Makes 36 squares

Dundee cake

275g/2½ cups flour
½ tsp baking powder
½ tsp ground allspice
250g/1⅓ cups raisins
125g/⅔ cup currants
60g/⅓ cup mixed candied fruit, chopped
60g/⅓ cup candied cherries
grated rind of 1 small orange
grated rind of 1 small lemon
½ tsp ground cinnamon
250g/1 cup butter
250g/1 cup sugar
5 eggs
60g/½ cup blanched almonds, halved

Sift the flour, baking powder, spice and cinnamon into a mixing bowl. Fold in the fruit and stir to coat each piece. Cream the butter and sugar together in another bowl until light and fluffy. Beat in the eggs, one at a time.

Fold the fruit and flour mixture into the creamed mixture.

Grease a deep 20cm/8in round spring form cake pan and line the bottom and sides with wax paper. Grease the paper lining. Spoon in the cake mixture and smooth the top. Arrange the almond halves on top in concentric circles, their pointed ends toward the center.

Bake in a warm oven (170°C/325°F) for 2 hours or until a skewer inserted in the center of the cake comes out clean. If the top of the cake is browning too quickly, cover it with brown paper. Turn off the oven and leave the cake inside for 10 to 15 minutes.

Allow to cool in the pan, then remove it from the pan and peel off the paper. The cake will keep for several weeks, stored in an airtight tin, (and, in fact, taste best after being stored for about 10 days).
Makes one 20cm/8in cake

Date cakes

6 Tbsp butter
2 Tbsp brown sugar
4 Tbsp clear honey
2 eggs, lightly beaten
125g/1 cup plus 2 Tbsp self-rising flour
1 tsp ground allspice
4-6 Tbsp milk
60g/⅓ cup dates, pitted and finely chopped

Cream the butter and sugar together until the mixture is fluffy. Beat in the honey, then the eggs. Sift in all but 2 tablespoons of the flour and the spice and fold in. Stir in enough of the milk to give the batter a

A rich Scottish fruit cake, Dundee Cake makes a lovely treat for an autumn afternoon.

Appetizing, home-baked Dried Fruit Scones should be served piping hot with butter and jam.

dropping consistency.

Coat the date pieces with the remaining flour and add to the batter. Mix well and spoon into 12 greased muffin tins. Bake in a fairly hot oven (200°C/400°F) for 15 to 20 minutes or until risen and golden brown.

Remove the cakes from the tins and cool on a wire rack.

Makes 12

Dried fruit scones

250g/2 cups self-rising flour
1 tsp baking powder
¼ tsp salt
3 Tbsp shortening
60g/¼ cup sugar
60g/⅓ cup raisins
2 Tbsp currants
1 large egg
75ml/⅓ cup milk

Sift the flour, baking powder and salt into a mixing bowl. Rub in the shortening until the mixture resembles breadcrumbs. Stir in the sugar, raisins and currants. Mix together the egg and milk and stir gradually into the fruit mixture until it is stiff and glossy. Knead lightly to a dough.

Roll out the dough to approximately 1cm/½in thick. Cut into 5cm/2in circles

and place these on a greased baking sheet. Bake in a very hot oven (230°C/450°F) for 10 to 15 minutes or until the scones are golden brown and risen.

Serve hot or cold, with butter and jam.

Makes 12

Banana walnut loaf

150g/⅔ cup sugar
3 Tbsp butter or margarine
3 eggs
4 bananas, mashed
250g/2 cups flour
1 tsp baking powder
½ tsp salt
¼ tsp baking soda
175g/1½ cups walnuts, chopped

Cream together the sugar, butter or margarine and eggs. Beat until the mixture is light, then beat in the bananas. Sift the flour, baking powder, salt and soda into the bowl and mix well. Fold in the walnuts.

Pour the batter into a greased small loaf pan. Bake in a moderate oven (180°C/350°F) for 1 hour, or until a skewer inserted into the center of the loaf comes out clean. Turn out of the pan onto a wire rack and cool before serving.

Makes one loaf

Desserts

Apple dumplings

PASTRY
350g/1½ cups flour
½ tsp salt
6 Tbsp butter
6 Tbsp shortening
4-5 Tbsp cold water
FILLING
6 large tart apples, cored
125g/⅔ cup brown sugar
grated rind of 1 lemon
6 cloves
milk
sugar

Sift the flour and salt into a mixing bowl. Add the butter and shortening and cut into small pieces. Rub the fat into the flour until the mixture resembles breadcrumbs. Stir in enough water to bind the mixture and knead to a dough. Chill for 20 minutes.

Roll out the dough and cut into six squares large enough to enclose the apples. Reserve some of the dough for decoration. Place one apple on each dough square and fill the center cavity of the apple with brown sugar, lemon rind and a clove. Brush the edges of the squares with water or milk and bring the dough up around the apple to enclose it and seal the edges.

Decorate with the reserved dough, cut into leaves. Brush with the milk and sprinkle with the sugar. Bake on a baking sheet in a hot oven (200°C/400°F) for 30 30 minutes. Serve hot.
Serves 6

Chocolate and rum fondue

250g/8oz semisweet chocolate, broken into pieces
6 Tbsp heavy cream
2 Tbsp rum
60g/⅓ cup confectioners' sugar, sifted
fresh fruit (banana, pear and apple slices, berries, etc.) and cubes of cake

Melt the chocolate in the cream in the top of a double boiler. Stir in the cream. Remove from the heat and stir in the rum and confectioners' sugar. Pour into a fondue pot or chafing dish set over a small flame. Serve with the fruit and cake.
Serves 6-8

A traditional English dessert, Apple Dumplings makes the most of autumn's scrumptious fruit crop.

Steamed orange pudding

125g/½ cup butter
125g/½ cup sugar
2 large eggs
175g/1½ cups flour
1 tsp baking powder
1 Tbsp finely grated orange rind
1 orange, peel and pith removed and segmented
3 Tbsp orange juice

Cream the butter and sugar together until the mixture is light and fluffy. Beat in the eggs, one at a time, then sift in the flour and baking powder. Fold in with the orange rind, then stir in the orange segments and juice. Spoon into a greased 1 liter/2 pint capacity steaming mold. Cover with a lid of pleated greased wax paper and foil and tie on securely with string.

Steam the pudding for 2½ hours, replenishing the boiling water as it is necessary.

Turn the pudding out of the mold onto a warmed serving dish and serve hot, with custard sauce.

Serves 4-6

Berry cheesecake

175g/2¼ cups graham crackers, crushed
175g/¾ cup sugar
6 Tbsp butter, melted
700g/3 cups cream cheese
4 eggs, lightly beaten
1 tsp lemon juice
2 tsp grated lemon rind
2 tsp cornstarch
3 Tbsp water
350g/12oz berries (blueberries, black-berries, loganberries, raspberries)

Mix together the graham crackers, ⅓ cup of the sugar and the melted butter. Press into the bottom of a greased, loose-bottomed 20cm/8in round cake pan.

Beat the cream cheese until it is soft. Beat in 125g/½ cup of the sugar, the eggs (gradually), lemon juice and half the lemon rind. Pour into the cake pan and bake in a moderate oven (180°C/350°F) for 35 minutes. Allow to cool, then put into the refrigerator to chill.

Put the remaining sugar in a saucepan with the berries, remaining lemon rind and 2 tablespoons of the remaining water.

Cream cheese in a crumb crust topped with any of autumn's soft fruits, mouthwatering Berry Cheesecake makes a lovely rich dessert.

Poach for 3 minutes. Meanwhile, dissolve the cornstarch in the remaining water. Stir in a little of the poaching liquid. Stir the cornstarch mixture into the poaching liquid and simmer for 2 to 3 minutes or until the liquid has thickened. Remove from the heat, set aside at room temperature and allow to cool.

Spoon the berry mixture onto the center of the cheesecake and serve.

Serve 6

Blackberry and apple pie

PASTRY
175g/1½ cups flour
2 tsp sugar
pinch salt
3 Tbsp butter
3 Tbsp shortening
1-2 Tbsp iced water
FILLING
150ml/⅔ cup water
500g/1lb cooking apples, peeled, cored and thickly sliced
1kg/2lb blackberries, hulled
250g/1 cup plus 1 Tbsp sugar

Sift the flour, sugar and salt into a mixing bowl. Add the butter and shortening and cut into small pieces. Rub the fat into the into the flour until the mixture resembles breadcrumbs. Stir in enough water to bind the mixture and knead to a dough. Chill for 20 minutes.

To make the filling, bring the water to a boil in a saucepan. Add the apples, blackberries and all but 1 tablespoon of the sugar. Cover and simmer for 10 minutes, then pour into a deep pie plate.

Roll out the dough. Cut a narrow strip long enough to go around the edge of the pie plate. Brush with water. Cover with the rest of the pastry and press edges to seal. Trim and crimp edges. Brush with water and sprinkle with the remaining sugar. Bake in a hot oven (220°C/425°F) for 25 to 30 minutes or until the pastry is golden brown.

Serve hot or cold.

Serves 6

Hazelnut cream

125g/¾ cup hazelnuts, peeled
1 envelope unflavored gelatin
2 Tbsp cold water
300ml/1¼ cups milk
4 egg yolks
125g/½ cup sugar
2 Tbsp coffee flavoring
300ml/1¼ cups heavy cream

Coarsely crush the nuts in the grinder attachment of a blender or using a pestle and mortar. Dissolve the gelatin in the water. Scald the milk with the nuts in a saucepan. Remove from the heat.

Beat the egg yolks and sugar together until the mixture is pale and thick. Pour on the milk and nut mixture, beating constantly. Return to the saucepan and cook, stirring constantly, until the mixture thickens. Do not boil or the custard will curdle. Remove from the heat and strain in the gelatin. Mix well. Stir in the coffee flavoring. All to cool.

Whip the cream until it is thick. When the hazelnut mixture is cold, but not yet set, fold in the cream. Pour into a 1.2 liters/2½ pint capacity soufflé dish or individual dishes and chill until set.

Serves 4-6

Jam, sour cream and hazelnut crêpes

175g/½ cup apricot jam
3 Tbsp brandy
25g/¼ cup confectioners' sugar, sifted
60g/½ cup hazelnuts, chopped
250ml/1 cup sour cream
CRÊPE BATTER
150g/1¼ cups flour
1 Tbsp sugar
3 egg yolks
5 Tbsp butter, melted
250ml/1 cup milk
2 Tbsp vegetable oil

First make the crêpe batter. Sift the flour and sugar into a mixing bowl. Make a well in the center and add the egg yolks and melted butter. Mix together, then gradually stir in the milk, beating until the batter is smooth.

Grease a crêpe pan or frying pan with a little of the oil. Pour in about 4 tablespoons of the batter and tilt the pan to cover the bottom completely. Cook over high heat for about 1 minute, then turn the crêpe over and cook the other side for about 30 seconds. Slide the crêpe out of the pan. Keep hot while you cook the remaining crêpes in the same way. Keep them hot, interleaved with wax paper.

Warm the jam and brandy in a saucepan. When the jam has melted remove from the heat and keep hot. Mix together the confectioners' sugar and hazelnuts. Put the sour cream in a serving bowl.

Lay the crêpes on a flat surface and cover each one with the jam mixture. Roll up the crêpes and arrange on a warmed serving dish. Sprinkle with the sugar and nut mixture and serve immediately, with the sour cream.

Serves 4

Whether added to apple pies, or served with cheesecake, blackberries are always popular.

Apple and caramel mold

125g/½ cup sugar
4 Tbsp water
1.5kg/3lb cooking apples, peeled, cored
and sliced
½ tsp ground allspice
¼ tsp ground cloves
60g/¼ cup sugar
4 Tbsp Calvados *or* applejack
60g/¼ cup butter
3 eggs
1 egg white, lightly beaten

Put the sugar and water in a saucepan and stir over gentle heat to dissolve the sugar. Bring to a boil and boil until the syrup turns a rich brown. Remove from the heat and pour into a warmed 1 liter/2 pint capacity mold. Tilt the mold so the sides and bottom are evenly coated.

Put the apples, allspice and cloves in a saucepan. Cover and cook gently for 20 to 25 minutes or until the apples are very soft. Remove from the heat and mash the apples to a purée. Return to the heat, uncovered, and cook for a further 10 to 15 minutes or until the purée is stiff and dry. Remove from the heat.

Beat the sugar into the apple purée, then stir in the Calvados or applejack, butter and eggs. Fold in the egg white and spoon into the caramel-lined mold. Cover with foil and place in a roasting pan. Pour enough boiling water into the pan to come halfway up the sides of the mold. Bake in a fairly hot oven (190°C/375°F) for 1¼ to 1½ hours or until set.

Remove from the oven and allow to cool for 15 minutes. Then, to serve hot, unmold onto a serving dish. Or allow to cool, and chill before unmolding.
Serves 4-6

Honey baked pears

4 large pears, peeled, halved and cored
4 Tbsp lemon juice
4 Tbsp brandy
125ml/½ cup clear honey
½ tsp ground cinnamon
¼ tsp grated nutmeg
2 Tbsp butter, cut into small pieces

Arrange the pear halves, cut sides down, in a greased baking dish. Warm the lemon juice, brandy and honey in a small saucepan. Remove from the heat and stir in the cinnamon and nutmeg. Pour over the pears. Dot with the pieces of butter and bake in a moderate oven (180°C/350°F) for 30 to 35 minutes or until the pears are tender but still firm. Serve with whipped cream.
Serves 4

Maple and orange mousse

3 large egg yolks
60g/⅓ cup brown sugar
2 envelopes unflavored gelatin
4 Tbsp dark rum
75ml/⅓ cup maple syrup
finely grated rind of 1 orange
75ml/⅓ cup orange juice
300ml/1¼ cups heavy cream
1 orange, peeled and sliced

Put the egg yolks and sugar in the top of a double boiler or in a heatproof bowl over a pan of hot water. Beat over gentle heat until the mixture is pale and thick and leaves a ribbon trail on itself when the beater is lifted. Remove from the heat.

Dissolve the gelatin in the rum and strain into the egg yolk mixture. Mix well. Stir in the maple syrup, orange rind and juice. Leave until at the point of setting.

Whip the cream until it is thick. Fold into the maple syrup mixture. Pour into a chilled 1 liter/2 pint capacity mold or dish. Chill for at least 3 hours or until set.

Unmold the mousse onto a serving dish. Garnish with the orange slices and serve.
Serves 4

Peach cobbler

10 peaches, peeled, pitted and sliced
60g/¼ cup sugar
½ tsp ground cinnamon
1 Tbsp butter, cut into small pieces
2 Tbsp brandy (optional)
PASTRY TOPPING
175g/1½ cups flour
1½ tsp baking powder
½ tsp salt
2 Tbsp butter
2 Tbsp shortening
6 Tbsp milk

Put the peaches in a 20cm/8in square cake pan that is 5cm/2in deep. Sprinkle with the sugar, cinnamon and butter.

Sift the flour for the pastry into a mixing bowl with the baking powder and salt. Add the butter and shortening and cut into small pieces. Rub the fat into the flour until the mixture resembles breadcrumbs. Stir in the milk and mix to a dough.

Roll out the dough to a 20cm/8in square, about 6mm/¼in thick. Place over the peaches in the pan. Bake in a fairly hot oven (200°C/400°F) for 40 minutes or until the pastry is golden brown. If you are using the brandy, carefully lift up the pastry crust and sprinkle the brandy over the peaches. Replace the crust and serve hot, with cream.
Serves 4-6

Spiced up with cinnamon and nutmeg, Honey Baked Pears make an extremely tasty dessert.

Normandy pear tart

PASTRY
275g/2½ cups flour
½ tsp salt
6 Tbsp butter
60g/¼ cup shortening
125g/½ cup plus 2 Tbsp sugar
60g/½ cup walnuts, finely chopped
2 egg yolks, finely beaten
3 Tbsp iced water
1 egg white, lightly beaten

FILLING
60g/¼ cup sugar
150ml/⅔ cup water
4 large pears, peeled, halved and cored
150ml/⅔ cup heavy cream
2 Tbsp walnuts, chopped

Sift the flour and salt into a mixing bowl. Add the butter and shortening and cut into small pieces. Rub the fat into the flour until the mixture resembles breadcrumbs. Stir in all but 2 tablespoons of the sugar and the walnuts, then the egg yolks and enough of the water to bind the mixture. Knead to a dough. Chill in the refrigerator for 30 minutes.

To make the filling, dissolve the sugar in the water in a saucepan over gentle heat. Bring to a boil and boil for 4 minutes. Add the pear halves and poach for 10 to 15 minutes or until they are just tender. Remove from the heat.

Roll out two-thirds of the dough and use to line a 23cm/9in loose-bottomed tart pan. Drain the pears and arrange them in a ring in the pastry case, narrow ends toward the middle and cut sides down. Roll out the remaining dough to a circle large enough to cover the top of the tart. Cut an 8cm/3in hole in the center and place the dough ring on top of the tart. Press the edges together to seal. Brush generously with the egg white and sprinkle over the remaining sugar.

Bake in a fairly hot oven (190°C/375°F) for 30 to 35 minutes or until the pastry is firm to the touch. Remove from the oven and allow to cool.

Carefully remove the tart pan and place the tart on a serving plate. Whip the cream until it is thick and pile in the center of the tart. Sprinkle with the chopped walnuts and serve.
Serves 4-6

Melting walnut pastry and tender pears combine to make Normandy Pear Tart a delicious dessert. Serve cold with extra cream.

Crab apples can be found growing wild in some parts of the country.

Preserves

Crab apple preserve

1 Tbsp whole cloves
5cm/2in cinnamon stick
1 Tbsp allspice berries
pared rind of 2 lemons
1.2l/2½ pints dark vinegar
1kg/2lb brown sugar
2.5kg/2lb crab apples, peeled

Tie the cloves, cinnamon, allspice berries and lemon rind in a piece of cheesecloth. Put the vinegar and sugar in a saucepan and stir over gentle heat to dissolve the sugar. Add the bag of spices and bring to a boil. Boil for 5 minutes.

Add the crab apples and simmer gently for 1 hour or until the fruit is just tender. Do not overcook or it will be mushy. Discard the bag of spices.

Pack the apples loosely into jam jars, being careful not to squash them.

Boil the liquid in the saucepan for 15 minutes or until it is thick and syrupy. Allow to cool, then pour into the jars. Cover the jars with vinegar-proof covers and secure with rubber bands. Label and store in a cool, dry dark place.
Makes 2-2.5kg/4-5lb

Piccalilli

1 medium cauliflower, broken into small flowerets
1 cucumber, quartered lengthwise and cut into 1cm/½in pieces
250g/8oz pickling onions
1 large Bermuda onion, chopped
4 green tomatoes, peeled and chopped
175g/½ cup coarse salt
625ml/2½ cups dark vinegar
SAUCE
625ml/2½ cups dark vinegar
3 Tbsp mustard seed, bruised
5cm/2in piece green ginger, peeled and chopped
4 garlic cloves, halved
1 Tbsp black peppercorns, bruised
1 Tbsp tumeric
1 Tbsp dry mustard
125g/½ cup sugar
3 Tbsp flour
4 Tbsp water

Put the vegetables in a large bowl and sprinkle with the salt. Leave for 4 hours, then drain well.

Bring the vinegar to a boil in a large saucepan. Add the vegetables and cover the pan. Simmer for 15 minutes or until the vegetables are almost tender. Drain the vegetables and place them in a large mixing bowl.

To make the sauce, put the vinegar, mustard seed, ginger, garlic, peppercorns, tumeric, mustard and sugar in a saucepan. Bring to a boil, stirring to dissolve the sugar, and simmer for 15 minutes. Remove from the heat and strain the liquid. Return the strained liquid to the rinsed-out saucepan and bring back to a boil.

Mix together the flour and water to make a smooth paste. Add a little of the hot liquid. Add to the strained liquid and bring to a boil, stirring. Cook, stirring for 2 minutes or until the sauce is thickened and smooth. Pour the sauce over the vegetables and toss well to coat.

Ladle the piccalilli into warmed jars with screwtop lids lined with vinegar-proof paper. Fill the jars completely. Allow to cool completely, before sealing. Label and store in a cool, dry place.
Makes about 1.5kg/3lb

Norfolk fruit chutney

1kg/2lb dried apricots, soaked overnight, drained and chopped
1kg/2lb cooking apples, peeled, cored and chopped
4 medium peaches, peeled, halved, pitted and chopped
2 medium onions, finely chopped
250g/1⅓ cups raisins
5cm/2in piece green ginger, peeled and finely diced
¾ tsp grated nutmeg
¾ tsp ground allspice
¾ tsp dry mustard
finely grated rind of 1 large lemon
juice and finely grated rind of 2 oranges
750ml/3 cups white wine vinegar
500g/2 cups sugar
500g/2⅔ cups soft brown sugar

Put the apricots, apples, peaches, onions, raisins, ginger, nutmegs, allspice, mustard, lemon rind, orange juice and rind and 500ml/1 pint of the vinegar in a large saucepan. Bring to a boil, stirring, then simmer gently for 1 to 1½ hours, stirring from time to time, or until the fruit mixture is soft and pulpy.

Stir in the sugars and remaining vinegar and simmer, stirring occasionally, for a further 45 to 50 minutes or until the chutney is very thick.

Ladle into warmed jam jars. Seal with vinegar-proof covers and secure with rubber bands. Label the jars and store in a cool, dry, dark place for 6 weeks before serving.
Makes about 3.5kg/8lb

Green tomato chutney

500g/1lb onions, chopped
4 Tbsp water
2.5kg/5lb green tomatoes, sliced
½ tsp salt
1 Tbsp pickling spices
625ml/2½ cups dark vinegar
500g/1lb (2⅔ cups) brown sugar

Simmer the onions in the water in a large saucepan until they are soft. Remove from the heat and drain well. Return the onions to the pan and add the tomatoes, salt and pickling spices. Return to the heat and bring to a boil, stirring occasionally and adding just enough vinegar from time to time to prevent the mixture sticking to the pan. Cook for 1½ hours, stirring from time to time with a wooden spoon, or until the chutney is very thick.

Stir in the remaining vinegar and the sugar. Simmer for a further 20 to 25 minutes, stirring occasionally, or until the chutney is very thick.

Ladle into warmed jam jars. Seal with vinegar-proof covers and secure with bands. Label the jars and store in a cool, dry place.

Makes about 3kg/6lb

A traditional English mustard pickle, Piccalilli adds a special zest to cold meats.

Winter

Fortunately, Winter no longer means living on what we managed to harvest and preserve earlier in the year. Meat, game (furred and feathered) and vegetables are all freely available. Now is the time for steaming soups made from cheap, fresh root vegetables; hot, hearty pies topped with crisp pastry; and rich fruit desserts served with sweet, warm sauces.

Get into the habit of eating a hot breakfast of bacon and eggs, hot cereals, pancakes or waffles with maple syrup and you'll feel ready to face the outside world – whatever the weather.

The seasonal fruits are all citrus, and Winter is traditionally the time for making marmalades. Use lemons and oranges for giving flavor and color to warming punches, too, to cheer guests at parties – remember, Winter is also a festive season.

What's best in season

Fruit:

Apples	Grapes	Mandarins	Pears
Apricots	Grapefruit	Melons	Persimmons
Bananas	Lemons	Oranges (especially	Pomegranates
Cranberries	Limes	Sevilles)	Rhubarb
Dates	Lychees	Passion fruit	Tangerines

Vegetables:

Avocados	Cucumbers	Leeks	Potatoes
Beets	Curly endive	Lettuces	Radishes
Broccoli	Eggplant	Mushrooms	Rutabaga
Brussels sprouts	Fennel	Okra (ladies' fingers)	Shallots
Cabbages	French or Belgian endive	Onions	Spinach
Carrots	Jerusalem artichokes	Oyster plant	Sweet potatoes
Cauliflowers	Kale	Parsnips	Turnips
Celeriac	Kohlrabi	Peppers	Watercress
Celery			

Herbs:

Bay	Parsley	Sage	Thyme
Mint	Rosemary	Winter savory	

Nuts:

Almonds	Brazil nuts	Chestnuts	Walnuts

Fish:

Bass	Haddock	Oysters	Sole
Carp	Hake	Perch	Sprats
Cockles	Halibut	Pike	Trout
Cod	Herring	Prawns	Tuna
Clams	Mackerel	Red snapper	Turbot
Eels	Mullet	Scallops	Whiting
Flounder	Mussels	Shrimp	
Grouper			

Poultry:

Available fresh or frozen
all year round

Game:

Bear	Muskrat	Quail	Wild ducks
Beaver	Opossum	Rabbit	Woodcock
Grouse	Partridge	Snipe	Other small game birds
Hare	Pheasant	Squirrel	
Hazel hen	Pigeon	Venison	

Meat and variety meats

Available fresh or frozen
all year round

Appetizers

Clams in tomato and garlic sauce

2 eggs, hard cooked
3 Tbsp olive oil
1 large onion, chopped
2 garlic cloves, crushed
45g/¾cup fresh white breadcrumbs
700g/1½lb tomatoes, peeled and chopped
salt and black pepper
4 dozen clams
500ml/1 pint dry white wine
2 Tbsp parsley, freshly chopped
lemon wedges, to serve

Separate the egg whites from the yolks. Finely chop the whites. Push the yolks through a strainer.

Heat the oil in a frying pan. Add the onion and garlic and fry until the onion is soft but not brown. Stir in the breadcrumbs, tomatoes, egg yolks and salt and pepper to taste. Mash the mixture to a purée. Remove from the heat.

Put the clams in a heavy saucepan. Pour over the wine and bring to a boil. Cover and simmer for 10 minutes or until the clams have opened.

Transfer the clams to a warmed serving dish. Keep hot. Strain the cooking liquid into the tomato mixture and return to the heat. Bring to a boil and pour over the clams. Sprinkle with the parsley and serve with the lemon wedges.
Serves 4

Scallops with garlic and basil

750g/1½lb scallops, cut into 1cm/½in pieces
juice of ½ lemon
salt and white pepper
75ml/⅓ cup vegetable oil
3 shallots, finely chopped
3 garlic cloves, crushed
½ tsp dried basil
2 Tbsp butter
1 Tbsp parsley, freshly chopped

Sprinkle the scallops with lemon juice and salt and pepper, then coat with the flour. Heat enough of the oil in a frying pan just to cover the bottom. Add the scallops and fry until browned.

Stir in the shallots, garlic and basil and cook for a further 2 minutes. Remove from the heat and stir in the butter and parsley. Spoon into four dishes and serve hot.
Serves 4

Gnocchi alla romana

625ml/2½ cups milk
1 onion, chopped
1 tsp salt
¼ tsp grated nutmeg
150g/1 cup semolina
2 eggs
125g/1 cup Parmesan cheese, grated
3 Tbsp butter, melted

Put the milk, onion, salt and nutmeg in a saucepan and bring to a boil. Remove from the heat and leave for 15 minutes. Strain the milk and return to the saucepan. Bring to a boil again and gradually stir in the semolina. Cook, stirring, for 2 minutes or until the mixture is very thick.

Remove from the heat and beat in the eggs and half the cheese. Pour into a greased 20cm/8in square baking dish. Allow to cool, then chill for 30 minutes.

Cut the gnocchi mixture into squares and triangles. Place these in a shallow baking dish and pour over the melted butter. Sprinkle the rest of the cheese on top. Bake in a fairly hot oven (200°C/400°F) for 20 to 25 minutes or until golden brown. Serve hot.
Serves 2-3

Scallops with Garlic and Basil – an exquisite first course for a dinner party accompanied by French bread.

A classic French dish, Snails in Garlic Butter make a sophisticated appetizer for a special occasion.

Skim the fat from the liquid in the mixing bowl and place it in a saucepan. Melt the fat and pour over the meat in the terrine. Cover and chill for at least 2 hours before serving.
Serves 10

Stuffed mushrooms

12 large mushrooms
salt and black pepper
1 Tbsp butter, melted
2 Tbsp butter
2 shallots, finely chopped
1 Tbsp flour
125ml/½ cup light cream
3 Tbsp parsley, freshly chopped
1½ Tbsp/1½ Tbsp Parmesan cheese, grated

Remove the stems from the mushrooms and set aside. Rub the caps with salt and pepper and brush with the melted butter. Arrange in one layer, hollow side up, in a greased shallow baking dish.

Finely chop the mushroom stems. Melt the butter in a frying pan. Add the mushrooms stems and shallots and fry for 4 to 5 minutes. Sprinkle over the flour and cook, stirring, for 1 minute. Remove from the heat and stir in the cream. Return to the heat and simmer, stirring, until thickened. Stir in the parsley and salt and pepper to taste.

Fill the mushroom caps with the cream mixture. Top each with a little grated cheese. Bake in a fairly hot oven (190°C/375°F) for 15 minutes or until the mushrooms are tender and the topping lightly browned. Serve hot.
Serves 4

Potted hare or rabbit

1kg/2lb hare or rabbit meat, cut into
2.5cm/1in pieces
125ml/½ cup red wine
1 Tbsp red wine vinegar
250g/1 cup pork fat back, diced
625ml/2½ cups boiling water
salt and black pepper
½ tsp grated nutmeg
1 tsp tyme, freshly chopped
¼ tsp dried marjoram

Put the meat in a mixing bowl and pour over the wine, vinegar and enough water just to cover the meat. Leave to soak for 2 hours. Drain the meat and pat dry with paper towels.

Cook the pork fat back in a frying pan until it has rendered most of its fat. Add the meat and brown on all sides. Transfer the meat mixture to a baking dish. Stir in the boiling water, salt and pepper to taste, the nutmeg and herbs. Cover the dish and bake in a cool oven (150°C/300°F) for 2½ hours or until the meat is very tender.

Drain the meat in a strainer over a mixing bowl. Chill the liquid in the mixing bowl for 20 minutes. Finely chop the meat and place in a terrine.

Snails in garlic butter

185g/¾ cup butter, softened
2 Tbsp parsley, freshly chopped
2 garlic cloves, crushed
salt and black pepper
2 Tbsp brandy
24 snail shells
24 snails

Mix together the butter, parsley, garlic, salt and pepper to taste and 1 tablespoon of the brandy. Push a little of the butter mixture into each snail shell and follow with a snail. Seal with more of the garlic butter.

Place the filled shells in a shallow baking dish or *escargotiere* and pour over the remaining brandy. Bake in a fairly hot oven (190°C/375°F) for 15 to 20 minutes or until the butter is bubbling and beginning to brown. Serve immediately.
Serves 4

Soups

Goulash soup

salt and black pepper
2 Tbsp paprika
500g/1lb lean chuck steak, cut into
2.5cm/1in cubes
60g/¼ cup butter
2 medium onions, thinly sliced
½ tsp ground cumin
1 garlic clove, crushed
2 Tbsp flour
1.9l/7½ cups beef stock
2 large potatoes, peeled and cubed
400g/14oz can tomatoes, chopped

Mix together salt and pepper and the paprika and coat the meat cubes with the mixture. Melt the butter in a saucepan. Add the meat cubes, in batches, and brown on all sides. Add the onions and cook for a further 5 minutes. Stir in the cumin, garlic and flour. Cook, stirring, for 1 minute.

Gradually stir in the stock and bring to a boil. Cover and simmer for 2 hours.

Add the potatoes and tomatoes with the can juice. Re-cover and simmer for a further 1 hour or until the meat and potatoes are tender. Serve hot.

Serves 6

Bean and vegetable soup

500g/1lb (1½ cups) dried white navy
beans, soaked overnight and drained
1 small head cabbage, shredded
6 medium potatoes, quartered
2 medium onions, thinly sliced
2 carrots, scraped and sliced
2 celery stalks, sliced
2 garlic cloves, crushed
125g/4oz bacon, in one piece
1 bouquet garni
1 tsp salt
1.5l/3 pints water

Put the beans in a saucepan and cover with water. Bring to a boil and simmer for 1 to 1½ hours or until the beans are cooked and tender.

Halfway through the beans' cooking time, put the remaining ingredients in another saucepan. Bring to a boil, then simmer for 30 to 45 minutes or until the bacon and vegetables are cooked and tender. Remove the bacon and chop it finely. Return to the saucepan. Remove and discard the bouquet garni from the mixture.

Drain the beans and add to the soup, stirring well. Cook for a further 3 minutes. Remove from the heat, transfer to a warmed tureen and serve.

Serves 4-6

Bean and Vegetable Soup – hearty and satisfying enough to be a meal in itself.

Leeks, parsnips and turnips – three winter vegetables which can be used in many ways and delicious in all of them.

Kidney bean and frankfurter soup

450g/1¼ cups dried kidney beans, soaked overnight and drained
1.9l/7½ cups water
1 medium onion, very finely chopped
1 bay leaf
1 tsp winter savory, freshly chopped
¼ tsp dried basil
salt and black pepper
250g/8oz frankfurters, cut into 6mm/¼in thick slices
1 Tbsp Worcestershire sauce
1 tsp dry mustard

Cook the beans in boiling salted water for 1½ to 2 hours or until they are tender. Drain well.

Bring the measured water to a boil in a saucepan. Add the beans and onion, then the bay leaf, savory, basil and salt and pepper to taste. Simmer for 20 minutes.

Add the remaining ingredients and simmer for a further 10 minutes or until the frankfurters are heated through. Serve hot.
Serves 8

Parsnip and tomato soup

2 Tbsp butter
2 medium onions, thinly sliced
1 garlic clove, crushed
500g/1lb parsnips, peeled and chopped
3 Tbsp flour
salt and black pepper
1 tsp thyme, freshly chopped
1l/2 pints chicken stock
150ml/⅔ cup milk
1 bay leaf
400g/14oz can tomatoes

Melt the butter in a saucepan. Add the onions and garlic and fry until they are soft but not brown. Add the parsnips and fry for 4 minutes. Sprinkle over the flour, salt and pepper to taste and the thyme and cook, stirring, for 1 minute. Remove from the heat and gradually stir in the stock and milk. Add the bay leaf and tomatoes with the can juice and stir well.

Return to the heat and bring to a boil, stirring. Cover and simmer for 40 minutes or until the parsnips are cooked through and very tender.

Remove from the heat, discard the bay leaf and allow to cool slightly. Purée the soup in an electric blender or by pushing it through a strainer. Return the puréed soup to the saucepan and reheat gently without boiling.

Serve hot.
Serves 6

Leek and cress soup

4 bacon slices, diced
1 Tbsp butter
500g/1lb leeks, thinly sliced
500g/1lb potatoes, peeled and chopped
2 Tbsp flour
salt and black pepper
¼ tsp cayenne pepper
¼ tsp grated nutmeg
1.2 liters/2½ pints chicken stock
300ml/1¼ cups milk
1 bunch watercress, coarsely chopped
8 Tbsp garden cress, chopped
1 bay leaf
150ml/⅔ cup sour cream

Fry the bacon in a saucepan until it is crisp and has rendered most of its fat. Remove the bacon from the pan with a slotted spoon and drain on paper towels. Crumble the bacon and keep hot.

Add the butter to the saucepan. When it has melted add the leeks and potatoes. Fry the vegetables until they are golden. Sprinkle over the flour, salt and pepper to taste, the cayenne and nutmeg and cook, stirring, for 1 minute.

Remove the pan from the heat and gradually stir in the stock and milk. Add the watercress, garden cress and bay leaf and stir well. Return to the heat and bring to a boil, stirring. Cover and simmer for 30 minutes.

Remove from the heat, discard the bay leaf and allow the soup to cool slightly. Purée in an electric blender or push through a strainer. Return the puréed soup to the saucepan and stir in the sour cream. Heat through gently without boiling.

Pour the soup into a warmed tureen or individual soup bowls and sprinkle over the crumbled bacon. Serve hot.
Serves 6-8

Mushroom soup

2 Tbsp butter
1 small onion, finely chopped
3 Tbsp flour
salt and black pepper
¼ tsp dried oregano
pinch cayenne pepper
1l/2 pints chicken stock
500g/1lb mushrooms, sliced
1 bay leaf
150ml/⅔ cup heavy cream

Melt the butter in a saucepan. Add the onion and fry until it is soft but not brown. Sprinkle over the flour, salt and pepper to taste, the oregano and cayenne. Cook, stirring, for 1 minute. Remove from the heat and gradually stir in the stock. Stir in the mushrooms and bay leaf.

Return to the heat and bring to a boil, stirring: Cover and simmer for 30 minutes.

Stir in the cream and heat through gently without boiling. Remove the bay leaf and serve.

Serves 4-6

Split pea soup

1 ham bone
2.5 liters/5 pints water
500g/1lb dried split peas, soaked overnight and drained
1 bay leaf
salt and black pepper
60g/¼ cup butter
2 medium onions, chopped
2 celery stalks, chopped
2 carrots, scraped and thinly sliced
2 leeks, cut into 1cm/½in pieces

Put the ham bone in a saucepan and pour over the water. Bring to a boil, then simmer for 1 hour.

Add the split peas, bay leaf and salt and pepper to taste and continue to simmer for 1 hour.

Meanwhile, melt the butter in a frying pan. Add the vegetables and fry until they are just beginning to soften. Add to the saucepan and stir well. Cover the saucepan

and simmer the mixture gently for a further 45 minutes.

Remove from the heat and allow the soup to cool. Skim off any fat from the surface. Remove the ham bone and cut any meat from the bone. Chop the meat and return to the saucepan. Bring the soup back to a boil, then serve.

Serves 6-8

Oyster soup

625ml/2½ cups light cream
300ml/1¼ cups milk
24 oysters, shucked and liquid from the shells reserved
250g/1⅓ cups shrimp (shelled, deveined and chopped)
salt and black pepper
½ tsp paprika

Scald the cream and milk in a saucepan. Remove from the heat and keep hot.

Put the oysters and their liquid in another saucepan. Add the shrimp and cook, stirring, for 2 to 3 minutes, or until the shellfish are heated through. Remove from the heat and stir in the cream and milk mixture, salt and pepper to taste and the paprika.

Serve hot.

Serves 4-6

Mushroom Soup – a creamy delight for a chilly winter day.

Main Dishes

Cullen skink

500g/1lb smoked haddock
water, boiling
2 onions, finely chopped
3 large potatoes, sliced
white pepper
500ml/1 pint milk
1 Tbsp butter

Place the haddock in a pan. Pour over enough boiling water to cover and leave for 10 to 15 minutes. Strain the liquid and pour 300ml/10fl oz into a saucepan. Add the onions, potatoes and pepper to taste. Cover and cook for 20 minutes or until the potatoes are tender.

Meanwhile, remove the skin and bones from the haddock and flake the flesh.

Remove the pan from the heat and mash the potatoes with the onions and cooking liquid. Gradually stir in the milk. Return to the heat and add the flaked haddock and butter. Heat through gently. Taste and add salt if necessary. Serve hot.
Serves 4

Flounder fillets with mushroom sauce

300ml/1¼ cups dry white wine
125ml/½ cup water
1 Tbsp lemon juice
1 bay leaf
6 black peppercorns
1 small onion, thinly sliced
salt
8 flounder fillets
60g/¼ cup butter
500g/1lb button mushrooms, thickly sliced
2 Tbsp flour
4 Tbsp heavy cream
1½ tsp dried chervil
pinch cayenne pepper
60g/½ cup Cheddar cheese, grated

Mix together the wine, water, lemon juice, bay leaf, peppercorns, onion and salt to taste in a baking dish. Place the fillets in the dish and turn to coat them with the wine mixture. Cover the dish and bake in a moderate oven (180°C/350°F) for 25 to 30 minutes or until the fish is cooked. Test with a fork: the flesh should flake easily.

Transfer the fish to a flameproof serving dish. Keep hot. Strain the cooking liquid and reserve 300ml/1¼ cups.

Melt 3 tablespoons of the butter in a saucepan. Add the mushrooms and cook for 3 minutes. Remove the saucepan from the heat, set aside and keep hot.

Melt the remaining butter in another saucepan. Stir in the flour and cook, stirring, for 1 minute. Remove from the heat and gradually stir in the reserved cooking liquid. Return to the heat and bring to a boil, stirring. Simmer, stirring, until thickened and smooth. Remove from the heat and stir in the cream, chervil, cayenne and salt to taste. Stir in the mushrooms.

Pour the mushroom sauce over the fish and sprinkle over the cheese. Broil for 5 minutes or until the cheese has melted and is lightly browned.

Serve hot.
Serves 4

Fish pie

300ml/1¼ cups milk
1 shallot, sliced
½ tsp dried marjoram
¼ tsp dried dill
1 bay leaf
salt and black pepper
2 Tbsp butter
30g/¼ cup flour
500g/1lb cod or other white fish fillets, skinned
8 Tbsp parsley, freshly chopped
1 tsp lemon juice
PASTRY
375g/3 cups flour
¼ tsp salt
375g/3 cups unsalted butter, chilled
6 Tbsp iced water
1 egg yolk
2 Tbsp milk

First make the pastry. Sift the flour and salt into a mixing bowl. Add one-third of the butter and cut into small pieces. Rub the butter into the flour until the mixture resembles breadcrumbs. Stir in enough of the water to bind the mixture and knead to a dough. Chill for 15 minutes. Form the remaining butter into a slab about 2cm/¾in thick.

Roll out the dough to a rectangle about 6mm/¼in thick. Place the slab of butter in the center and fold the dough over it to make a package. Chill for a further 10 minutes.

Place the dough, folds down, on a floured surface and roll out into a rectangle in three, then turn so the open end is facing you. Roll out again, fold and chill for 15 minutes. Repeat the rolling and folding twice more and leave to chill while making the filling.

Put the milk, shallot, marjoram, dill, bay leaf and salt and pepper to taste in a saucepan. Infuse over low heat for 10

Opposite, above: Economical, warming and filling, Cullen Skink is a traditional Scottish dish of smoked haddock and potatoes.
Opposite, below: A light, tasty main meal, Flounder Fillets with Mushroom Sauce may be served with croquette or creamed potatoes and a well-chilled white wine.

Mushrooms and parsley are just two of the ingredients in the delicious, Beef, Kidney and Oyster Pie.

minutes. Strain. Poach the cod fillets in the strained milk for about 15 minutes. Test with a fork: the flesh should flake easily. Drain, then remove any bones. Flake the fish.

Melt the butter in a saucepan. Add the flour and cook, stirring, for 1 minute. Remove from the heat and gradually stir in the strained milk. Return to the heat and simmer, stirring, until thickened and smooth. Remove from the heat and stir in the flaked fish pieces, chopped parsley and lemon juice.

Roll out the dough to a square about 6mm/¾in thick. Trim the edges to straighten them. Lift the dough onto a greased baking sheet. Spoon the fish filling into the center and lift up the four corners of the dough over the filling. Pinch them together in the center to seal. Mix together the egg yolk and milk and, using a pastry brush, brush generously over the dough.

Bake in a fairly hot oven (190°C/375°F) for 30 to 40 minutes or until the pastry is golden brown.

Serve hot.

Serves 4

Pike or perch fillets with mustard and green peppercorn sauce

1kg/2lb pike or perch fillets, skinned
juice of 1 lemon
salt and black pepper
185g/¾ cup butter
1 onion, finely chopped
1 tsp green peppercorns, crushed
1 Tbsp prepared German mustard
2 Tbsp heavy cream
1 Tbsp parsley, freshly chopped

Put the fillets in a shallow dish and sprinkle with the lemon juice. Leave for 10 minutes, then pat dry with paper towels. Rub the fillets with salt and pepper.

Melt ¼ cup of the butter in a frying pan. Add the fillets and fry for 5 minutes on each side or until cooked. Test with a fork: the flesh should flake easily. Transfer the fillets to a warmed serving dish and keep hot.

Add the remaining butter to the cleaned-out frying pan. When it has melted, add the onion. Fry until it is soft but not brown. Stir in the peppercorns and mustard and cook for 2 minutes. Stir in the cream. Remove from the heat and pour this sauce over the fillets. Sprinkle with the parsley.

Serve hot.

Serves 4-6

Beef, kidney and oyster pie

30g/¼ cup flour
salt and black pepper
¼ tsp dry mustard
1kg/2lb lean chuck steak, cut into
2.5cm/1in cubes
250g/8oz/kidney, skinned, cored and
cut into small pieces
4 Tbsp vegetable oil
2 medium onions, chopped
250ml/1 cup beef stock
150ml/⅔ cup sherry or Madeira
1 tsp Worcestershire sauce
1 bouquet garni
125g/1 cup mushrooms, quartered
2 Tbsp parsley, freshly chopped
12 oysters, shucked
PASTRY
185g/1½ cups flour
pinch salt
125g/½ cup butter
3-4 Tbsp iced water
1 egg, lightly beaten

First make the pastry. Sift the flour and salt into a mixing bowl. Add the butter and cut into small pieces, then mix in enough of the water to bind the mixture to a dough which should be lumpy. Roll out the dough to an oblong and fold in three. Turn so that the open end faces you and roll out again. Fold and turn twice more, then chill for 15 minutes.

Mix together the flour, salt and pepper and the mustard in a plastic bag. Add the beef cubes and kidney pieces and shake the bag so they become well coated with the flour mixture. Remove from the bag and set aside.

Heat the oil in a frying pan. Add the beef and kidney and fry until they are browned on all sides. Transfer the meat mixture to a deep baking dish, using a slotted spoon.

Add the onions to the frying pan and fry until they are soft but not brown. Stir in the stock, sherry or Madeira, salt and pepper to taste, the Worcestershire sauce and bouquet garni. Bring to a boil and pour over the meat in the pie dish. Stir in the mushrooms, parsley and oysters. Leave to cool.

Place an upturned egg cup in the center of the baking dish. Roll out the pastry to 6mm (¼in) thick. Cut a long strip 2.5cm (1kn) wide and place around the edge of the baking dish. If it is not long enough, cut and then join. Brush with beaten egg. Roll out the remaining pastry to fit the top of the dish. Lift on with a rolling pin. Press the edges together, trim and finish with the blade of a knife. Crimp edges. Brush pastry with beaten egg. Make leaf shapes with dough trimmings and decorate the top of the pie crust.

Bake in a fairly hot oven (200°C/400°F) for 1 hour or until the pastry is golden brown. Serve hot.
brown.

Serve hot.

Serves 4-6

Italian beef braised in red wine

1 × 1.2kg/2½lb top round of beef,
rolled and tied
2 garlic cloves, halved
salt and black pepper
2 Tbsp plus 1 tsp butter
1 Tbsp vegetable oil
1 medium onion, thinly sliced
3 celery stalks, chopped
4 small carrots, scraped and sliced
3 large tomatoes, peeled, seeded
and chopped
¼ tsp ground cloves
300ml/1¼ cups dry red wine,
preferably Italian
1 Tbsp flour

Rub the beef all over with the cut sides of

the garlic, then discard the garlic. Rub the beef with salt and pepper.

Melt all but 1 teaspoon of the butter with the oil in a flameproof casserole. Add the beef and brown it on all sides. Remove the beef from the casserole and set aside on a plate.

Add the onion, celery and carrots to the casserole and fry until the onion is soft but not brown. Stir in the tomatoes and cloves and return the beef to the casserole. Pour over the wine and bring to a boil. Cover and transfer to a moderate oven (180°C/350°F). Braise for 3 hours or until the meat is very tender.

Transfer the meat to a warmed serving dish. Keep hot. Skim any fat from the surface of the liquid in the casserole. Strain into a saucepan, pressing down well on the vegetable to extract the juices. Bring the strained liquid to a boil and boil for 3 minutes.

Blend the flour with the remaining butter to make a paste. Add to the cooking liquid, in small pieces, and simmer, stirring, until thickened and smooth. Pour this sauce into a sauceboat and serve with the meat.

Serves 4

Italian Beef Braised in Red Wine is a simple, succulent dish, perfect for a dinner party.

Well worth the time and trouble spent in preparation, Spiced Brisket of Beef tastes really fabulous.

Spiced brisket of beef

90g/½ cup brown sugar
1 × 2.75kg/6lb brisket of beef
15g/½oz saltpeter
100g/⅓ cup rock salt
2 Tbsp black peppercorns
2 Tbsp juniper berries
1 Tbsp allspice berries
300ml/1¼ cups water

Rub the sugar all over the beef. Place the beef in a heavy earthenware pot, cover with cheesecloth and leave in a cool place for 2 days.

Crush the saltpeter, salt, peppercorns, juniper berries and allspice berries using a pestle and mortar. Each day for the next 10 days, rub the sugared beef with the salt mixture.

Shake any excess sugar and salt mixture off the beef and place it in a heavy casserole. Add the water and cover the pot with three layers of wax paper and then the lid. Bake in a very cool oven (140°C/275°F) for 5 hours.

Remove from the oven and leave to cool for 2 hours.

Remove the beef from the casserole and wrap it in foil. Place a plate with a heavy weight on top. Leave for 24 hours before slicing thinly and serving.
Serves 12

Russian meat and potato pie

1kg/2lb potatoes
60g/¼ cup butter
4 Tbsp milk
salt and black pepper
2 eggs, lightly beaten
2 Tbsp vegetable oil
2 medium onions, thinly sliced
125g/1 cup mushrooms, sliced
500g/1lb ground beef
½ tsp caraway seeds
60g/½ cup Cheddar cheese, grated

Cook the potatoes in boiling salted water until they are tender. Drain well. Return to the saucepan and add half of the butter, the milk and salt and pepper to taste. Mash well until smooth. Allow to cool for 10 minutes.

Stir half the beaten egg into the potato mixture.

Melt the remaining butter with the oil in a frying pan. Add the onions and fry until they are soft but not brown. Add the mushrooms and fry for 3 minutes. Add the meat, salt and pepper to taste and the caraway seeds and cook until the meat is browned.

Cover the bottom of a baking dish with half the potato mixture. Spoon over the meat mixture and cover with the remaining potato mixture. Brush the top with the remaining beaten egg. Sprinkle over the cheese.

Bake in a moderate oven (180°C/350°F) for 30 to 40 minutes or until the top is golden borwn.

Serve hot.

Serves 4

Beef stew with garbanzos

3 bacon slices, chopped
1.5kg/3lb lean chuck steak, cut into
2.5cm/1in cubes
2 Tbsp vegetable oil
2 large onions, thinly sliced
2 garlic cloves, crushed
1 Tbsp flour
1.2l/2½ pints water
2 Tbsp tomato paste
375g/12oz tomatoes, peeled
and quartered
1 tsp dried basil
½ tsp dried chervil
salt and black pepper
185g/1 cup dried garbanzos, soaked
overnight, cooked and drained

Fry the bacon in a frying pan until it is crisp and golden brown. Transfer the bacon to an ovenproof casserole using a slotted spoon.

Add the meat cubes to the frying pan, in batches, and brown on all sides. Transfer to the casserole. Add the oil to the frying pan and when it is hot add the onions and garlic. Fry until the onions are golden brown. Sprinkle over the flour and cook, stirring with a spatula until the mixture becomes a deep golden brown and the flour has been incorporated.

Transfer to an ovenproof casserole and gradually stir in the water. Set over medium heat and bring to a boil, stirring. Stir in the tomato paste, tomatoes, basil, chervil and salt and pepper to taste. Pour into the casserole and stir well until the ingredients are blended.

Cover the casserole and bake in a warm oven (170°C/325°F) for 2 hours.

Add the garbanzos, stir well and continue baking for 30 minutes or until the meat is tender. Remove the dish from the oven and serve hot, from the casserole.

Serves 6

Beef Stew with Garbanzos is a delicious, economical dish.

Allspice veal roll

1 x 1kg/1 x 2lb boned breast of veal
60g/⅔ cup fresh white breadcrumbs
1 Tbsp raisins
grated rind of 1 orange
1 Tbsp parsley, freshly chopped
1 tsp sage, freshly chopped
1 tsp thyme, freshly chopped
1 Tbsp onion, finely chopped
salt and black pepper
3 Tbsp butter, cut into small pieces
1 Tbsp ground allspice
6 Tbsp butter
3 Tbsp orange juice
watercress and orange slices, to garnish

Mix together the breadcrumbs, raisins, orange rind, parsley, sage, thyme, onion and salt and pepper to taste. Lay the veal out flat and cover with the breadcrumb mixture. Dot with the pieces of butter. Roll up like a jelly roll and tie at 2.5cm/1in intervals with string.

Cream together the allspice and 2 tablespoons of the butter. Spread this mixture all over the rolled veal. Melt the remaining butter and pour it into a roasting pan. Place the veal roll in the pan and turn to coat it with the butter. Pour over the orange juice. Roast in a moderate oven (180°C/350°F) for 1¼ hours or until the veal is cooked through.

Transfer to a warmed serving dish and remove the string. Garnish with the watercress and orange slices.
Serves 4

Osso Buco

90g/¾ cup flour
salt and black pepper
1.5kg/3lb veal shank, sawn into
8cm/3in pieces
125g/½ cup butter
1 large onion, thinly sliced
400g can/14oz can tomatoes
2 Tbsp tomato paste
185ml/¾ cup dry white wine
1 tsp sugar
GREMOLADA
1 Tbsp finely grated lemon rind
2 garlic cloves, crushed
1½ Tbsp parsley, freshly chopped

Mix together the flour and salt and pepper and use to coat the veal pieces. Melt the butter in a flameproof casserole. Add the veal pieces and brown on all sides. Remove from the casserole.

Add the onion to the casserole and fry until it is soft but not brown. Stir in the tomatoes with the can juice, the tomato paste, wine and sugar. Bring to a boil.

The juice and grated rind of orange give this Allspice Veal Roll a really individual flavor.

Pork chops with Mushroom and Parsley Stuffing will grace any table. Serve with carrots and onions.

stuffing onto them. Roll up and tie each roll with string.

Melt 2 tablespoons of the remaining butter in the same pan. Add the pork rolls and brown on all sides. Transfer the rolls to a flameproof casserole and pour over the cider. Cover and bake in a moderate oven (180°C/350°F) for 1 hour or until tender.

Transfer the pork rolls to a warmed serving dish. Remove the string. Keep hot.

Place the casserole over heat on top of the stove and bring to a boil. Blend together the remaining butter and the flour to make a smooth paste. Add in small pieces to the cooking liquid and simmer until thickened. Pour over the pork rolls.
Serves 4

Pork chops with mushroom and parsley stuffing

4 double loin pork chops
1 Tbsp parsley, freshly chopped
30g/⅓ cup fresh white breadcrumbs
¼ tsp cayenne pepper
salt and black pepper
2 Tbsp butter
1 small onion, finely chopped
1 garlic clove, crushed
60g/½ cup mushrooms, finely chopped
1 Tbsp vegetable oil
MAITRE D'HOTEL BUTTER
60g/¼ cup butter
2 tsp parsley, freshly chopped
1 tsp lemon juice
salt and white pepper

First make the maître d'hôtel butter. Cream the butter until it is soft and beat in the remaining ingredients with salt and pepper to taste. Roll the butter on a sheet of wax paper into a sausage shape. Chill for 45 minutes.

Make a slit in the meaty part of each chop to make a pocket. Mix together the parsley, breadcrumbs, cayenne and salt and pepper to taste.

Melt the butter in a saucepan. Add the onion and garlic and fry until the onion is soft but not brown. Stir in the mushrooms and fry for 3 minutes. Remove from the heat and stir in the parsley mixture. Stuff the chops with this mixture and secure the opening with wooden cocktail sticks.

Place the chops in a baking dish and brush with the oil. Cover and bake in a warm oven (170°C/325°F) for 1 hour. Uncover the dish and bake for 30 minutes.

Cut the chilled butter into eight slices.

Transfer the chops to a warmed serving dish. Discard the cocktail sticks and top each chop with pats of maître d'hôtel butter. Serve immediately.
Serves 4

Return the veal pieces to the casserole with salt and pepper to taste and stir well. Cover and simmer for 1½ to 2 hours or until the veal is so tender it is almost falling off the bone.

Meanwhile, make the gremolada. Mix together the lemon rind, garlic and parsley.

Stir the gremolada into the veal mixture and cook for a further 1 minute. Serve hot, from the casserole.
Serves 6

Normandy pork

1kg/2lb pork tenderloin, cut into
8 pieces
5 Tbsp butter
1 large onion, finely chopped
1 small apple, peeled, cored and
finely chopped
125g/½ cup pork sausagemeat
60g/⅔ cup fresh breadcrumbs
1 Tbsp parsley, freshly chopped
1 tsp sage, freshly chopped
salt and black pepper
1 egg, lightly beaten
300ml/1¼ cups hard cider
2 Tbsp flour

Have the butcher slit and pound the pieces of pork to make flat scalops. Melt 2 tablespoons of the butter in a frying pan. Add the onion and fry until it is soft. Transfer to a bowl.

Add the apple, sausagemeat, breadcrumbs, parsley, sage, salt and pepper to taste and the egg to the onion and mix well. Lay the pork pieces flat and spoon this

Loin of pork with dried fruit

16 dried pitted prunes
16 dried apricot halves
½ tsp ground allspice
juice and grated rind of ½ orange
juice and grated rind of ½ lemon
625ml/2½ cups dry white wine
1 × 2.5kg/5lb loin of pork
(boned weight), rolled and tied
salt and black pepper
1 Tbsp sage, freshly chopped
2 Tbsp butter
1 Tbsp brown sugar
1 garlic clove, crushed
2 large cooking apples, peeled, cored
and sliced
2 tsp cornstarch

Put the prunes and apricots in a mixing bowl. Sprinkle with the spice, orange juice

and rind, lemon juice and rind and half the wine. Cover and leave to soak overnight.

Rub the pork with salt and pepper and the sage. Melt the butter in a flameproof casserole. Add the pork and brown on all sides. Pour in the soaked fruit mixture. Sprinkle over the brown sugar and garlic and add all but 1 tablespoon of the remaining wine. Bring to a boil, cover and cook for 2 hours.

Skim off any fat from the surface of the cooking liquid. Add the apple slices, re-cover and cook for a further 20 minutes.

Transfer the pork to a carving board. Carve into thick slices and arrange on a warmed serving dish. Keep hot.

Dissolve the cornstarch in the remaining tablespoon of wine. Stir a little of the hot liquid into the cornstarch mixture, then stir into the casserole and simmer for 5 minutes. Pour over the meat.
Serves 6

Loin of Pork with Dried Fruit is a succulent and fruity casserole and makes an attractive main course.

Pork chili

1 Tbsp butter
1 Tbsp vegetable oil
2 medium onions, thinly sliced
1 green pepper, pith and seeds
removed and chopped
1kg/2lb pork shoulder (boned weight),
trimmed of excess fat and cut
into 2.5cm/1in cubes
400g/14oz can condensed tomato soup
1 large celery stalk, finely chopped
¼ tsp hot chili powder
400g/14oz can red kidney beans, drained
salt and black pepper

Melt the butter with the oil in a saucepan. Add the onions and fry until they are golden brown. Stir in the green pepper and pork cubes and fry until the pork cubes are browned on all sides. Cover and cook gently for 35 minutes.

Stir in the soup (undiluted), celery and chili powder and continue to cook, covered, for 15 minutes or until the pork is tender.

Stir in the kidney beans with salt and pepper to taste. Cook, uncovered, for 5 minutes. Serve hot.
Serves 4

Pork with red wine

125g/½ cup butter
4 Tbsp olive oil
1.5kg/3lb pork tenderloin, cut into
thick slices
2 large onions, chopped
salt and black pepper
375ml/1½ cups dry red wine
300g/2½ cups mushrooms, sliced
2 Tbsp flour
375ml/1½ cups heavy cream

Melt half the butter with the oil in a frying pan. Add the pork slices and fry until they are browned on all sides. Transfer the pork to a flameproof casserole, using a slotted spoon.

Add the onions to the frying pan and fry until they are soft but not brown. Transfer the onions to the casserole and sprinkle over salt and pepper to taste. Pour in the wine.

Place the casserole in a moderate oven (180°C/350°F) and cook for 1½ hours or until the pork is tender.

Fifteen minutes before the pork is ready, melt the remaining butter in a saucepan. Add the mushrooms and cook for 3 minutes. Transfer the mushrooms to the casserole with a slotted spoon. Continue cooking for 10 minutes.

Remove the pork slices from the casserole and keep hot. Mix together the flour and cream, adding the cream a little at a time. Stir a little of the hot cooking liquid into the mixture. Place the casserole over low heat. Add the cream mixture a little at a time, stirring constantly, until thickened. Return the meat to the casserole and serve, from the casserole.
Serves 6

Knockwurst and lentil casserole

500g/1lb lentils
1.2 liters/2½ pints beef stock
salt and black pepper
1 large onion, whole, skinned
1 bouquet garni
2 Tbsp butter
6 bacon slices, chopped
2 garlic cloves, chopped
6 knockwurst, cut into 2.4cm/1in
thick slices
125g/1 cup Cheddar cheese, grated

Put the lentils, stock, salt to taste, the onion and bouquet garni in a saucepan. Bring to a boil, then simmer for 1½ hours or until the lentils are tender. Drain the lentils, reserving the cooking liquid. Remove and discard the onion and bouquet garni.

Melt the butter in a frying pan. Add the bacon and garlic and fry until the bacon is lightly browned. Add the knockwurst and fry for 5 minutes. Remove from the heat and drain the bacon and knockwurst on kitchen paper towels.

Cover the bottom of a baking dish with half the lentils. Add the knockwurst and bacon and sprinkle with pepper. Top with the remaining lentils. Pour in the reserved lentil cooking liquid. Sprinkle the cheese on top and bake in a moderate oven (180°C/350°F) for 45 minutes to 1 hour or until the cheese is golden brown. Serve hot, from the dish.
Serves 6

Ham cooked in beer

625ml/2½ cups light beer
625ml/2½ cups dark beer
185g/1 cup brown sugar
1 × 4.5kg/10lb processed ham
1 Tbsp butter
2 Tbsp flour

Bring the beers and sugar to a boil in a roasting pan, stirring to dissolve the sugar. Remove from the heat.

Peel any excess fat from the ham and place it in the roasting pan. Baste with the beer mixture. Bake in a moderate oven (180°C/350°F) for 2 hours.

Transfer the ham to a warmed serving dish. Keep hot.

Strain the cooking liquid into a saucepan. Blend the butter with the flour to make a paste. Add this in small pieces to the cooking liquid, stirring, and bring to a boil. Simmer, stirring, until thickened and smooth. Pour this gravy into a warmed gravyboat.

Serve with the ham.

Serves 10-15

Stuffed cabbage leaves

750g/1½lb lean lamb, ground
4 shallots, finely chopped
3 tomatoes, peeled, seeded and chopped
5 Tbsp long-grain rice, cooked
salt
¼ tsp cayenne pepper
¼ tsp grated nutmeg
1 medium head cabbage, parboiled
and separated into leaves
1 Tbsp vegetable oil
300ml/1¼ cups dry white wine
juice of 1 lemon
1 Tbsp flour

Mix together the lamb, shallots, tomatoes, rice, salt to taste, the cayenne and nutmeg. Form into a thick sausage to enclose it completely. If necessary, tie with string at 5cm/2in intervals.

Heat the oil in a flameproof casserole. Put the cabbage roll in the casserole and pour over the wine. Bring to a boil, then cover the casserole and simmer the roll for 1 hour.

Transfer the cabbage roll to a warmed serving dish. Keep hot. Mix together the lemon juice and flour, stir in 2 tablespoons of the hot liquid from the casserole and then stir into the casserole. Simmer, stirring, until thickened and smooth. Pour this sauce into a sauceboat and serve with the stuffed cabbage.

Serve hot or cold.

Serves 4-6

Roast leg of lamb coated with mustard

125g/½ cup prepared French mustard
3 Tbsp soy sauce
2 garlic cloves, crushed
1½ Tbsp rosemary, freshly chopped
1 Tbsp olive oil
1 × 2.5kg/5lb leg of lamb
salt and black pepper

Mix together the mustard, soy sauce, garlic and rosemary. Beat in the oil. Place the lamb on a rack in a roasting pan and rub it with salt and pepper. Brush over the mustard mixture. Roast in a moderate oven (180°C/350°F) for 1½ hours or until the juices run only faintly pink when the lamb is pierced with a skewer. Transfer to a carving board and serve.

Serves 4-6

Knockwurst and Lentil Casserole is a tasty and filling family meal, ideal for cold winter days.

Country-style lamb

1 × 1kg/2lb rack of lamb
2 Tbsp butter
3 Tbsp vegetable oil
1 cooking apple, peeled, cored
and chopped
3 medium potatoes, peeled and cut
into 6mm/¼in thick slices
1 medium onion, thinly sliced
185ml/¾ cup beef stock
2 tsp tomato paste
½ tsp dried marjoram
salt and black pepper

Cut the loose flap, or chine, of bones from the lamb and cut the meat into strips. Put the butter and 1 tablespoons of the oil in a roasting pan. Add the meat, strips of meat and the apple. Roast in a fairly hot oven (190°C/375°F) for about 20 minutes, basting occasionally, or until the meat is well browned.

Heat the remaining oil in a frying pan. Add the potatoes and onion and fry until the potatoes are lightly browned and almost tender. Remove from the heat.

Remove the meat from the oven. When it is cool enough to handle, cut it between the rib bones into chops. Place about one-third of the potatoes and onion in a baking dish. Cover with half the chops and then another layer of potatoes and onion. Add the remaining chops with the apple and liquid, and remaining potatoes and onion.

Mix together the stock, tomato paste, marjoram and salt and pepper to taste. Pour into the baking dish. Cover and bake for 15 minutes or until the meat is tender. Serve hot, from the dish.
Serves 3-4

Braised oxtail

1 oxtail, skinned and cut into pieces
salt and black pepper
¼ tsp ground allspice
1 Tbsp brandy
2 Tbsp butter
2 medium onions, chopped
2 medium carrots, scraped and chopped
1 bouquet garni
185ml/¾ cup brown stock
185ml/¾ cup dry red wine
2 Tbsp tomato paste

Rub the oxtail pieces with salt and pepper and the spice. Sprinkle with the brandy and leave for 20 minutes.

Melt the butter in a flameproof casserole. Add the oxtail pieces and brown on all sides. Remove the oxtail pieces from the pot. Add the onions and carrots to the casserole and fry until the onions are soft but not brown. Return the oxtail pieces to the casserole with the bouquet garni, stock, wine and tomato paste. The liquid should almost cover the meat so add a little more stock if necessary.

Bring to a boil, skimming off any scum that rises to the surface. Cover and simmer for 4 hours or until the meat is very tender and falling off the bones. Remove from the heat and cool. Remove the bouquet garni.

Chill for at least 8 hours or overnight.

Remove the fat from the surface. Bring to a boil again and simmer for 10 minutes. Transfer the oxtail pieces to a warmed serving dish and keep hot.

Boil the braising liquid until it has reduced by one-third. Pour a little over the oxtail and the rest into a saucepan.
Serves 4

Deviled liver

60g/½ cup flour
salt and black pepper
½ tsp cayenne pepper
1 tsp dry mustard
1kg/2lb calf's or lamb's liver, sliced
6mm/¼in thick
60g/¼ cup butter
1 Tbsp olive oil
watercress, to garnish
SAUCE
2 Tbsp Worcestershire sauce
2 tsp paprika
1 Tbsp red wine vinegar
1 tsp dry mustard
2 tomatoes, peeled, seeded and chopped
1 Tbsp sugar
1 Tbsp onion, minced
1 Tbsp chutney
75ml/⅓ cup dry red wine
1 garlic clove, crushed
75ml/⅓ cup light cream

First make the sauce. Put all the ingredients, except the cream, in a saucepan. Bring to a boil, then simmer for 5 minutes. Remove from the heat.

Mix together the flour, salt and pepper, the cayenne, and mustard. Coat the liver slices in this seasoned flour. Reserve any leftover flour.

Melt the butter with the oil in a frying pan. Add the liver slices and cook for 2 to 3 minutes on each side, or until spots of blood appear on the surface. Transfer the liver to a warmed serving dish. Keep hot.

Stir any leftover flour into the fat in the frying pan. Gradually stir in the sauce and bring to a boil. Simmer, stirring, for 3 minutes. Stir in the cream and heat through without boiling. Spoon the sauce over the liver and garnish with the watercress.
Serves 4-6

Chicken and leek pie

1 × 2.5kg/5lb chicken
2 medium onions, halved
2 celery stalks, quartered
1 bouquet garni
salt
2.5 liters/5 pints water
1kg/2lb leeks, cut into 1cm/½in slices
1 tsp sugar
125g/4oz cooked ham, thinly sliced
1 Tbsp parsley, freshly chopped
4 Tbsp heavy cream
PASTRY
185g/1½ cups flour
pinch salt
150g/⅔ cup butter, cut into pieces
3-4 Tbsp iced water
1 egg, lightly beaten

Put the chicken, onions, celery, bouquet garni and salt in a saucepan. Add the water. The chicken should be completely covered, so, if necessary, add more water. Bring to a boil, skimming off any scum that rises to the surface. Cover and simmer for 1 to 1½ hours or until the chicken is tender.

Meanwhile, make the pastry. Sift the flour and salt into a mixing bowl. Add the butter and the water and mix quickly to a lumpy dough. Roll out the dough into an oblong and fold it in three. Turn so the open end faces you and roll out again into an oblong. Fold, turn and roll out twice more, then chill for 30 minutes.

Transfer the chicken to a carving board. Strain the cooking liquid and return 500ml/1 pint of it to the saucepan. Add the leeks and return to the heat. Bring to a boil, then partly cover and simmer for 15 to 20 minutes or until the leeks are tender. Remove from the heat.

Skin the chicken and remove the meat from the bones. Cut the meat into bite-size pieces and put them in a deep baking dish. Pour the leeks and stock into the dish. Sprinkle with salt and the sugar. Cover with a layer of ham slices, leaving a small gap in the center, and sprinkle over the parsley.

Roll out the dough and use to cover the baking dish, crimping the edges to seal. Cut a cross in the center. Brush the dough with the beaten egg. Use the dough trimmings to decorate the top.

Bake in a fairly hot oven (200°C/400°F) for 1 hour or until the pastry is golden.

Heat the cream gently in a saucepan. Open the cross in the pastry and pour in the cream. Serve hot or cold.
Serves 6

An economical idea for mid-week cooking, Braised Oxtail may be served with vegetables, sausages and buttered noodles for a really satisfying meal.

Chicken and Peanut Butter Stew – a spicy and colorful dish to brighten up those winter days.

Chicken and peanut butter stew

2 Tbsp peanut oil
1 medium onion, chopped
1 garlic clove, crushed
1 green pepper, pith and seeds removed and chopped
1 × 2kg/4lb chicken, cut into serving pieces
250g/1 cup peanut butter
625ml/2½ cups chicken stock
1 tsp turmeric
1 Tbsp ground coriander
1 tsp ground cumin
½ tsp hot chili powder
2 tomatoes, peeled and chopped

Heat the oil in a saucepan. Add the onion, garlic and green pepper. Fry until the onion is soft. Add the chicken pieces and brown well. Remove from the heat.

Mix together the peanut butter, 125ml/ ½ cup of the stock, salt and pepper to taste, the turmeric, coriander, cumin and chili powder. Stir into the chicken and cook, stirring, for 5 minutes. Stir in the remaining stock and the tomatoes. Cover and simmer for 30 minutes.

Uncover and cook for a further 15 minutes or until the chicken is tender.
Serves 4

Orange chicken with rosemary

4 large chicken quarters
salt and black pepper
6 Tbsp butter
2 large onions, thinly sliced
500ml/1 pint orange juice
1 Tbsp rosemary, freshly chopped
1 Tbsp grated orange rind
1½ Tbsp cornstarch
1 Tbsp water

Rub the chicken pieces with salt and pepper. Melt 4 tablespoons of the butter in a flameproof casserole. Add the chicken pieces and brown on all sides. Remove from the casserole.

Add the remaining butter to the casserole with the onions. Fry until they are soft but not brown. Stir in the orange juice and bring to a boil. Return the chicken pieces to the casserole with the rosemary and orange rind. Cover and simmer for 30 to 40 minutes or until the chicken is tender.

Transfer the chicken pieces to a warmed serving dish. Keep hot.

Dissolve the cornstarch in the water and stir gradually into the liquid in the casserole. Simmer, stirring, until thickened. Pour this sauce over the chicken and serve.
Serves 4

Stuffed boned turkey with chestnuts

2 Tbsp butter
1 large onion, finely chopped
1.5kg/3lb pork sausage meat
4 Tbsp fresh white breadcrumbs
1 Tbsp thyme, freshly chopped
salt and black pepper
1 tsp celery salt
¼ tsp grated nutmeg
2 eggs, lightly beaten
4 Tbsp milk
75ml/⅓ cup port
1 × 4.5kg/10lb turkey, boned
125g/½ cup butter, melted
1kg/2lb chestnuts
625ml/2½ cups water
2 tsp brown sugar

Melt half the butter in a saucepan. Add the onion and fry until it is golden brown. Add the sausage meat and cook, stirring, until it loses its pinkness. Stir in the breadcrumbs, thyme, pepper to taste, the celery salt and nutmeg. Cook for a further 5 minutes, then remove the pan from the heat.

Mix together the eggs, milk and port. Stir into the sausagemeat mixture. Return to the heat and cook, stirring, for 5 minutes. Remove from the heat.

Rub the turkey all over with salt and pepper. Lay it out flat and cover with the sausagemeat mixture. Form into a roll, securing where necessary with a trussing needle and string.

Place the turkey in a roasting pan and dot with the remaining butter, cut into small pieces. Roast in a fairly hot oven (190°C/375°F) for 2 to 2½ hours. Baste occasionally with the melted butter.

Meanwhile, split the skins of the chestnuts at the pointed end and put in a saucepan. Cover with water and bring to a boil. Boil for 30 seconds, then drain and peel.

Put the measured water and brown sugar in the saucepan and stir over gentle heat to dissolve the sugar. Add the peeled chestnuts and bring to a boil. Cover and simmer for 20 minutes or until the chestnuts are tender but still firm. Drain and refresh under cold running water. Drain again and pat dry with paper towels.

Ten minutes before the turkey is cooked, arrange the chestnuts around it in the roasting pan. Baste well with the cooking juices and continue roasting.

Transfer the turkey to a warmed serving dish. Remove the trussing string. Drain the chestnuts and arrange around the turkey.

Serve hot.
Serves 8-10

Duck with port and cherries

1 × 3kg/7lb duck
salt and black pepper
2 Tbsp butter
1 medium onion, chopped
2 small apples, peeled, cored and grated
125g/1 cup Granola
1 egg, lightly beaten
75ml/⅓ cup port
425g/15oz can bing cherries, pitted, drained and juice reserved
2 tsp cornstarch
1 tsp water

Prick the duck all over. Rub the cavity with salt and pepper.

Melt the butter in a saucepan. Add the onion and fry until lightly browned. Stir in the apples and Granola. Remove from the heat and stir in the egg. Spoon the stuffing into the duck and secure the opening with a skewer or trussing needle and string.

Place the duck on a rack in a roasting pan and roast in a moderate oven (180°C/350°F) for 1½ to 2 hours or until the juices run clear when the thigh is pierced with a skewer. Baste occasionally with the fat in the pan.

Transfer the duck to a warmed serving dish. Remove the skewer or string and keep hot.

Skim the fat from the surface of the cooking liquid in the pan. Pour the liquid into a saucepan and stir in the port and reserved cherry juice. Dissolve the cornstarch in the water and stir into the port mixture. Bring to a boil and simmer, stirring, until thickened and smooth. Stir in the cherries and heat through gently.

Arrange the cherries around the duck and pour the sauce into a sauceboat.
Serves 4

Rabbit hot pot

6 Tbsp flour
salt and black pepper
1 × 2kg/4lb rabbit, cut into serving pieces
2 large onions, thinly sliced
3 carrots, scraped and sliced
2 Tbsp parsley, freshly chopped
1 tsp thyme, freshly chopped
500g potatoes, peeled and thickly sliced
500ml/1 pint chicken stock

Mix the flour with salt and pepper and use to coat the rabbit pieces. Place half the sliced onion in a casserole. Cover with half the carrots, then with all the rabbit pieces. Sprinkle with the parsley and thyme and cover with the remaining onion and carrot slices. Arrange the potatoes on top,

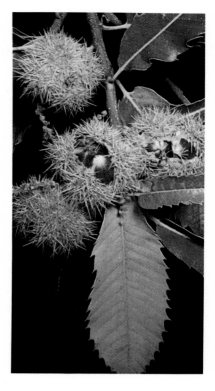

Usually chestnuts form part of a stuffing but here they are used to accompany Stuffed Boned Turkey.

slightly overlapping, to cover completely. Pour in the stock.

Cover the casserole and bake in a warm oven (170°C/325°F) for 2 hours or until the rabbit is tender. Increase the temperature to moderate (180°C/350°F). Uncover the casserole and bake for a further 30 minutes or until the potatoes are lightly browned and crisp.

Serve hot, from the casserole.

Serves 4-6

Pheasant and chestnut casserole

500g/1lb chestnuts
2 young pheasants
salt and black pepper
2 Tbsp grated orange rind
1 Tbsp thyme, freshly chopped
4 bacon slices
2 Tbsp butter
2 Tbsp vegetable oil
1 medium onion, finely chopped
2 garlic cloves, crushed
185g/1½ cups button mushrooms, sliced
250ml/1 cup chicken stock
2 Tbsp orange juice
1 bay leaf
2 Tbsp port
1 Tbsp flour

Split the skins of the chestnuts at the pointed end and put in a saucepan. Cover with water and bring to a boil. Boil for 30 seconds, then drain and peel.

Rub the pheasants inside and out with salt and pepper. Mix together the orange rind and thyme and place in the cavities in the pheasants. Cover the breasts with the bacon slices and truss the birds.

Melt half the butter with the oil in a frying pan. Add the pheasants and brown on all sides. Transfer to a flameproof casserole. Add the onion and garlic to the frying pan and fry until the onion is soft but not brown. Stir in the mushrooms and chestnuts and fry for 5 minutes. Remove from the heat.

Arrange the vegetables around the pheasants in the casserole. Pour in the stock and orange juice and add the bay leaf. Bring to a boil on top of the stove. Cover and simmer for 1 hour or until the pheasants are cooked. (The juices should run clear when the thigh is pierced.)

Transfer the pheasants to a warmed serving dish. Untruss and discard the bacon. Arrange the vegetables and chestnuts around the birds. Keep hot.

Strain the cooking liquid into a saucepan. Stir in the port and bring to a boil. Blend the remaining butter with the flour to form a smooth paste. Add in small pieces to the cooking liquid and simmer, stirring, until thickened and smooth. Pour this sauce over the pheasants and serve at once.

Serves 4

Roast pheasant

2 young pheasants
salt and black pepper
4 bacon slices (optional)
2 Tbsp butter, melted
watercress, to garnish

Rub the pheasants all over with salt and pepper. Truss them. If they have not been larded, cover the breasts with the bacon. Place in a roasting pan and roast in a moderate oven (180°C/350°F) for 1 hour or until the pheasants are cooked. Baste frequently with the melted butter.

Transfer the pheasants to a warmed serving dish and garnish with the watercress. Serve hot, with fried julienne potatoes and cranberry and bread sauces.

Serves 4

Roast stuffed goose

1 × 3.5-4kg/8-9lb goose, liver reserved
salt and black pepper
4 Tbsp clear honey
STUFFING
2 Tbsp butter
2 medium onions, finely chopped
1kg/2lb pork sausagemeat
90g/1 cup fresh white breadcrumbs
60g/⅓ cup black olives, pitted and chopped
2 Tbsp red wine
salt and black pepper
1 Tbsp thyme, freshly chopped

Prick the goose all over and rub with salt and pepper. Chop the goose liver.

To make the stuffing, melt the butter in a saucepan. Add the onions and fry until they are soft but not brown. Add the sausagemeat and fry, stirring, until it is well browned. Add the goose liver and cook for a further 2 to 3 minutes. Remove from the heat and stir in the remaining ingredients with salt and pepper to taste.

Stuff the goose with this mixture and secure the opening with a skewer or trussing needle and string. Place the goose, on its breast, on a rack in a roasting pan. Roast in a very hot oven (230°C/450°F) for 15 minutes. Reduce the temperature to moderate (180°C/350°F) and continue roasting for 2½ to 3 hours or until the goose is cooked. (The juices should run clear when the thigh is pierced with a skewer.) Turn the goose onto its back halfway through the cooking.

Tender Roast Pheasant is an ideal dinner-party dish. Here it is shown with the traditional European accompaniment of 'game' chips.

Remove all the fat from the roasting pan. Increase the oven temperature to very hot (230°C/450°F). Coat the goose with the honey and return to the oven. Roast for a further 8 to 10 minutes or until the skin is glazed and crisp. Untruss and serve the goose immediately.
Serves 4-6

Rabbit or hare chasseur

2 saddles of rabbit or hare, cut into thin fillets
salt and black pepper
1 Tbsp lemon juice
30g/¼ cup flour
60g/¼ cup butter
2 large shallots, finely chopped
2 slices cooked ham, cut into strips
250ml/1 cup dry white wine
125g/1 cup mushrooms
250ml/1 cup heavy cream
1 Tbsp parsley, freshly chopped

Rub the fillets with salt and pepper and the lemon juice. Coat them with the flour. Melt the butter in a frying pan. Add the shallots and ham. Fry until the shallots are soft but not brown.

Put the rabbit or hare fillets in the pan and brown on all sides. Pour over the wine and bring to a boil. Simmer gently for 10 minutes. Transfer the fillets to a baking dish using a slotted spoon.

Add the mushrooms and cream to the frying pan and stir well. Heat through gently without boiling. Pour this sauce over the fillets. Bake in a moderate oven (180°C/350°F) for 20 minutes.

Remove from the oven, sprinkle over the parsley and serve at once, straight from the dish.
Serves 6

Squab with cherry sauce

2 × 750g/1½ lb squab
salt and black pepper
125g/½ cup salt pork, diced
1 medium onion, finely chopped
1 tsp sage, freshly chopped
2 tsp grated orange rind
5 Tbsp long-grain rice, cooked
250ml/1 cup chicken stock
500g/1lb can bing cherries, pitted and drained
4 Tbsp heavy cream
1 Tbsp brandy

Rub the squab inside and out with salt and pepper. Fry the pork fat in a flameproof casserole until it is golden brown and has rendered most of its fat. Transfer the salt pork to a mixing bowl using a slotted spoon.

Add the onion to the casserole and fry until it is soft but not brown. Remove from the heat. Add the onion to the diced pork, using a slotted spoon. Stir the sage, orange rind, rice and salt and pepper to taste into the diced pork mixture. Stuff the squab with this mixture. Secure the openings with a skewer or trussing needle and string.

Reheat the pork fat in the casserole. Add the squab and brown on all sides. Pour in the stock and bring to a boil. Cover and cook for 50 minutes to 1 hour or until the birds are cooked through.

Transfer the squab to a warmed serving dish and keep hot.

Bring the liquid in the casserole to a boil and boil until it has reduced to about half the original quantity. Stir in the cherries, cream and brandy and heat through gently without boiling. Pour this sauce over the squab and serve.
Serves 4

Venison chops with sour cream and horseradish sauce

4 venison chops
salt and black pepper
2 garlic cloves, halved
4 Tbsp vegetable oil
185ml/¾ cup sour cream
1 tsp horseradish root, grated

MARINADE
125ml/½ cup dry white wine
4 Tbsp olive oil
1 onion, thinly sliced
1 garlic clove, crushed
6 black peppercorns
1 Tbsp thyme, freshly chopped

Mix together the marinade ingredients in a shallow dish. Add the venison chops and leave to marinate for 24 hours, basting occasionally.

Remove the chops from the marinade and pat dry with paper towels. Reserve the marinade. Rub the chops with salt and pepper and the cut sides of the garlic cloves. Discard the garlic.

Heat the oil in a frying pan. Add the chops and brown on each side. Pour in the reserved marinade and bring to a boil. Cover and simmer for 20 minutes or until the chops are tender.

Remove from the heat and allow to cool. Leave to marinate for a further 24 hours.

Return the pan to the heat and bring to a boil. Simmer for 15 minutes. Transfer the chops to a warmed serving dish. Keep hot. Strain the cooking juices into a saucepan and bring to a boil. Reduce the heat and stir in the sour cream and horseradish. Heat through gently without boiling. Pour the sauce over the chops and serve them at once.
Serves 4

Squab with Cherry Sauce makes a lovely, rich meal that is certain to impress dinner guests.

Vegetables

Gratin dauphinois

1 garlic clove, halved
2 Tbsp butter
1kg/2lb potatoes, peeled and cut into
6mm/¼in thick slices
salt and black pepper
185g/1½ cups Gruyère *or* Cheddar cheese,
grated
1 egg, lightly beaten
300ml/1¼ cups milk, scalded
pinch grated nutmeg

Rub a baking dish with the cut sides of the garlic. Discard the garlic. Grease the dish thickly with half the butter. Place about one-third of the potato slices in the dish and sprinkle with the salt and pepper and ¼ cup of the cheese. Add another layer and top with the remaining potato slices.

Put the egg, milk and nutmeg in a saucepan and bring to a boil, stirring. Pour into the baking dish. Sprinkle over the remaining cheese and dot with the remaining butter, cut into small pieces.

Bake in a fairly hot oven (190°C/375°F) for 45 to 50 minutes or until the potatoes are tender. Serve hot, from the dish.
Serves 6

This appetizing dish, Gratin Dauphinois, is a classic French recipe and is especially good served with roast lamb or veal.

Turnip, potato and carrot hash

1 large turnip, peeled and chopped
3 medium carrots, scraped and chopped
1 large onion, chopped
3 medium potatoes, peeled and chopped
250ml/8fl oz can beef consommé
salt and black pepper
1 Tbsp butter, cut into small pieces

Put the vegetables in a saucepan with the consommé and salt to taste. Bring to a boil, then simmer for 20 to 30 minutes or until the vegetables are tender and most of the liquid has evaporated.

Remove from the heat and pour off any excess liquid. Add pepper to taste and mash the vegetables to form a smooth, thick purée. Transfer the purée to a baking dish, smoothing the top. Dot with the pieces of butter and bake in a fairly hot oven (200°C/400°F) for 10 to 15 minutes or until the top is golden brown. Serve hot, from the baking dish.
Serves 6

Onions with lemon and marjoram sauce

6 medium onions
salt and black pepper
1 bouquet garni
500ml/1 pint milk
½ tsp dried marjoram
finely grated rind of 1 lemon
2 Tbsp butter
2 Tbsp flour
1 Tbsp lemon juice
1 Tbsp parsley, freshly chopped
lemon wedges, to serve

Blanch the onions in boiling water for 2 minutes. Drain well. Return to the saucepan and cover with fresh water. Add salt and the bouquet garni. Bring to a boil, then cover and simmer for 25 to 30 minutes or until the onions are tender.

Meanwhile, put the milk, marjoram and lemon rind in a saucepan. Infuse over low heat for 10 minutes. Strain the milk through a fine strainer.

Melt the butter in a saucepan. Stir in the flour and cook, stirring, for 1 minute. Remove from the heat and gradually stir in the milk. Return to the heat and cook, stirring, until thickened and smooth. Stir in salt and pepper to taste and the lemon juice and remove from the heat.

Drain the onions and place on a warmed serving dish. Pour over the sauce and sprinkle with the parsley. Garnish with the lemon wedges and serve.
Serves 4-6

Brussels sprouts with chestnuts

750g/1½lb Brussels sprouts
salt and black pepper
24 chestnuts
2 Tbsp arrowroot
1 Tbsp port *or* water
500ml/1 pint beef stock
125g/½ cup butter

Cook the sprouts in boiling salted water for 6 to 8 minutes or until they are almost tender. Drain and refresh under cold running water, then drain again.

Split the skins of the chestnuts at the pointed end and put in a saucepan. Cover with water and bring to a boil. Boil for 30 seconds, then drain and peel.

Put the peeled chestnuts in a flameproof casserole. Mix together the arrowroot and port or water, then stir in the stock. Pour this mixture over the chestnuts. Add 3 tablespoons of the butter. Put the casserole over the heat and bring to a boil. Cover and transfer to a warm oven (170°C/325°F). Cook for 45 to 60 minutes or until the chestnuts are tender.

Drain the chestnuts and return to the casserole. Add the Brussels sprouts, remaining butter and salt and pepper to taste. Cover the casserole with buttered wax paper and bake for 20 minutes.
Serves 6

Sweet potato and marshmallow bake

750g/1½lb sweet potatoes
salt
2 tsp clear honey
2 Tbsp butter
juice of 1 orange
2 eggs, well beaten
250g/8oz marshmallows

Bake the sweet potatoes in a moderate oven (180°C/350°F) for 1 hour or until they are tender. Remove from the oven and cool slightly, then peel off the skins.

Put the sweet potatoes, salt to taste, the honey, butter, orange juice and eggs in a mixing bowl. Mash together until a thick, smooth purée is formed. Transfer to a greased baking dish and smooth the top. Bake in the moderate oven for 10 minutes.

Remove from the oven and arrange the marshmallows over the top. (Halve the marshmallows if they are large.) Increase the temperature to fairly hot (200°C/400°F) and bake for a further 10 minutes or until the marshmallow topping has melted and is lightly browned. Serve hot, in the dish.
Serves 4

Cauliflower bread

2 medium cauliflowers, broken into flowerets
750g/1½lb potatoes, peeled and quartered
1 Tbsp butter
salt and white pepper
¼ tsp cayenne pepper
6 eggs
150g/1¼ cups Gruyère cheese, grated

Cook the cauliflowers in boiling salted water for 15 minutes or until tender. Meanwhile, cook the potatoes in boiling salted water for 15 minutes or until tender. Drain the potatoes and cauliflowers and place in a mixing bowl. Add the butter, salt and pepper to taste and the cayenne. Mash together to form a purée.

Beat the eggs into the purée, one at a time, then stir in all but 2 tablespoons of the cheese. Spoon into a greased 2.5l/5 pint baking mold and place the mold in a roasting pan. Pour enough boiling water into the pan to come halfway up the sides of the mold. Cover the mold tightly with foil and bake in a moderate oven (180°C/350°F) for 1 hour.

Remove the foil and turn the cauliflower bread out onto a warmed heatproof serving dish. Sprinkle over the remaining cheese and bake for a further 5 minutes or until the cheese is melted and lightly browned.
Serves 4-6

Braised celeriac

6 bacon slices, diced
1 large celeriac, peeled and sliced
1 Tbsp butter
1 small onion, chopped
300ml/1¼ cups beef stock
185ml/¾ cup dry white wine or additional stock
salt and black pepper
1 Tbsp parsley, freshly chopped

Blanch the bacon in boiling water for 10 minutes. Meanwhile, blanch the celeriac in boiling salted water for 5 minutes. Drain the bacon and celeriac.

Melt the butter in a flameproof casserole. Add the bacon and onion. Fry until the onion is soft but not brown. Remove the bacon and onion from the casserole.

Add the celeriac to the casserole and spoon the onion and bacon on top. Pour in the stock and wine and add salt and pepper to taste. Bring to a boil, cover and transfer to a moderate oven (180°C/350°F). Braise for 1 hour.

Sprinkle over the parsley and serve, from the casserole.
Serves 6

The sweet potato is an edible tuber native to South America. It has a floury texture and tastes sweet, hence its name.

Salads

Endive, almond and pepper salad

4 heads French or Belgian endive, sliced
150g/1 cup blanched almonds,
lightly toasted
2 red chili peppers, seeded and
finely chopped
1 red pepper, pith and seeds removed
and thinly sliced
DRESSING
6 Tbsp olive oil
2 Tbsp red wine vinegar
1 tsp lemon juice
salt and black pepper

Put the endive, almonds, chili peppers and red pepper in a salad bowl. Put all the dressing ingredients, with salt and pepper to taste, in a screwtop jar. Shake well and pour over the salad ingredients. Toss together and serve.

Serves 4

Beet and orange salad

6 medium beets, cooked and peeled
2 large oranges
2 bunches watercress
DRESSING
4 Tbsp olive oil
1½ Tbsp wine vinegar
1 tsp prepared mustard
¼ tsp dried tarragon
salt and black pepper
½ tsp sugar

Slice the beets. Grate the rind of one orange. Peel the oranges, removing all the white pith. Slice the oranges.

Arrange the watercress on a serving dish. Place the orange and beet slices alternately, slightly overlapping, in circles on the watercress.

Put all the dressing ingredients, with salt and pepper to taste, in a screwtop jar. Add the orange rind and shake well. Pour this dressing over the beet and orange slices and serve.

Serves 4

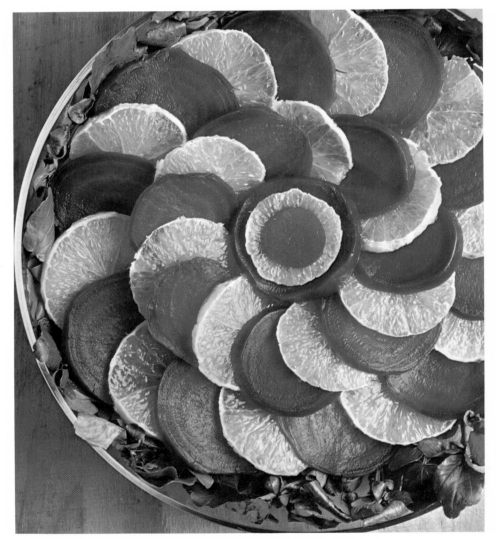

An unusual combination, Beet and Orange Salad has both color and flavor.

Breakfasts

Egg and bacon with sherry sauce

4 eggs
4 bacon slices
2 Tbsp butter
1 Tbsp flour
185ml/¾ cup milk
185ml/¾ cup heavy cream
salt and white pepper
60g/½ cup Cheddar cheese, grated
4 Tbsp dry sherry
2 egg yolks, lightly beaten
4 slices hot buttered toast
1 tsp paprika

Put the eggs in a saucepan and cover with water. Bring to a boil, then remove from the heat and leave to soft-cook for 5 minutes. While the eggs are cooking, broil the bacon until it is crisp.

Meanwhile, make the sauce. Melt the butter in a saucepan. Stir in the flour and cook, stirring, for 1 minute. Remove from the heat and gradually stir in the milk. Return to the heat and simmer, stirring, until thickened and smooth. Stir in the cream, salt and pepper to taste, the cheese and sherry. Heat through gently without boiling until the cheese melts. Remove from the heat and beat in the egg yolks.

Place a slice of hot toast on each of four warmed serving plates. Top each with a slice of bacon and an egg. Spoon over the sauce and sprinkle with paprika. Serve immediately.
Serves 4

Herrings in rolled oats

4 large herrings, filleted and halved
1 lemon, quartered
125g/1 cup rolled oats
salt and black pepper
1 egg, lightly beaten
125g/½ cup butter

Rub the herring fillets all over with the lemon quarters. Discard the lemon. Mix together the rolled oats and salt and pepper. Coat the herrings first in the beaten egg and then in the rolled oats.

Melt the butter in a frying pan. Add the herrings, in batches, and fry for 2 to 3 minutes on each side or until the fish is cooked. Test with a fork: the flesh should flake easily.

Transfer to a warmed serving dish and serve hot.
Serves 6-8

Buttermilk pancakes with maple syrup

300g/2½ cups flour
½ tsp salt
2 tsp baking powder
1 Tbsp sugar
2 eggs, separated
500ml/1 pint buttermilk
60g/¼ cup butter, melted
4 Tbsp vegetable oil
250ml/1 cup maple syrup

Sift the flour, salt, baking powder and sugar into a mixing bowl. Add the egg yolks, buttermilk and melted butter and beat well until smooth. Beat the egg whites until they will hold a soft peak and fold into the buttermilk mixture.

Lightly grease a frying pan with a little of the oil. Drop tablespoonsful of the batter onto the pan, well spaced, and cook for about 1 minute or until the pancakes bubble on the surface. Turn over and cook the other sides for 30 seconds or until lightly browned. Transfer the pancakes to a warmed serving dish and keep hot while you cook the remaining pancakes in the same way.

Meanwhile, gently heat the maple syrup until it is hot.

Serve the pancakes hot, with the maple syrup.
Serves 4-6

Sand waffles

60g/½ cup cornstarch
250g/2 cups flour
½ tsp salt
½ tsp ground cinnamon
125g/½ cup butter
60g/¼ cup sugar
2 eggs
4 Tbsp sour cream
375ml/1½ cups milk
grated rind of ½ lemon

Sift together the cornstarch, flour, salt and cinnamon. Cream the butter with the sugar. Beat in the eggs, one at a time, then fold in the flour mixture. Stir in the sour cream and milk to form a fairly thick but pouring batter. Stir in the lemon rind. Heat a waffle iron.

Spoon a few tablespoonfuls of the batter into the hot waffle iron and press the lid down firmly. Bake until the waffle is golden brown and crisp. Transfer to a warmed serving dish and keep hot while you make the remaining waffles.

Serve hot with maple syrup or clear or orange blossom honey.
Serves 4-6

A tasty mixture of cooked fish, rice and hard-boiled eggs, Kedgeree is a traditional British breakfast dish of Anglo-Indian origin that makes a good start to a winter's day.

Kidney and mushroom croûtes

4 large slices of bread cut 2cm/¾in
thick, crusts removed
5 eggs
150ml/⅔ cup milk
60g/¼ cup butter
4 bacon slices, chopped
4 lamb kidneys, skinned, cored
and chopped
250g/2 cups mushrooms, chopped
1 Tbsp lemon juice
salt and black pepper
4 Tbsp vegetable oil

Slightly hollow out the centers of the bread slices, making a 1cm/½in deep indentation in each one. Mix together one of the eggs and the milk in a shallow dish. Put the bread slices in the dish and soak.

Melt 2 tablespoons of the butter in a frying pan. Add the bacon and fry until it is crisp and brown. Add the kidney pieces and cook for 5 minutes. Stir in the mushrooms and cook for 3 minutes. Stir in the lemon juice and salt and pepper to taste and simmer gently for 2 minutes. Remove from the heat and keep hot.

Poach the remaining four eggs in simmering water.

Meanwhile, melt the remaining butter in

another frying pan. Add the bread slices and fry for 4 minutes, turning once, or until they are golden brown and crisp. Drain on paper towels.

Place the bread croûtes on warmed serving dishes and fill with mixture.

Top each bread croûte with a poached egg and serve immediately.
Serves 4

Kedgeree

125g/½ cup butter
300g/2 cups cooked smoked haddock,
skinned, boned and flaked
300g/1½ cups long-grain rice, cooked
2 eggs, hard-cooked and finely chopped
salt and black pepper
¼ tsp cayenne pepper
2 Tbsp light cream
1 Tbsp parsley, freshly chopped

Melt three-quarters of the butter in a frying pan. Add the fish, rice, eggs, salt and pepper to taste and the cayenne. Stir in the cream. Heat through gently without boiling, then pile onto a warmed serving dish. Cut the remaining butter into small pieces and dot over the top.

Sprinkle the top of the mixture with the chopped parsley and serve at once.
Serves 4

Light Dishes

Broccoli soufflé

750g/1½lb broccoli, cut into small pieces
salt and black pepper
1 garlic clove
2 Tbsp butter
60g/¼ cup flour
250ml/1 cup heavy cream
4 eggs, separated
60g/¼ cup Parmesan cheese, grated

Cook the broccoli in boiling salted water, with the garlic, for 15 minutes. Drain well and discard the garlic. Finely chop the broccoli.

Melt the butter in a saucepan. Stir in the flour and cook, stirring, for 1 minute. Remove from the heat and gradually stir in the cream. Return to the heat and cook, stirring, until thickened. Remove from the heat and allow to cool slightly.

Lightly beat the egg yolks and stir into the cream sauce. Add salt and pepper to taste, then stir in the broccoli. Beat the egg whites until they will hold a stiff peak. Fold into the broccoli mixture. Spoon into a greased ring mold. Place the mold in a roasting pan and add enough boiling water to come halfway up the sides of the mold.

Bake in a moderate oven (180°C/350°F) for 35 to 40 minutes or until the soufflé is puffed and set. Turn out onto a warmed serving dish and fill the center with cooked carrot slices or any hot cooked vegetable. Sprinkle over the cheese.
Serves 6

Chef's salad

1 medium head lettuce
75g/½ cup cooked chicken, cut into strips
75g/½ cup cooked tongue *or* ham, cut into strips
75g/½ cup Gruyère cheese, cut into strips
1 egg, hard-cooked and thinly sliced
1 Tbsp onion, finely chopped
3 Tbsp black olives, pitted and chopped
75ml/⅓ cup olive oil
2 Tbsp red wine vinegar
½ tsp lemon juice
¼ tsp prepared French mustard
salt and black pepper

Break the lettuce into leaves and arrange in a large salad bowl. Add the chicken, tongue, cheese, egg, onion and olives. Chill for 10 minutes.

Put the remaining ingredients, with salt and pepper to taste, in a screwtop jar. Shake well. Just before serving, pour this dressing over the salad ingredients.
Serves 4

An unusual and colorful vegetable dish, Broccoli Soufflé is delicious decorated with parsley and served with new potatoes.

Top : Spaghetti Carbonara – one of the great Italian pasta dishes is excellent served with a green salad and a glass of Valpolicella.
Above : Omelet Arnold Bennett – one of the classics of French cookery – is a meal in itself; light yet satisfying.

Omelet Arnold Bennett

3 Tbsp butter
125g/¾ cup smoked haddock, cooked and flaked
150ml/⅔ cup heavy cream
6 eggs, separated
3 Tbsp Parmesan cheese, grated
salt and black pepper
1 Tbsp parsley, freshly chopped

Melt 2 tablespoons of the butter in a frying pan. Add the haddock and 2 tablespoons of the cream. When the cream is hot, remove from the heat and allow to cool.

Beat the egg yolks with half the cheese, salt and pepper to taste and the parsley. Stir in the haddock mixture. Beat the egg whites until they will hold a stiff peak. Fold into the haddock mixture.

Melt the remaining butter in a frying pan or omelet pan. Pour in the haddock mixture and cook for 2 minutes or until the bottom is set and lightly browned.

Sprinkle over the remaining cheese and pour over the remaining cream. Transfer the pan to the broiler and broil for 30 seconds. Slide onto a serving dish.
Serves 2-3

Spaghetti carbonara

500g/1lb spaghetti
3 Tbsp butter
6 bacon slices, chopped
3 Tbsp heavy cream
3 eggs
125g/1 cup Parmesan cheese, finely grated
salt and black pepper

Cook the spaghetti in boiling salted water for 8 to 12 minutes or until it is *al dente* (just tender to the bite).

Meanwhile, melt 1 tablespoon of the butter in a frying pan. Add the bacon and fry until it is crisp and golden brown. Remove from the heat and stir in the cream. Keep hot.

Beat the eggs and 50g/½ cup of the grated cheese together. Stir in salt and pepper to taste.

Drain the spaghetti and transfer it to a warmed mixing bowl. Add the remaining butter and toss well to coat the strands. Stir in the bacon mixture, then the egg mixture, tossing the spaghetti thoroughly.

Serve at once, with the remaining grated cheese.
Serves 4

Desserts

Spotted Dick

250g/2 cups flour
1 tsp salt
2 Tbsp sugar
2 tsp baking powder
pinch ground cloves
90g/⅓ cup shredded beef suet
125g/⅔ cup currants
60g/⅓ cup raisins
6-8 Tbsp water
3 Tbsp milk
6 Tbsp strawberry jam

Sift the flour, salt, sugar, baking powder and cloves into a mixing bowl. Stir in the suet, currants and raisins. Stir in enough water to bind the mixture and knead to a dough. Roll out the dough to a rectangle about 6mm/¼in thick. Brush the edges with milk. Spread over the jam and roll up the dough like a jelly roll. Press the edges together to seal.

Wrap the roll loosely in foil or cheese-cloth, making a pleat to allow for expansion, and steam for 2½ hours.

Unwrap the pudding and transfer to a warmed serving dish.

Serve hot.

Serves 6-8

Apples baked in brandy and vermouth

4 cooking apples, cored
5 Tbsp butter
2 Tbsp sugar
125ml/½ cup dry white vermouth
125ml/½ cup water
75ml/⅓ cup brandy
4 white bread slices, crusts removed
2 Tbsp redcurrant jelly

Make a shallow slit all around the center of the apples. Put 1 teaspoon of butter in the cavity of each and place in a flameproof baking dish. Sprinkle over the sugar, vermouth, water and 2 tablespoons of the brandy. Bake in a moderate oven (180°C/350°F) for 30 to 35 minutes or until the apples are tender.

Meanwhile, cut the bread slices into circles about 8cm/3in in diameter. Melt the remaining butter in a frying pan. Add the bread slices and fry until crisp and golden brown on both sides. Drain the bread slices thoroughly and then arrange on a serving dish. Place an apple on each slice.

Place the baking dish over the heat on top of the stove and stir in the remaining brandy and redcurrant jelly. Bring to a boil and boil until reduced to about half the original quantity. Pour this sauce over the apples and serve.

Serves 4

This traditional British dessert, Spotted Dick, made with suet, dried fruits and filled with strawberry jam is a great favorite. Served steaming hot, it is a perfect choice for a cold winter's day.

Rhubarb and orange pie

PASTRY
300g/2½ cups flour
¼ tsp salt
185g/¾ cup butter
6 Tbsp iced water
2 Tbsp milk
2 Tbsp sugar
FILLING
750g/1½lb rhubarb, in 5cm/2in pieces
juice and finely grated rind of 2 oranges
2 Tbsp cornstarch
185g/1 cup brown sugar

Sift the flour and salt into a mixing bowl. Add the butter and cut into small pieces, then rub the fat into the flour until the mixture resembles breadcrumbs. Stir in enough water to bind the mixture, then knead to a dough. Chill for 30 minutes.

Put the rhubarb in a mixing bowl and pour over the orange juice. Leave to marinate for 30 minutes.

Roll out two-thirds of the dough and use to line a 23cm/9in deep pie plate. Drain the rhubarb, discarding the orange juice. Arrange half the rhubarb in the pie plate and sprinkle with half the orange rind, half the cornstarch and half the brown sugar. Add the remaining rhubarb, orange rind, cornstarch and brown sugar. Roll out the remaining dough and use to cover the pie plate. Press the edges together to seal and cut a cross in the center.

Brush the pie with the milk and sprinkle over the sugar. Bake in a fairly hot oven (190°C/375°F) for 30 to 40 minutes or until the pastry is golden brown. Serve hot or cold.
Serves 4-6

Guards' pudding

250g/2⅔ cups fresh white breadcrumbs
250g/1 cup shredded beef suet
185g/1 cup brown sugar
4 Tbsp strawberry or raspberry jam
2 eggs
1½ tsp baking soda

Mix together the breadcrumbs, suet and sugar. Stir in the jam. Beat the eggs with the soda and stir into the breadcrumb mixture. Spoon into a greased 2 liter/4 pint capacity steaming mold. Cover with a lid of greased wax paper and foil and tie on securely with string, making a pleat across the center to allow for expansion.

Steam for 3 hours, adding more boiling water when necessary.

Turn the pudding out onto a serving dish and serve hot, with whipped cream.
Serves 4-6

Dried fruit compôte

750g/1½lb mixed dried fruit (apples, apricots, raisins, prunes, etc.)
425ml/1¾ cups water
185ml/¾ cup dry red wine
250g/1 cup sugar
5cm/2in cinnamon stick
finely pared rind of 1 lemon, cut into thin strips

Soak the fruit in cold water to cover for 12 hours or overnight. Remove the fruit from the bowl and drain well.

Put the water, wine, sugar, cinnamon and lemon rind in a saucepan and heat gently stirring to dissolve the sugar. Bring to a boil. Add the fruit and simmer for 10 to 15 minutes or until the fruit is tender and rather pulpy.

Transfer the fruit to a serving dish using a slotted spoon. Keep hot if serving the compôte hot.

Remove the cinnamon stick from the liquid and return to a boil. Boil for 30 minutes or until reduced and slightly thickened. Pour the syrup over the fruit and serve.

Alternatively, allow to cool and chill well in the refrigerator before serving.
Serves 6-8

Steamed chocolate pudding

4 squares semisweet chocolate, broken into small pieces
2 Tbsp strong black coffee
125g butter
150g/⅔ cup sugar
5 eggs, separated
125g/1 cup walnuts, finely chopped

Melt the chocolate with the coffee gently in a saucepan. Remove from the heat and allow to cool.

Cream the butter and the sugar together until the mixture is light and fluffy. Beat in the egg yolks, one at a time. Stir in the chocolate mixture, then the walnuts. Beat the egg whites until they will hold a stiff peak. Fold into the chocolate mixture using a metal spoon.

Spoon into a greased 1 liter/2 pint capacity steaming mold and cover with a lid of greased wax paper and foil. Make a pleat in the center to allow for expansion. Tie the lid onto the mold securely with string.

Steam the pudding for 1 to 1¼ hours, replenishing the boiling water when necessary.

Serve hot, from the mold.
Serves 4

Above: Cooked in red wine with a delicate, aromatic flavor, this original winter fruit salad – Compote of Dried Fruits – makes an attractive dessert. Below: This rich chocolate steamed dessert from Germany – Schokoladen Pudding is made with chocolate, walnuts, eggs and coffee and is especially good served with whipped cream.

Mincemeat and apple crumble

500g/1lb cooking apples, peeled, cored
and sliced
2 Tbsp sugar
250g/1 cup mincemeat
2 tsp grated lemon rind
½ tsp ground allspice
2 Tbsp brandy
TOPPING
185g/1½ cups flour
6 Tbsp butter
125g/½ cup sugar
2 tsp grated lemon rind
½ tsp ground allspice

Put the apples and sugar in a saucepan and
add enough water just to cover. Bring to a
boil, then poach gently until the apples are
tender but still firm. Drain the apple slices
and mix with the mincemeat, lemon rind,
allspice and brandy. Spoon into a greased
baking dish.

To make the topping, sift the flour into a
mixing bowl. Add the butter and cut into
small pieces, then rub into the flour until
the mixture resembles breadcrumbs. Stir
in the remaining ingredients. Spoon the
topping over the mincemeat mixture and
smooth the top.

Bake in a fairly hot oven (200°C/400°F)
for 30 to 40 minutes or until the topping is
browned and crisp. Serve hot with cream
or custard sauce.
Serves 4

Cranberry mousse

250g/8oz cranberries
75g/⅓ cup sugar
2 Tbsp water
4 egg yolks
1 Tbsp orange juice
2 egg whites
150ml/⅔ cup heavy cream

Put the cranberries, 2 tablespoons of the
sugar and the water in a saucepan. Cook
gently until the fruit is just tender. Remove from the heat. Drain the cranberries,
reserving the juice. Add enough bottled or
canned cranberry juice to make up to
125ml/½ cup, if necessary.

Put the egg yolks in the top of a double
boiler or heatproof bowl over a pan of hot
water and beat with the remaining sugar
over heat until they are thick and pale. Beat
in the cranberry juice. Continue beating
until the mixture will make a ribbon trail
on itself when the beater is lifted. Remove
from the heat and stir in the cranberries
and orange juice. Chill for 30 minutes.

Beat the egg whites until they will hold a
stiff peak. Whip the cream until it is thick.
Fold the cream into the cranberry mixture,
then fold in the egg whites. Spoon into a
serving dish or individual dishes and chill
for at least 6 hours.
Serves 4

German cheesecake

185g/2¼ cups graham crackers, crushed
6 Tbsp butter, melted
125g/½ cup sugar
1 tsp ground cinnamon
2 eggs, lightly beaten
¼ tsp salt
juice and grated rind of ½ lemon
125ml/½ cup light cream
250g/1 cup cottage cheese
90g/¾ cup mixed chopped nuts

Mix together the cracker crumbs, melted
butter, 2 tablespoons of the sugar and the
cinnamon. Press into the bottom and sides
of a greased 20cm/8in round cake pan,
reserving 2 tablespoons of the crumb mixture.

Beat the eggs, salt, lemon juice and rind
together until well-mixed. Stir in the
cream, cottage cheese and half the nuts.
Spoon into the crumb shell and sprinkle
over the reserved crumb mixture and
remaining nuts.

Bake in a moderate oven (180°C/350°F)
for 35 to 45 minutes or until the filling is
set. Turn off the oven and leave the cake
inside, with the door open, for 10 minutes.

Remove from the oven and allow to cool
completely.

Serve cold.
Serves 6-8

Bananas baked in rum and cream

6 bananas
1 Tbsp sugar
6 Tbsp white rum
125g/1 cup macaroons, crushed
1 Tbsp butter, melted
300ml/1¼ cups heavy cream

Put the bananas in a greased baking dish.
Sprinkle with the sugar and rum. Bake in a
moderate oven (180°C/350°F) for 15
minutes.

Remove from the oven and allow to cool
for 10 minutes.

Reset the oven to warm (170°C/325°F).
Mix the macaroons with the butter. Pour
the cream over the bananas and sprinkle
over the macaroon mixture. Bake for a
further 20 minutes. Serve hot, in the baking
dish.
Serves 4

*Above: Cranberry Mousse, a
refreshing cold dessert with a
difference, is best made during
Christmas when cranberries are
readily available and makes a superb
treat for a special dinner party.
Below: A traditional German
cheesecake, Kasekuchen has a crunchy
cinnamon biscuit base with a smooth
cream, egg, lemon, cheese and nut
filling.*

Drinks

Hot toddy

300ml/1¼ cups water
150ml/⅔ cup whiskey or brandy
1 tsp lemon juice
2 strips lemon rind
pinch ground allspice
2 Tbsp brown sugar

Put all the ingredients in a saucepan and stir over gentle heat to dissolve the sugar. Heat through without boiling. Discard the lemon rind and pour into a pitcher. Serve immediately.
Serves 4

Festive and spicy, Mulled Wine is guaranteed to warm up any winter party and will prove highly popular with the guests.

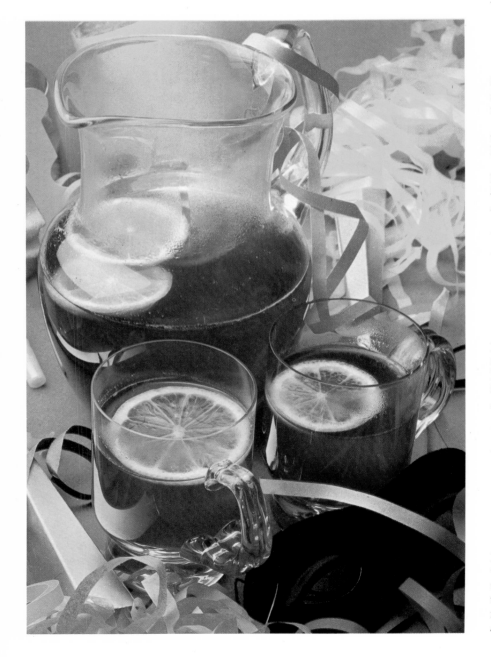

Mulled wine

1 bottle dry red wine
juice and thinly pared rind of 1 lemon
½ tsp grated nutmeg
5cm/2in cinnamon stick
3 Tbsp sugar
1 lemon, thinly sliced

Put the wine, lemon rind and juice, grated nutmeg, cinnamon stick and sugar in a saucepan. Stir over gentle heat to dissolve the sugar. Heat through without boiling, then strain into a pitcher. Garnish with the lemon slices and serve.
Serves 6-8

Archbishop

1 Seville orange
20 whole cloves
1 Tbsp brown sugar
1 bottle medium dry sherry

Stud the orange with the cloves. Bake in a moderate oven (180°C/350°F) for 30 minutes or until the orange is brown.
    Cut the orange in half and sprinkle with the sugar. Put the halves in the bottom of a heatproof punch bowl.
    Warm the sherry in a saucepan until it is hot but not boiling. Pour into the punch bowl and serve hot.
Serves 4-6

Hot apple drink

500ml/1 pint apple juice
2 Tbsp orange-flavored liqueur
2 strips lemon rind
1 Tbsp brown sugar
pinch grated nutmeg

Put all the ingredients in a saucepan and stir over gentle heat to dissolve the sugar. Heat through without boiling, then strain into a pitcher and serve.
Serves 4

Hot buttered rum

185ml/¾ cup hard cider or water, boiling
1 Tbsp butter
4 Tbsp dark rum
1 tsp sugar
pinch grated nutmeg

Mix together 4 tablespoons of the cider or water and the butter in a mug. Stir to melt the butter. Stir in the rum and sugar, then the remaining cider or water. Sprinkle the nutmeg on top and serve.
Serves 1

Marmalades

Marmalade

Marmalade is a preserve made with citrus fruit – oranges, lemons, limes, grapefruit and tangerines – and the ideal time to make it is in winter when the bitter Seville oranges have their short season. Other fruit, such as apples, pineapples and pears, may be added to give a pleasant combination, and the marmalade may be flavored with ginger and other spices such as cinnamon and cloves.

Marmalade is made in the same way as jam (see Summer section), with one difference – because the peel of citrus fruit is tough, it has to be softened either by soaking or cooking. The softening of the peel also releases the pectin, which is contained in the pith and seeds.

There are three basic methods of making marmalade. One is to squeeze the juice into a pan and add the chopped peel (with pith) and the seeds tied in a piece of cheesecloth. Acid (lemon juice or citric or tartaric acid) and a measured amount of water are stirred in and the mixture is simmered for 2 hours. The bag of seeds is discarded and sugar stirred in. When it has dissolved, the marmalade is boiled until setting point is reached.

For the second method, the fruit is finely pared and the rind is shredded. The rind, acid and half the water are simmered together for 2 hours. Meanwhile, the fruit pulp is cooked with the pith in the remaining water for 2 hours. The fruit pulp is drained and all seeds, pith and coarse tissue discarded. The remaining pulp is strained and added to the rind mixture with sugar, and the marmalade is boiled until setting point is reached.

The third method uses whole fruit. They are put in the pan with the water and simmered for 2 hours or until tender. The fruit is then removed from the pan, chopped and the seeds are returned to the pan tied in cheesecloth. After a further simmering of 15 minutes, the seeds are discarded and the chopped fruit returned to the pan. Sugar is stirred in until it has completely dissolved and the marmalade boiled until setting point is reached.

To can marmalade, remove from the heat and skim off the scum. Allow to cool slightly until a skin forms on top, then ladle into warmed jam jars. Cover with wax paper discs and when cold, seal with jam covers. Alternatively, use canning jars. Label the jars and store in a cool, dry, dark place.

Seville orange marmalade

1.5kg/3lb Seville oranges
juice of 2 lemons
2.5-3.75l/5-7½ pints water
2.75kg/6lb sugar

Scrub the fruit and use method one, two or three.
Makes about 4.5kg/10lb.

Five fruit marmalade

1 orange
1 grapefruit
1 lemon
1.5l/3 pints water
1 large cooking apple, peeled, cored and diced
1 pear, peeled, cored and diced
1.5kg/3lb sugar

Scrub the orange, grapefruit and lemon and prepare according to method one, two or three. Add the apple and pear and continue as specified.
Makes about 2.25kg/5lb

Grapefruit marmalade

1.5kg/3lb grapefruit
2 tsp citric acid
3.75l/7½ pints water
2.75kg/6lb sugar

Scrub the grapefruit and proceed as method one, two or three.
Makes about 4.5kg/10lb

An interesting variation, Five Fruit Marmalade made from orange, grapefruit, lemon, apple and pear, has a distinctive, delicate flavor of its own.

Feast Days

When agriculture, and the consequent provision of food, were more closely linked to the seasons of the calendar, special days of fasting and feasting were as much a matter of practical necessity as of spiritual celebration. Although the seasons have become extended and blurred, religious and historical feast days and festivals are still celebrated, however, and enjoyed, throughout the world.

The Lenten feast and the harvest festival, for example, remind us of the cycle of nature but are now more closely linked to religion than the scarcity or abundance of fresh food.

Each country and religion has its own celebrations and special days set aside to remember great events, no matter what seasonal calendar they follow. By trying to understand the meaning behind them and enjoying the food traditionally eaten on those days we can all enjoy them no matter what our religion or nationality.

January 1-
New Year's Day

On the stroke of Midnight, on the 31st of December, the New Year begins and, with it, our hopes for prosperity, health and happiness. As the clock chimes, and "Auld Lang Syne" is sung, thoughts turn to family and friends gathered together. An ideal centerpiece for the New Year's Day buffet table would be a baked ham glazed with bourbon.

Bourbon-glazed ham

4.5kg/10lb smoked ham, well scrubbed,
soaked overnight and drained
1 bouquet garni
8 peppercorns
1 onion, quartered
1 carrot, scraped and quartered
1 celery stalk, quartered
375g/2 cups brown sugar
2 tsp dry mustard
150ml/⅔ cup Bourbon
12 whole cloves
2 oranges, peeled and segmented

Put the ham in a saucepan and cover with water. Add the bouquet garni, peppercorns, onion, carrot and celery. Bring to a boil, then simmer for 4½ hours.

Remove from the heat and leave the ham to cool in the liquid.

Mix together the brown sugar, mustard and 4 tablespoons of the bourbon. Drain the ham and cut away the rind. Score the fat in a diamond pattern, making cuts all the way through the fat to the meat. Put the ham on a rack in a roasting pan and coat with the remaining bourbon. Spread over the sugar mixture. Push the cloves into the fat and arrange the orange segments on top, securing each segment with a wooden cocktail stick.

Bake in a moderate oven (180°C/350°F) for 45 minutes to 1 hour.
Serve hot or cold.
Serves 10-12

January 6-
Twelfth Night

Twelfth Night, or the Feast of the Epiphany, commemorates the visit of the Magi to the infant Jesus. In Latin America, for instance, children put out shoes to receive gifts from the passing kings. Throughout the Catholic world, a fruit bread or cake is baked with a dried bean inside. Whoever finds the bean is king or queen for the evening's festivities.

Twelfth night cake

375g/1½ cups butter
375g/1½ cups sugar
6 eggs
375g/3 cups flour
½ tsp grated nutmeg
1 tsp ground cinnamon
1 tsp ground ginger
375g/2 cups raisins
375g/2 cups currants
90g/¾ cup ground almonds
275g/1½ cups mixed candied peel, chopped
3 Tbsp whiskey

Cream the butter and sugar together in a mixing bowl until the mixture is light and fluffy. Beat in the eggs, one at a time, adding a little flour with each egg to prevent curdling. Sift together the remaining flour and spices and fold into the creamed mixture with the fruit. Stir in the whiskey.

Spoon the cake mixture into a 23cm/9in diameter springform cake pan which has been lined with greased wax paper. Bake in a cool oven (150°C/300°F) for 4 to 4½ hours or until a skewer or toothpick inserted into the center comes out clean.

Leave to cool in the pan for 1 hour, then

turn out onto a wire rack to cool completely. Store in an airtight tin.
Makes one 23cm/9in cake

January 25 - Burns Night

Scottish people throughout the world celebrate the birth of their famous poet, Robert Burns, born on January 25, 1759, with a banquet. The celebration begins with the famous grace:

> *"Somehae meat that canna eat,*
> *And some wad eat that want ile,*
> *But we hae meat, and we can eat,*
> *And sae the Lord be than Kit."*

"The Skirl o' the Pipes" announces the arrival of the haggis, the highlight of the meal, at the table and it is slit open with a *skean d'hu* (ceremonial knife) while Burns' salutation is recited. For true Scots, the haggis is drenched with Scotch whiskey!

Traditional haggis recipes call for the savory meat mixture to be boiled in a sheep's paunch, but as this is difficult for modern cooks, we give a version of haggis steamed in a mold. Haggis is traditionally served with chappit (mashed) potatoes and bashed neeps (mashed rutabaga).

Haggis

250g/8oz liver
185g/1 cup oatmeal
2 medium onions
250g/1 cup lean ground beef
185g/¾ cup shredded beef suet
salt and black pepper
pinch grated nutmeg

Put the liver in a saucepan and cover with cold water. Bring to a boil and boil for 5 minutes. Drain the liver, reserving 4 tablespoons of the water.

Toast the oatmeal under the broiler or in the oven until it is golden brown. Allow to cool slightly. Meanwhile, grind the liver with the onions. Add the oatmeal, beef, suet, salt and pepper to taste, the nutmeg and the reserved liver cooking liquid to the ground mixture and combine thoroughly. Spoon into a greased steaming mold and tie a lid of greased wax paper and foil on top. Make a pleat in the lid to allow for expansion.

Steam the haggis for 3 hours, replenishing the boiling water when necessary.

Remove the haggis from the heat and serve it at once.
Serves 6-8

Fresh root ginger is a common ingredient in Chinese dishes.

January/February - Chinese New Year

The renewal of the Chinese lunar calendar falls between January 21 and February 19 on the Gregorian calendar. This colorful and exciting two-week celebration ends with the Lantern Festival (Yüan Hsiao) when children parade with beautiful lighted lanterns. Rice is a symbol of life and fertility, and in some parts of China it is customary to "present the New Year's rice," that is, to place a wooden bowl of rice on the altar dedicated to the family ancestors. One day of the New Year festivities commemorates the first planting of rice, five thousand years ago. Chinese Fried Rice, Red-Cooked Pork and Crabmeat Dumplings will give a taste of the Chinese New Year.

Feng kuo (crabmeat dumplings)

6 dried Chinese mushrooms, soaked
for 30 minutes and drained
2 Tbsp sesame or vegetable oil
1 Tbsp scallions, chopped
1 tsp green ginger, peeled and finely
chopped
250g/1⅓ cups crabmeat, flaked
salt and black pepper
¼ tsp sugar
1 tsp soy sauce
1 Tbsp dry sherry
DUMPLING DOUGH
250g/2 cups flour
125ml/½ cup boiling water

Remove and discard the mushroom stalks. Finely chop the caps. Heat the oil in a frying pan. Add the mushrooms, scallions, ginger and crabmeat. Fry stirring, for 3 minutes. Stir in salt and pepper, the sugar, soy sauce and sherry and cook, stirring, for 1 minute. Remove from the heat.

Sift the flour into a mixing bowl and gradually stir in the boiling water. Knead the dough for 5 minutes or until smooth and elastic. Return to the bowl, cover and leave for 30 minutes.

Roll the dough into a sausage about 2.5cm/1in in diameter. Cut into slices 2.5cm/1in thick. Flatten the slices until they are about 8cm/3in in diameter. Place a teaspoonful of the crabmeat filling on one half of each dough circle and fold over the other half to make half-moon shapes. Press the edges together to seal.

Steam the dumplings, in batches, if necessary, for about 10 minutes. Serve hot.
Serves 4

Chinese fried rice

250g/2 cups long-grain rice, soaked in
cold water for 30 minutes and drained
500ml/1⅓ pint water
salt
2 Tbsp vegetable oil
2 medium onions, finely chopped
250g/1 cup cooked ham, finely chopped
2 Tbsp peas, cooked
2 medium tomatoes, peeled and
quartered
250g/1⅓ cups shrimp (shelled), deveined
1 Tbsp soy sauce
1 egg, lightly beaten

Put the rice, water and 1 teaspoon salt in a saucepan and bring to a boil. Cover and simmer for 15 minutes or until all the water has been absorbed. Remove from the heat.

A classic Chinese dish – Hung Shao Chu Jo is also one of the most popular. The skin of the pork is considered to be an integral part of the delicacy of the dish.

Heat the oil in another saucepan. Add the onions and cook, stirring, for 2 minutes. Add the ham, peas, tomatoes, shrimp and salt to taste and cook, stirring, for 1 minute.

Stir in the rice and cook, stirring, for 2 minutes. Add the soy sauce and egg and cook, stirring, for a further 2 minutes.
Serves 4

Hung shao chu jo (Red-cooked pork)

2kg/4lb pork shoulder (boned weight)
75ml/⅓ cup vegetable oil
7 Tbsp soy sauce
1 Tbsp sugar
150ml/⅔ cup chicken or beef stock
150ml/⅔ cup red wine

Cut the pork into twelve pieces. Heat the oil in a flameproof casserole. Add the pork pieces and brown on all sides. Remove from the heat and pour off the oil. Add 4 tablespoons of the soy sauce, half the sugar and 75ml/⅓ cup each of the stock and wine. Turn the meat over in this sauce several times, continually basting the meat thoroughly with a spoon.

Return to the heat and bring to a boil. Transfer to a warm oven (170°C/325°F) and bake for 1 hour, turning the meat once during cooking.

Add the remaining soy sauce, sugar, stock and wine to the casserole. Turn the meat over several times, then return to a cool oven (150°C/300°F). Continue baking for 1 hour, turning the meat once. Remove the casserole from the oven and serve hot, straight from the casserole.
Serves 4

February 14 - St. Valentine's Day

The origins of this day may be traced to the old Roman feast, Lupercalia, in February, at which young men and maidens drew partners by lot. A later festival custom was associated with the Christian bishop, Valentine, who was martyred on February 14, 271AD. Another idea relates this holiday to the mating season for birds! Whatever its origin, it is a day for exchanging promises of love, in the form of anonymous greeting cards, chocolates, flowers – or a heart-shaped cake.

Valentine cake

CAKE
300g/1¼ cups sugar
8 eggs, at room temperature
½ tsp vanilla extract
250g/2 cups flour
250g/1 cup unsalted butter, melted
FILLING AND FROSTING
185g/¾ cup strawberry jam
750g/3 cups sugar
500ml/1 pint water
pinch cream of tartar
½ tsp red food coloring
250g/1⅓ cups confectioners' sugar

To make the cake, put the sugar, eggs and vanilla in a heatproof bowl over a pan of hot water. Beat until the mixture is pale and thick and will make a ribbon trail on itself when the beater is lifted. (If using an electric beater, no heat is required.) Remove from the heat and sift the flour into the bowl. Fold it in, then gradually stir in the melted butter. Pour into a greased and floured deep heart-shaped cake pan (20cm/8in across at its widest point) or two heart-shaped layer cake pans.

Bake in a fairly hot oven (190°C/375°F) for 20 to 30 minutes or until the cake springs back when lightly pressed in the center. Allow to cool in the pan for 5 minutes, then turn out onto a wire rack and leave to cool completely.

If baked in a deep cake pan, slice the cake into two layers. Spread one layer with the jam and carefully place the other layer on top.

Put 500g/2 cups of the sugar and 225ml/⅞ cup of the water in a saucepan. Stir over gentle heat to dissolve the sugar, then bring to a boil. When the mixture boils, sprinkle over the cream of tartar and boil until the mixture reaches 115°C/240°F on a sugar or candy thermometer (that is, the soft ball stage).

Remove from the heat and pour the fondant onto a marble or enamel surface which has been sprinkled lightly with water. Do not scrape out the pan as sugar crystals will have formed and will make the frosting uneven. Sprinkle the surface of the fondant with water and leave aside to cool for 3 minutes.

Using a metal spatula or a sugar scraper, start working the fondant by bringing the mixture in from the edges to the middle and form it into a large ball shape. When the fondant "turns" or goes white and opaque, knead it with your hands to make it smooth.

Put the remaining sugar and 250ml/1 cup of the remaining water in a saucepan. Stir over gentle heat to dissolve the sugar, then bring to a boil. Boil until the mixture reaches 105°C/220°F on a sugar thermometer. Remove the saucepan from the heat and set aside to allow the sugar syrup to cool slightly.

Cut off one-quarter of the fondant and roll it out to about 3mm/⅛in thick. Carefully cut out three small heart shapes and a long strip, then twist the strip into a ribbon bow.

Put the remaining fondant into a heatproof bowl over a pan of hot water. Heat until the fondant is very soft (do not let the water boil). Beat in 125ml/½ cup of the sugar syrup, a tablespoon at a time. Stir in the food coloring, adding more if necessary to make the frosting a deep red.

Remove from the heat and spread the frosting over the top and sides of the cake. When the cake is covered with frosting, dip a knife in boiling water and use to make the frosting smooth. Arrange the hearts and ribbon bow on top, as in the picture opposite.

Dissolve the confectioners' sugar in enough of the remaining water to make a stiff mixture. Pipe in small rosettes around the top and bottom edges of the cake. It is now ready to serve.
Makes one heart-shaped cake

February/March - Shrove Tuesday

Shrove Tuesday, or Fastnacht, Carnival or Mardi Gras, is a day of feasting before the Lenten fast begins on Ash Wednesday. Eggs, milk and other food not permitted during the fast are to be used up. In England, these are made into crêpe batter and the crêpes are most often served simply with sugar and lemon juice, on what they call "Pancake Day". A well-known and very delicious crêpe recipe is Crêpes Suzette.

Crêpes Suzette

BATTER
150g/1¼ cups flour
1 Tbsp sugar
3 egg yolks
5 Tbsp butter, melted
125ml/½ cup milk
125ml/½ cup cold water
2 Tbsp vegetable oil
FILLING
4 sugar lumps
2 medium oranges
4 Tbsp sugar
185g/¾ cup unsalted butter, softened
75ml/⅓ cup orange juice
5 Tbsp orange-flavored liqueur
3 Tbsp brandy

To make the batter, sift the flour and sugar into a mixing bowl. Make a well in the center and add the egg yolks and melted butter. Mix together, then gradually draw in the flour. Stir in the milk and water and beat to a smooth dough.

Grease a crêpe pan or frying pan with a little of the oil. Pour in a few tablespoonfuls of the batter and tilt the pan so the bottom is evenly covered. Cook the crêpe for about 1 minute, then turn it over and cook the other side for about 30 seconds. Slide the crêpe out of the pan and keep hot while you cook the remaining crêpes in the same way. Interleave the crêpes with wax paper. Keep hot.

Rub the sugar lumps over the rind of the oranges so they absorb the zest (oil). Put the sugar lumps in a mixing bowl and mash them with a wooden spoon. Peel the oranges, removing all the white pith from the rind. Finely chop the orange rind and add to the sugar lumps with half the sugar and the softened butter. Cream the mixture together until it is light and fluffy. Stir in the orange juice and 3 tablespoons of the orange-flavored liqueur.

Melt the orange butter in a frying pan. Dip the crêpes in, one at a time, until well soaked, then fold into quarters. Arrange in a warmed shallow serving dish. Sprinkle the remaining sugar over the crêpes and carefully pour over any remaining orange butter.

Warm the remaining orange-flavored liqueur and the brandy in a small saucepan. Pour over the crêpes and ignite. Shake the dish gently and serve when the flames have died away.
Serves 4-6

This decorative Valentine's Cake makes a unique present for someone special on St. Valentine's Day.

Mothering Sunday

Falling on the fourth Sunday in Lent, this is named for the custom of the faithful attending the mother church in which they had been baptized. Gifts were offered at the altar to the church, and to their mothers as tokens of love and gratitude.

The Simnel Cake, traditionally baked for Mothering Sunday, is topped by almond paste balls said to represent the Apostles. Interestingly, in ancient Rome, Roman matrons honored Juno and her son Mars during the festival of Matronalia by baking ball-topped cakes.

The cake has a central layer of marzipan which is cooked with the cake mixture. The top, which is decorated with another layer of marzipan, is broiled or baked until it turns golden brown.

Simnel cake

185g/1½ cups flour
25g/¼ cup rice flour
1 tsp baking powder
185g/¾ cup sugar
185g/¾ cup butter
3 eggs
185g/1 cup raisins
185g/1 cup currants
125g/⅔ cup candied cherries,
finely chopped
grated rind of 1 lemon
2 Tbsp candied lemon peel,
finely chopped
1 tsp grated orange rind
ALMOND PASTE
500g/4 cups ground almonds
375g/2 cups confectioners' sugar
125g/½ cup sugar
2-3 egg yolks
½ tsp almond extract
APRICOT GLAZE
4 Tbsp apricot jam
75ml/⅓ cup water
1 tsp lemon juice

Sift the flour, rice flour and baking powder into a mixing bowl. In another bowl, cream the sugar and butter together until the mixture is light and fluffy. Beat in the eggs, one at a time, with a tablespoon of the flour mixture between each. Fold in half the remaining flour. Mix the remaining flour with the raisins, currants, candied cherries, lemon rind, candied lemon peel and grated orange rind, stirring to coat the fruit well. Carefully fold the flour and fruit mixture into the batter, using a wooden spoon.

To make the almond paste, sift the almonds, confectioners' sugar and sugar into a mixing bowl. Add two of the egg yolks and the almond extract and mix together with your fingertips. Add the remaining egg yolk if the mixture is too dry. Turn the almond paste out onto a surface dusted with confectioners' sugar or cornstarch and knead the mixture for 5 minutes or until it is very smooth and rather shiny.

Cut off one-third of the almond paste and shape into a 16cm/6½in circle. Spoon half the cake mixture into a deep 18cm/7in diameter cake pan that has been lined with greased wax paper. Smooth the surface of the cake mixture and place the almond paste circle on top. Cover with the remaining cake mixture and smooth the surface. Bake in a moderate oven (180°C/350°F) for 1½ hours. Reduce the temperature to cool (150°C/300°F) and continue baking for 1 to 1¼ hours or until a skewer inserted into the center comes out clean and the cake is firm.

Allow the cake to cool in the pan for 5 minutes, then turn out onto a wire rack and set aside at room temperature to cool completely.

Meanwhile, make the apricot glaze. Put the jam and water in a saucepan and cook gently for 5 minutes. Stir in the lemon juice, then remove from the heat and strain well.

Brush the top of the cake with most of the apricot glaze. Cut off half the remaining almond paste and roll out to a circle the same diameter as the top of the cake. Lay on top of the cake. Roll the remaining almond paste into 11 balls. Brush the balls with the remaining apricot glaze and gently and carefully press around the edge of the almond paste top.

Place the cake on an ovenproof dish and bake in a hot oven (220°C/425°F) for 5 to 8 minutes or until the tops of the balls are golden brown.
Allow to cool before serving.
Makes one 18cm/7in cake

Opposite: Simnel Cake – a traditional British cake originally given to mothers by girls in domestic service as a gift on Mothering Sunday, although nowadays it is often served at Easter.
Left: Each of the eleven glazed marzipan balls represents one of the Apostles.

Passover

This Jewish festival runs from the fifteenth to the twenty-second day of the lunar month Nisan. It gives thanks for the deliverance of the Hebrews from Egyptian bondage in the thirteenth century BC. On the first and second nights of Passover, there is a ceremony called a Seder with unleavened bread, or matzo, and bitter herbs symbolizing the Exodus. Matzo Brei and the carrot candies, Ingber, are made with ingredients symbolically linked to the Passover.

Ingber (carrot candies)

450g/1¾ cups sugar
3 Tbsp water
500g/1lb carrots, scraped and grated
½ tsp green ginger, peeled and finely chopped
60g/½ cup walnuts, finely chopped
2 Tbsp lemon juice

Dissolve the sugar in the water in a saucepan over low heat. Stir in the carrots, then bring to a boil. Boil for 30 minutes or until the mixture is very thick.

Remove from the heat and stir in the ginger, walnuts and lemon juice. Pour into a greased 15cm/6in square cake pan. Allow to cool, then cut into 2.5cm/1in squares. When the candies are completely cool and set, remove from the pan.
Makes about 20

Matzo brei (scrambled eggs with matzos)

2 matzos, broken into 5cm/2in pieces
125ml/½ cup milk
2 eggs, lightly beaten
salt
pinch grated nutmeg
2 Tbsp vegetable fat or oil

Put the matzo pieces in a mixing bowl and pour over the milk. Leave to soak for 5 minutes. Pour off any excess milk and add the eggs, salt to taste and the nutmeg. Mix well.

Melt the butter in a saucepan. Pour in the matzo mixture and cook, stirring occasionally, until the eggs are lightly scrambled. Serve hot.
Serves 2

April/May - Good Friday

The cross on the Hot Cross Bun, traditionally baked for this holy day, is said to symbolize Christ's cross. Originally, the Greeks and Romans had similar cakes for festivals, with the sun symbol – a circle – divided into quarters by a cross, to represent the four seasons. Serve Hot Cross Buns, split and toasted, with lots of butter.

Hot cross buns

½ cake compressed yeast
250ml/1 cup milk, lukewarm
500g/4 cups flour
½ tsp salt
1 tsp ground allspice
1 tsp ground cinnamon
60g/¼ cup sugar
2 eggs
60g/¼ cup butter, melted
60g/⅓ cup raisins
60g/⅓ cup mixed candied peel, chopped
CROSSES
1 Tbsp butter
30g/¼ cup flour
1 tsp cold water
GLAZE
2 Tbsp milk
1 tsp sugar

Mash the yeast to a paste with 2 tablespoons of the milk. Set aside in a warm, draft-free place until frothy. Sift the flour, salt, spice, cinnamon and sugar into a mixing bowl. Make a well in the center and add the yeast mixture, remaining milk, eggs and melted butter. Gradually draw the flour mixture into the liquids and continue mixing until the flour is incorporated and the dough comes away from the bowl.

Turn out of the bowl and knead for 10 minutes or until the dough is smooth and elastic. Return to a greased bowl, cover and leave to rise in a warm, draft-free place for 1 hour or until almost doubled in bulk.

Punch down the dough and knead again. Knead in the raisins and candied peel. Divide the dough into sixteen pieces and form into bun shapes. Place on two greased baking sheets, leaving 5cm/2in space between each bun, and let rise for 15 to 20 minutes.

Meanwhile, make the dough for the crosses. Rub the butter into the flour until the mixture resembles breadcrumbs. Stir in the cold water to bind the mixture, then knead to a dough. Roll out to a rectangle about 3mm/⅛in thick and cut into 32 strips 5cm/2in long. Press two strips, in a cross, on the top of each bun.

Mix together the milk and sugar for the glaze and brush over the buns. Bake in a very hot oven (230°C/450°F) for 15 minutes or until the buns are a deep golden.
Makes 16

Above, right: Traditionally eaten during Passover, Ingber or Ingberlach are unusual carrot and walnut candies. Old carrots are best for this recipe.
Below, right: Decorated with a cross, Hot Cross Buns are a traditional British treat eaten on Good Friday.

April/May – Easter Sunday

A moveable feast day, Easter Sunday falls on the first Sunday after the first full moon after the vernal or Spring equinox. Called Ostern in Germany, Pasqua in Italy, Pâques in France, Pasha in Greece and Paske in Norway, it is, along with Christmas, the most important Christian religious festival. The recipes given are traditional for Easter – Cassata alla Siciliana, an Italian chocolate cake, Greek Easter lamb, Russian Kulich (a fruit bread) and finally, our American Easter Bunny cookies.

Cassata alla Siciliana (Italian chocolate cake)

1 pound cake, 23cm/9in long and
8cm/3in wide
500g/1lb ricotta cheese
2 Tbsp heavy cream
60g/¼ cup sugar
2½ Tbsp orange-flavored liqueur
2 Tbsp mixed candied fruit, chopped
1 Tbsp pistachio nuts, chopped
2 squares semi sweet chocolate, grated
CHOCOLATE FROSTING
12 squares semisweet chocolate,
broken into small pieces
185ml/¾ cup black coffee
250g/1 cup unsalted butter, cut into
small pieces and chilled

Cut the cake lengthwise into 1cm/½in slices. Press the ricotta through a strainer into a mixing bowl. Beat until it is smooth, then beat in the cream, sugar and liqueur. Fold in the candied fruit, nuts and grated chocolate.

Place one slice of cake on a flat plate and spread with one-third of the ricotta mixture. Place another slice of cake on top and spread with another third of the ricotta mixture. Make another layer in this way and finish with the last slice of cake. Gently press the loaf together. Wrap the cake in foil and chill in the refrigerator for 3 hours.

Melt the chocolate with the coffee in a saucepan. Remove from the heat and beat in the butter, a piece at a time. Continue beating until the mixture is smooth, then allow to cool until the frosting is thick enough to spread.

Cover the top and sides of the cake with the frosting, reserving a little for decoration. Pipe the reserved frosting on top in swirls. Chill the cake for at least 12 hours before serving.
Serves 8-10

Kulich (Russian Easter bread)

1½ cakes compressed yeast
225ml/⅞ cup lukewarm milk
60g/⅓ cup raisins
3 Tbsp rum
750g/6 cups flour
275g/1½ cups confectioners' sugar
½ tsp salt
½ tsp vanilla extract
9 egg yolks
250g/1 cup unsalted butter, softened
½ tsp saffron powder
1 Tbsp hot water
60g/½ cup blanched almonds, shredded
60g/⅓ cup candied peel, chopped
FROSTING
250g/1⅓ cups confectioners' sugar
3 Tbsp cold water
1 tsp lemon juice

Mash the yeast and 1 tablespoon of the milk to make a paste. Leave in a warm, draft-free place until frothy. Meanwhile, soak the raisins in the rum for 15 minutes.

Sift the flour, confectioners' sugar and salt into a mixing bowl. Make a well in the center and add the yeast mixture and remaining milk. Gradually mix the flour into the liquid. Beat in the vanilla, then the egg yolks, one at a time. Gradually beat in the softened butter.

Dissolve the saffron in the hot water and stir into the dough. Turn out of the bowl and knead for 10 minutes or until smooth and elastic. Return to a greased bowl and leave to rise in a warm place for 1 to 1½ hours or until doubled in bulk.

Toast the almonds under the broiler until they are golden brown. Add to the soaked raisins with the candied peel. Punch down the dough. Add the fruit and nuts and knead to distribute them evenly. Put the dough into a greased and lined coffee can or tall cylindrical mold that is about 15cm/6in in diameter and 18cm/7in tall. Leave to rise in a warm place for 30 minutes.

Bake in a fairly hot oven (200°C/400°F) for 40 minutes. Reduce the temperature to moderate (180°C/350°F) and continue baking for 1 hour.

Cool in the can for 10 minutes, then cool completely, standing upright, on a wire rack.

To make the frosting, sift the confectioners' sugar into a mixing bowl. Add the water and lemon juice and mix to a thin paste. Pour this frosting over the top of the cooled bread and allow it to trickle down the sides. Allow the frosting to set before serving.
Makes one 1.5kg/3lb bread

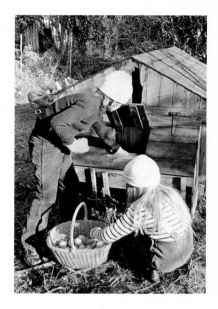

Left: Topped with icing, Kulich is one of the traditional foods cooked for the Russian Orthodox Easter celebrations and is rich with rum, almonds, eggs and fruit.
Above: Eggs are universal symbols of creation. Decorating them for gifts and festive occasions is a traditional and favorite pastime with children at Easter.

Easter bunnies

6 Tbsp butter
60g/¼ cup plus 1 Tbsp sugar
1 egg, separated
185g/1½ cups flour
1½ tsp baking powder
¼ tsp salt
2 Tbsp warm milk

Cream the butter and all but 1 tablespoon of the sugar together until the mixture is light and fluffy. Beat in the egg yolk. Sift together the flour, baking powder and salt and fold into the creamed mixture. Stir in the milk. Chill the dough for 1 hour.

Roll out the dough to 6mm/¼in thick. Cut out ten 5cm/2in circles, ten 2.5cm/1in circles, twenty 2cm/¾in circles and ten 1cm/½in circles. Make up the bunnies on a greased baking sheet, using the 5cm/2in circles for the bodies, the 2.5cm/1in circles for the heads and the 1cm/½in circles for the tails. Shape the 2cm/¾in circles into ovals for the ears.

Bake the bunnies in a fairly hot oven (200°C/400°F) for 10 minutes. Coat the bunnies with the lightly beaten egg white and sprinkle with the remaining sugar. Bake for a further 10 minutes or until the bunnies are golden brown. Cool.

For an extra touch you might pipe the names of your children on the bunnies.
Makes 10

Greek Easter lamb

1 × 2.5kg/5lb leg of lamb
2 garlic cloves, cut into slivers
1 Tbsp rosemary, freshly chopped
salt and black pepper
60g/¼ cup butter
250g/1 cup lima beans (shelled)
4 small onions
6 medium potatoes, peeled and thinly sliced
625ml/2½ cups chicken stock

Make several incisions in the lamb and insert the garlic slivers in them. Rub the meat with the rosemary and salt and pepper and lay the rosemary sprigs over the fat. Put the meat on a rack in a roasting pan and cover with the butter. Roast in a very hot oven (230°C/450°F) for 10 minutes.

Baste the lamb with the fat in the pan and arrange the beans, onions and potatoes around the meat. Pour the stock over the vegetables. Return to a moderate oven (180°C/350°F) and continue roasting to 2 to 2¼ hours or until the lamb is cooked.

Transfer the lamb to a warmed serving dish and surround with the vegetables.
Serves 6

July 4 - Independence Day, U.S.A.

On July 4, 1776, the Continental Congress adopted the Declaration of Independence, thereby severing the ties between England and the American colonies. Every year on this day, we celebrate with fireworks, parades and patriotic fervor. Why not celebrate by making two typically American recipes, Southern-fried Chicken and Devil's Food Cake.

Devil's food cake

4 squares semisweet chocolate
250ml/1 cup milk
185g/1 cup brown sugar
3 egg yolks
300g/2½ cups flour
1 tsp baking soda
pinch salt
125g/½ cup butter
185g/¾ cup sugar
4 Tbsp water
1 tsp vanilla extract
2 egg whites
CHOCOLATE FUDGE FROSTING
250ml/1 cup light cream
500g/2 cups sugar
pinch salt
2 squares semisweet chocolate, grated
3 Tbsp butter
½ tsp vanilla extract
60g/½ cup walnuts, chopped

Put the chocolate, milk, brown sugar and one egg yolk in the top of a double boiler or in a heatproof bowl over a pan of hot water. Heat gently, stirring, until the chocolate melts and the sugar dissolves. Remove from the heat. Sift the flour, soda and salt into a mixing bowl.

Cream the butter and sugar together in another mixing bowl until the mixture is light and fluffy. Beat in the remaining egg yolks, one at a time. Mix in one-third of the flour, then half the water. Add the remaining flour and water and beat until the batter is smooth. Stir in the vanilla extract and chocolate mixture until they are well blended.

Beat the egg whites until they will hold a stiff peak. Fold into the chocolate batter. Spoon into three greased 20cm/8in layer cake pans. Bake in a moderate oven (180°C/350°F) for 25 minutes or until a skewer inserted into the centers comes out clean. Turn the cake layers out onto a wire rack and allow to cool.

To make the frosting, scald the cream in a saucepan. Remove from the heat and stir in the sugar, salt and grated chocolate. Return to the heat and stir to melt the chocolate, then cover and cook for 3 minutes. Uncover the pan and boil until the mixture reaches 115°C/238°F on a sugar thermometer (the soft ball stage). Remove from the heat and place the bottom of the pan in cold water.

When the mixture has cooled to 43°C/110°F, beat in the butter and vanilla. Continue beating until the frosting is thick and of a spreading consistency. Stir in the walnuts.

Sandwich the three cake layers together with three-quarters of the frosting and cover the tops and sides with the remainder.

Serves 8-10

Southern fried chicken

350ml/1½ cups milk
5 Tbsp flour
salt and black pepper
4 chicken breasts
1 egg
1 tsp water
90g/1 cup fresh white breadcrumbs
125g/½ cup butter
3 Tbsp vegetable oil
½ tsp sugar

Put 3 tablespoons of milk in a saucer. Mix together 4 tablespoons of the flour with salt and pepper on a plate. Dip the chicken breasts in the milk and then in the seasoned flour. Leave to dry for 10 minutes.

Lightly beat the egg with the water on a plate. Put the breadcrumbs on another plate. Dip the chicken breasts in the egg and then in the breadcrumbs, coating well.

Melt three-quarters of the butter with the oil in a frying pan. Add the chicken breasts and cook, turning occasionally, for 20 minutes. Drain the chicken on paper towels and transfer to a warmed serving dish. Keep hot.

Melt the remaining butter in a saucepan. Stir in the sugar and cook, stirring, until the mixture turns dark brown. Stir in the remaining flour and cook, stirring, for 1 minute. Remove from the heat and gradually stir in the remaining milk. Return to the heat and bring to a boil. Simmer, stirring, until thickened and smooth. Pour this into a gravyboat and serve with the chicken.

Serves 4

This famous American dish has almost as many 'correct' versions as there are states. Here, Southern Fried Chicken is served with fried bananas, bacon rolls and horseradish sauce although other accompaniments may include corn fritters, potato pancakes, boiled rice, or mashed potatoes – so it's up to you to choose!

The pumpkin is an autumn fruit which is traditionally served on Thanksgiving.

September 29 – Michaelmas Day

Michaelmas is the feast day of the arch-angel, St. Michael. It marked the end of the agricultural hire year when men were free to seek fresh employment – and when tenants had to pay their quarterly rent. To appease the landlord, it was the custom to give a fat goose, which had fed on corn stubble after the harvest. In Ireland there is an old saying that if you eat goose on Michaelmas Day, you will never want for money all the year round! So here, to help you celebrate Michaelmas, is a recipe for a succulent stuffed goose.

Michaelmas goose

1 × 3.5-4kg/8-9lb goose
1 lemon, quartered
salt and black pepper
STUFFING
6 large potatoes, peeled
1 medium onion, chopped
4 bacon slices, finely diced
salt and black pepper
375g/12oz pork sausagemeat
1 Tbsp parsley, freshly chopped
1 tsp thyme, freshly chopped
1 tsp sage, freshly chopped
ONION SAUCE
4 medium onions, chopped
150ml/⅔ cup water
150ml/⅔ cup milk
2.5cm/1in thick slice of turnip
60g/¼ cup butter
1 tsp grated nutmeg
salt and black pepper
4 Tbsp light cream
APPLE SAUCE
2 large cooking apples, peeled, cored and chopped
125ml/½ cup water
2 Tbsp butter
2 Tbsp sugar
1 tsp lemon juice
pinch salt

Prick the goose all over and rub the skin with three of the lemon quarters. Squeeze the juice from the remaining lemon quarter into the cavity in the goose. Rub the skin with salt and pepper.

To make the stuffing, cook the potatoes in boiling salted water for 15 to 20 minutes or until they are tender. Drain well and mash to a smooth purée. Allow to cool, then stir in the remaining stuffing ingredients with salt and pepper to taste. Spoon the stuffing into the goose and close the opening with a skewer or trussing needle and string.

Place the goose, on its breast, on a rack in a roasting pan. Roast in a very hot oven (230°C/450°F) for 30 minutes. Reduce the temperature to moderate (180°C/350°F) and continue roasting for 3 hours 20 minutes. Remove the fat from the pan occasionally. To test if the goose is cooked, pierce the thigh with a skewer: the juices should run clear.

Meanwhile, prepare the sauces. To make the onion sauce, put the onions, water, milk and turnip in a saucepan and bring to a boil. Simmer for 20 minutes or until the onions are very soft and beginning to pulp. Remove from the heat and beat in the butter, nutmeg and salt and pepper to taste. When the mixture is smooth, stir in the cream. Keep hot.

To make the applesauce, put the apples and water in a saucepan and cook until the apples are soft and pulpy. Remove from the heat and purêe in a food mill or by pushing through a strainer. Stir in the remaining sauce ingredients and keep hot.

Transfer the goose to a carving board and serve with the onion- and applesauces. *Serves 6-8*

November 5 – Guy Fawkes' Day

In 1605, the hapless Guy Fawkes and his fellow Roman Catholic conspirators attempted to blow up the British Parliament. The Gunpowder Plot, as it became known, was discovered, and Guy Fawkes is still being punished today – once a year, on November 5, all over England he is burned as a straw effigy at the top of a bonfire. Gingerbread, often in the shape of a man – Guy Fawkes again? – and toffee are enjoyed during the festivities.

Gingerbread

250g/2 cups flour
½ tsp baking soda
1½ tsp ground ginger
¼ tsp ground cloves
½ tsp ground cinnamon
¼ tsp salt
6 Tbsp butter
125g/½ cup sugar
1 egg
185ml/¾ cup molasses
250ml/1 cup sour cream

Sift the flour, soda, ginger, cloves, cinnamon and salt into a mixing bowl. Cream the butter and sugar together in another bowl until the mixture is light and fluffy. Beat in the egg and molasses, then stir in the sour cream. Gradually stir the flour mixture into the molasses mixture.

Pour into a greased large loaf pan. Bake in a moderate oven (180°C/350°F) for 1¼ hours or until a skewer inserted into the centre comes out clean. Allow to cool on a wire rack.

Makes one 1kg/2lb bread

Toffee

375g/2 cups brown sugar
6 Tbsp butter
1 Tbsp light corn syrup
2 tsp dark vinegar
3 tbsp water

Put all the ingredients in a saucepan and stir over gentle heat to dissolve the sugar. Bring to a boil and boil until the mixture reaches 163°C/325°F on a sugar or candy thermometer (the hard crack stage). Alternatively, test by dripping a little of the mixture into cold water. If it sets and is hard and crunchy, the toffee is ready. Remove from the heat and allow to cool for 10 minutes.

Pour the toffee into a greased 15cm/6in square cake pan. Leave until cool but not set. Cut into 2.5cm/1in squares with an oiled knife. Leave until completely cold, them remove from the pan and break into pieces. Wrap each in a piece of wax paper and store in an airtight tin.

Makes 60

November -
Thanksgiving

On the fourth Thursday in November, we celebrate the feast of Thanksgiving, which harks back to the first harvest feast enjoyed by the Pilgrims, having survived their first winter in the New World. Foods that are traditional Thanksgiving fare were eaten then – turkey, corn, sweet potatoes, pumpkins – and here are recipes for a delicious and unusual roast stuffed turkey and pumpkin pie.

Pumpkin pie

PASTRY
185g/1½ cups flour
¼ tsp salt
6 Tbsp butter
2-3 Tbsp iced water
FILLING
125g/⅔ cup brown sugar
pinch salt
1½ tsp ground cinnamon
½ tsp ground ginger
¼ tsp ground cloves
750g/1½lb can pureed pumpkin
3 eggs, lightly beaten
300ml/1¼ cups light cream

To make the pastry, sift the flour and salt into a mixing bowl. Add the butter and cut into small pieces, then rub the fat into the flour until the mixture resembles breadcrumbs. Stir in enough of the water to bind the mixture, then knead to a dough. Chill for 30 minutes.

Roll out the dough and use to line a 23cm/9in pie plate.

Mix together all the ingredients for the filling. Pour into the dough-lined pie plate. Bake in a fairly hot oven (190°C/375°F) for 45 to 50 minutes or until a knife inserted into the filling comes out clean. Allow to cool before serving.

Serves 6-8

A favorite with children – and many adults, too – toffee is easy to make; but it is important to use a large saucepan, as the syrup boils up quickly.

Roast turkey with pumpkin and pork and cranberry stuffings

1 × 4.5kg-10lb turkey, liver reserved and
finely chopped
salt and black pepper
125g/½ cup butter, melted
4 Tbsp apricot jam
150ml/⅔ cup white wine
2 Tbsp flour
1 Tbsp butter
PUMPKIN STUFFING
60g/¼ cup butter
2 medium onions, finely chopped
300g/2½ cups pumpkin, peeled, seeded
and grated
2 large carrots, scraped and grated
salt and black pepper
2 tsp sugar
½ tsp grated nutmeg
4 Tbsp heavy cream

PORK AND CRANBERRY STUFFING
2 Tbsp butter
1 medium onion, finely chopped
300g/10 oz pork sausagemeat
125g/½ cup cranberry jelly
1½ tsp dried basil
salt and black pepper
60g/½ cup blanched almonds, chopped

Rub the turkey, inside and out, with salt and pepper.

To make the pumpkin stuffing, melt the butter in a saucepan. Add the onions, pumpkin and carrots and fry until the onions are soft but not brown. Stir in salt and pepper to taste, the sugar, nutmeg and cream. Cook gently for 10 minutes or until the pumpkin is tender and most of the liquid has evaporated. Remove from the heat and allow to cool.

To make the pork and cranberry stuffing, melt the butter in a frying pan. Add the onion and fry until it is soft but not brown. Stir in the sausagemeat and fry until the meat loses its pinkness. Add the turkey liver, cranberry jelly, basil, salt and pepper to taste and the almonds. Cook for a further 3 minutes. Remove the frying pan from the heat, set aside and allow the mixture to cool.

Fill the neck end of the turkey with as much of the pumpkin stuffing as it will hold. Secure the flap with a skewer or trussing needle and string. Put any remaining pumpkin stuffing in the vent end and follow with the pork and cranberry stuffing. Secure that opening with a skewer or trussing needle and string.

Brush the turkey with some of the melted butter. Place it, breast side down, in a roasting pan. Pour over the remaining melted butter. Roast in a hot oven (220°C/425°F) for 15 minutes. Reduce the temperature to moderate (180°C/350°F) and continue roasting for 2¼ hours, basting occasionally with the melted butter in the pan.

Turn the turkey onto its back and brush with the jam. Pour over the wine and roast for a further 30 minutes or until the skin is golden brown and the turkey is cooked. To test, pierce the thigh with a skewer or a sharp fork: the juices that run out should be clear.

Transfer the turkey to a carving board and remove the skewers or string. Pour 350ml/1½ cups of the liquid from the pan into a saucepan. Bring to a boil and boil for 5 minutes. Blend the flour and butter together to make a paste and add in small pieces to the cooking liquid. Simmer, stirring, until the mixture is thickened and smooth. Keep warm. Pour into a gravy-boat and serve this delicious gravy as an accompaniment to the turkey.
Serves 8-10

Below, left : This mouth-watering recipe for Roast Turkey will certainly turn a Thanksgiving dinner into a feast. It should be served with sweet potatoes and is delicious with chilled white wine.
Below, right : Corn dollies, made as long ago as 5000 years, were generally made as fertility symbols. After the last sheaf of harvest was cut it would be made into a corn dolly and great feasting and celebration would take place.

December 25 - Christmas Day

Christmas is surely the happiest and most welcomed of all Christian celebrations. All over the Christian world, Christmas Day feasting is long and joyous. From Britain we have a recipe for steamed Christmas pudding, from Germany a rich yeast fruit cake, from West India a spicy meat mold and, enjoyed everywhere, mincemeat pies and a wassail bowl. The wassail bowl takes its name from the Saxon toast, "Waes Hael" – Good Health.

It is traditional, when making a Christmas Pudding, for each member of the family to take a turn stirring the pudding mixture, wishing for health and prosperity for the family. The stirring must be done clockwise as that is the direction the sun moves around an earth at the center of the universe – to stir "widdershins" invites trouble. Tokens may be added to the mixture – a silver coin signifying wealth, a ring for marriage, a thimble for spinsterhood, a button for bachelorhood. Whoever finds a token when eating the pudding has his or her future predicted!

Christmas pudding

250g/2 cups self-raising flour
1 tsp salt
1 tsp grated nutmeg
1 tsp ground cinnamon
1 tsp ground cloves
375g/4 cups fresh breadcrumbs
357g/1½ cups shredded beef suet
500g/2⅔ cups brown sugar
500g/2⅔ cups currants
1kg/8 cups raisins
125g/⅔ cup candied peel, chopped
60g/⅓ cup candied cherries, chopped
60g/⅓ cup blanched almonds, shredded
2 medium cooking apples, peeled, cored and grated
finely grated rind and juice of 1 orange
finely grated rind and juice of ½ lemon
6 eggs
150ml/⅔ cup milk
75ml/⅓ cup brandy (optional)

Sift the flour, salt, nutmeg, cinnamon and cloves into a mixing bowl. Add the breadcrumbs, suet, sugar, currants, raisins, candied peel, cherries and almonds. Mix well, then stir in the apples and lemon and orange rinds.

Lightly beat the eggs, milk, orange juice and lemon juice together. Stir into the dry ingredients until they are thoroughly moistened. Spoon into two greased 2¼

pint capacity steaming molds, carefully packing down well and slightly coming the tops.

Cover the molds with a lid of greased wax paper and foil, making a pleat in the center to allow for expansion. Tie on securely with string. Steam for 6 hours, replenishing the boiling water when necessary.

Allow the puddings to cool, then re-cover with fresh wax paper and foil. Set aside and store in a cool, dry place until Christmas.

To prepare for serving, steam the puddings for a further 3 hours, replenishing the boiling water when necessary. Turn out the puddings onto a warmed serving dish and pour over the brandy, if you are using it. Set alight and serve while still flaming.

Makes two large puddings

Stollen (German fruit bread)

½ cake compressed yeast
1 Tbsp lukewarm water
125g/½ cup butter
185ml/¾ cup milk
500g/4 cups flour
1tsp salt
½ tsp ground cinnamon
¼ tsp ground mace
¼ tsp ground cardamom
185g/¾ cup sugar
2 eggs, lightly beaten
185g/1 cup candied peel, chopped
90g/½ cup raisins
60g/½ cup walnuts, chopped
FROSTING
2 Tbsp butter, melted
250g/1⅓ cups confectioners' sugar
2 Tbsp water
¼ tsp vanilla extract
DECORATION
16 walnut halves

Mash the yeast and water to a paste and set aside in a warm, draft-free place until the mixture is frothy. Meanwhile, scale the milk. Remove from the heat and add the butter. When it has melted, set aside to cool to lukewarm.

Sift the flour, salt and spices into a mixing bowl. Make a well in the center and add the sugar, yeast mixture, milk mixture and eggs. Mix well, gradually drawing the flour into the liquid. Turn the dough out of the bowl and knead for 10 minutes or until it is smooth and elastic. Return to a greased bowl and leave to rise in a warm place for 1 to 1½ hours or until doubled in bulk.

Punch down the dough and knead for 4

Above: Evergreen trees are traditionally set up at Christmas and hung with candles, presents and decorations.
Left: This delicious spicy fruit bread – Stollen – is a German speciality and is traditionally served at Christmas.

minutes. Knead in the candied peel, raisins and walnuts to distribute them evenly. Shape the dough into a rounded crescent and place on a greased baking sheet. Leave in a warm place for 30 to 45 minutes to rise.

Bake in a fairly hot oven (200°C/400°F) for 15 minutes. Reduce the temperature to moderate (180°C/350°F) and continue baking for 30 minutes. To test if the stollen is cooked, rap the bottom with your knuckles: it should sound hollow like a drum. Allow to cool on a wire rack.

To make the frosting, beat all the ingredients together until the mixture is smooth. Spread the frosting over the top of the stollen and allow it to drip down the sides. Decorate the top with the walnut halves.
Makes one 1.5kg/3lb loaf

Wassail bowl

2l/4 pints beer
300ml/1¼ cup medium sweet sherry
¼ tsp grated nutmeg
pinch ground cinnamon
pinch ground ginger
pared rind of 2 lemons
125g/⅔ cup brown sugar
4 red-skinned apples, baked for 10 minutes and kept warm
4 Tbsp brandy

Put the beer, sherry, nutmeg, cinnamon, ginger, lemon rind and brown sugar in a saucepan and stir over gentle heat to dissolve the sugar. Bring to just below boiling point, then remove the pan from the heat.

Put the apples in a heatproof punch bowl. Warm the brandy in a ladle and ignite it. Pour it flaming over the apples, then pour over the beer mixture. Serve hot.
Serves 18-20

Mince pies

500-700g/1-1½lb mincemeat
3 Tbsp milk
2 Tbsp sugar
PASTRY
375g/3 cups flour
¼tsp salt
6 Tbsp butter
6 Tbsp shortening
2-3 Tbsp iced water

To make the pastry, sift the flour and salt into a mixing bowl. Add the butter and shortening and cut into small pieces, then rub the fat into the flour until the mixture resembles breadcrumbs. Stir in enough water to bind the mixture and knead to a dough. Chill in the refrigerator for 30 minutes.

Roll out two-thirds of the dough to about 6mm/¼in thick. Cut out sixteen 8cm/3in circles. Use to line sixteen muffin pans. Place a spoonful of mincemeat in each dough-lined pan. Roll out the remaining dough to 6mm/¼in thick and cut out sixteen 6cm/2½in circles. Use these as lids and carefully press the edges together to seal.

Brush the pies with milk and bake in a fairly hot oven (200°C/400°F) for 20 minutes or until the pastry is golden brown. Sprinkle with the sugar and serve warm or cold.
Makes 16

Mincemeat

125g/½ cup beef suet, ground or finely chopped
125g/⅔ cup currants
250g/1⅓ cups raisins
1 medium cooking apple, peeled, cored and grated
2 Tbsp mixed candied peel, chopped
½ tsp grated orange rind
½ tsp grated lemon rind
1 Tbsp orange juice
1 tsp lemon juice
3 Tbsp dry sherry
pinch grated nutmeg
pinch ground cinnamon
pinch ground allspice
pinch ground mace
1½ Tbsp ground almonds
1½ Tbsp brandy

Mix together all the ingredients except the brandy. Spoon the mincemeat into clean dry jam or canning jars, filling them to within 2.5cm/1in of the tops. Sprinkle a little brandy over each and cover the jars. Leave in a cool, dark, dry place for at least 1 month before using.
Makes about 750g/1½lb

December 31-Hogmanay

The last day of the year is called Hogmanay in Scotland and some parts of the North of England and, as may be expected, is observed with much sampling of Scotland's fine whiskey. Also traditional on this day are Black Bun, a rich fruit cake encased in pastry, and Shortbread.

Shortbread is often formed into shapes in special shortbread molds. These are made of wood and have a thistle pattern imprinted on the bottom.

Black bun

PASTRY
350g/3 cups flour
¼ tsp salt
6 Tbsp butter
2 Tbsp sugar
2 small eggs, lightly beaten
4-6 Tbsp iced water
FILLING
250g/2 cups flour
1 tsp baking soda
1½ tsp baking powder
125g/⅔ cup brown sugar
1 tsp ground allspice
½ tsp ground cinnamon
½ tsp ground ginger
¼ tsp ground mace
350g/2 cups raisins
350g/2 cups currants
125g/1 cup almonds, chopped
125g/1 cup walnuts, chopped
125g/⅔ cup mixed candied peel, chopped
grated rind and juice of 1 lemon
185ml/¾ cup milk
1 Tbsp brandy
1 egg, lightly beaten

First make the pastry. Sift the flour and salt into a mixing bowl. Add the butter and cut into small pieces, then rub the fat into the flour until the mixture resembles breadcrumbs. Stir in the sugar. Stir in the eggs with enough of the water to bind the mixture and knead to a dough. Chill for 30 minutes.

Roll out just over two-thirds of the dough to a circle about 1cm/½in thick. Use to line a deep 18cm/7in diameter cake pan. Chill while you make the filling.

Sift the flour, soda and baking powder into a mixing bowl. Stir in the brown sugar, spices, raisins, currants, almonds, walnuts, candied peel and lemon rind and juice. Mix in the milk and brandy. Spoon into the dough-lined cake pan and smooth the top.

Roll out the remaining piece of dough to a circle large enough to cover the top of the pan. Place over the filling and press the edges together to seal. Cut a cross in the center of the dough top and brush with the beaten egg. Bake in a fairly hot oven (200°C/400°F) for 15 minutes. Cover with foil and reduce the temperature to warm (170°C/325°F). Continue baking for 3½ hours or until a skewer inserted into the center cross comes out clean.

Turn the cake out of the pan and cool on a wire rack. Wrap in foil and leave for at least 1 week before serving.
Makes one 18cm/7in cake

A Scottish specialty, this unusual, rich fruit cake encased in a sweet crisp pastry is a great favorite at Hogmanay.

Shortbread is another favorite at Hogmanay, and is offered to every guest in a Scottish home on New Year's Eve – along with a glass of whiskey.

Shortbread

250g/2 cups flour
125g/1 cup rice flour
125g/½ cup plus 1 Tbsp sugar
250g/1 cup butter

Sift the flour and rice flour into a mixing bowl. Stir in all but 1 tablespoon of the sugar. Add the butter and cut it into small pieces, then rub the fat into the dry ingredients until the mixture resembles breadcrumbs. Knead gently to form a smooth dough.

Divide the dough in half and form each piece into a circle about 1cm/½in thick and 15cm/6in in diameter. Transfer the circles to a greased baking sheet. Crimp the edges to make a decorative effect and prick the top with a fork. Chill for 20 minutes.

Bake the shortbread in a moderate oven (180°C/350°F) for 10 minutes. Reduce the temperature to cool (150°C/300°F) and continue baking for 30 to 40 minutes or until the shortbread is crisp and lightly browned.

Cut the shortbread circles into triangles and allow to cool slightly on the baking sheet. Sprinkle with the sugar and cool completely on a wire rack.
Makes two 15cm/6in circles

Index

Pictures supplied by:
Bernard Alfieri: 118T; 199T
Heather Angel: 94B
Rex Bamber: 107
Steve Bicknell: 193
Pat Brindley: 57T
Barry Bullough: 87L
Camera Press: 195
Patrick Cocklin: 178
Delu/PAF International: 18; 37; 62;
72; 103
Alan Duns: 9; 12; 17; 22; 26; 31;
34L; 34R; 39T; 46; 49; 59TR;
66L; 68; 69; 75B 78; 81B; 82T;
88; 99; 105; 109; 116; 117R;
118B; 119B; 121; 123; 127; 129;
138T; 138B; 146/147; 161; 181;
197T&B
V Finnis: 23
P Hunt: 86
George Hyde: 171
Paul Kemp: 13; 16; 27; 31B;
38; 44; 55; 56; 67; 154; 185
Don Last: 14; 102; 125; 126
Michael Leale: 80
John Lee: 81
Max Logan: 76; 167T
David Meldrum: 19; 35; 42/3; 73;
75T; 104; 162
M. Nimmo: 155
Stanli Opperman: 53; 149
Roger Phillips: FC; 6/7; 10; 11;
20/1; 28; 30; 32; 33; 40; 47; 48; 50;
57B; 58; 60/1; 63; 66R; 70; 74; 77;
79T; 79B; 82B; 83; 85; 87R; 89;
90/1; 93; 95; 96; 97; 100; 101; 111;
112; 114; 115; 117; 120; 124; 128;
131; 132/3; 135; 139; 141; 144; 145;
153; 156; 158/9; 164; 165; 166T&B;
168B; 170T; 172; 173; 174/5;
176/7; 178/9; 182; 185B; 186; 191;
191; 192/3; 194; 198
Iain Reid: 25; 45; 64; 106; 110;
137; 140; 151; 167; 170B; 189
David Smith: 140T; 148; 190
Harry Smith: 130
Jerry Tubby: 187
John Turner: 136
Unwins Limited: 65
George Wright: 94T